TAKING THE CRIME OUT OF SEX WORK

New Zealand sex workers' fight for decriminalisation

Edited by Gillian Abel, Lisa Fitzgerald and Catherine Healy
with Aline Taylor

This edition published in Great Britain in 2010 by

The Policy Press
University of Bristol
Fourth Floor
Beacon House
Queen's Road
Bristol BS8 1QU
UK

t: +44 (0)117 331 4054
f: +44 (0)117 331 4093
e: tpp-info@bristol.ac.uk
www.policypress.co.uk

North American office:
The Policy Press
c/o International Specialized Books Services
920 NE 58th Avenue, Suite 300
Portland, OR 97213-3786, USA
t: +1 503 287 3093
f: +1 503 280 8832
e: info@isbs.com

British Library Cataloguing in Publication Data
A catalogue record for this book is available from the British Library.

Library of Congress Cataloging-in-Publication Data
A catalog record for this book has been requested.

ISBN 978 1 84742 334 4 hardcover

Cover design by The Policy Press
Front cover: image kindly supplied by Matías Sánchez
Printed and bound in Great Britain by Cromwell Press Group, Trowbridge

Contents

List of tables and figures

Tables

Figure

Notes on contributors

Gillian Abel is a senior public health lecturer and researcher at the University of Otago, Christchurch, New Zealand. She has been researching in the field of sex work for 13 years. She was the principal investigator in a major study of the impact of decriminalisation on the health and safety practices of sex workers in New Zealand. Her research uses mixed methods approaches and her other research interests include youth health, social network analysis and sexual health.

Tim Barnett is the Global Programme Manager for World AIDS Campaign based in Cape Town, South Africa. Until 2008, he was a Labour MP in New Zealand and represented the inner-city Christchurch Central electorate. He was appointed Senior Government Whip after the 2005 election. In his first term of parliament, he was the parliamentary private secretary to the Associate Minister of Justice on human rights issues, the Minister for the Community and Voluntary Sector and the Minister of Social Development. He was also chair of the Justice and Electoral Select Committee. He sponsored the Prostitution Law Reform Bill, which was introduced to parliament in 2000 and became law in 2003.

Calum Bennachie is the Pride and Unity for Male Prostitutes (PUMP) coordinator for the New Zealand Prostitutes' Collective (NZPC), having worked for the collective since 1999. PUMP is the male sex worker project of NZPC. Calum has been involved in lesbian and gay politics since the early 1990s, and was a volunteer with the New Zealand AIDS foundation for five years from 1993. He recently completed his PhD which looked at controlling anti-gay hate speech in New Zealand.

Cheryl Brunton is a public health physician and senior lecturer at the University of Otago, Christchurch, and has a strong interest in harm reduction approaches. Her research interests include injecting drug use and hepatitis C. She was a co-investigator in the major study of the impact of decriminalisation on the health and safety practices of sex workers in New Zealand. She also works for the local public health service and is a designated medical officer of health under the 1956 Health Act. In this latter role, she became an inspector of brothels under the 2003 Prostitution Reform Act.

Lisa Fitzgerald is a public health sociologist and has an interest in qualitative social research and health. She was a co-investigator in the major study of the impact of decriminalisation on the health and safety practices of sex workers in New Zealand. She is currently a lecturer in social science related to population health, in the Epidemiology and Social Medicine Division of the School of Population Health, University of Queensland, Australia.

Paul Fitzharris was appointed to chair the Prostitution Law Review Committee by the Ministry of Justice in December 2003. Prior to his retirement in 2001, he was acting deputy commissioner and periodically acting commissioner for the New Zealand police force. Since his retirement, he has served on the Establishment Board for the proposed New Zealand Transport Agency, the Board of Land Transport in New Zealand and the Legal Aid Review Panel. He is also a management consultant.

Catherine Healy is a founding member of the New Zealand Prostitutes' Collective and is currently the national coordinator. She was a member of the Prostitution Law Review Committee charged with reviewing the operation of the 2003 Prostitution Reform Act.

Jan Jordan is currently senior lecturer in the Institute of Criminology, Victoria University of Wellington. She has over 20 years' experience of teaching and researching in the area of women and crime, and has undertaken projects for various government departments over this time. Currently, she is completing a book based on interviews with 15 women attacked by the same serial rapist, focusing in particular on the ways they survived the attack and managed the resultant police and court processes. She was also a member of the Prostitution Law Review Committee.

Dean Knight is a legal scholar in the Faculty of Law, Victoria University of Wellington, with particular expertise in local government law, along with public and administrative law generally. He is the co-author of *LexisNexis local government* and has written a number of articles on local government and regulation by local authorities. Before joining the faculty he spent eight years in private practice, during which time he advised and represented numerous local authorities in relation to governance and regulatory issues.

Alison Laurie is Programme Director of Gender and Women's Studies at Victoria University of Wellington, where she teaches courses on feminist thought, auto/ biography and oral history, and queer studies. She has published nationally and internationally on lesbian, gay and feminist topics. She is currently writing a social history of lesbianism in New Zealand, and co-editing (with Linda Evans) *Twenty years on: Histories of homosexual law reform in New Zealand* and (with Graham Willett) *Wolfenden 50*.

Elaine Mossman is a senior lecturer in the Crime and Justice Research Centre, Victoria University of Wellington, and has carried out several pieces of research on the decriminalisation of prostitution in New Zealand. In 2005, she assisted the Prostitution Law Review Committee in the development of an evaluation framework to review the 2003 Prostitution Reform Act. Her other research interests include adolescent mental health, juvenile youth justice, adventure therapy and mixed methods research design.

Anna Reed is the regional coordinator of NZPC in Christchurch. A sex worker for 25 years, she has participated in field research with the University of Otago, Christchurch School of Medicine.

Aline Taylor comes from a background in anthropology, with a particular interest in researching issues on development, sport and gender. She has undertaken fieldwork in a variety of different contexts and written a number of ethnographic accounts within her areas of interest. Her most recent fieldwork was carried out in Tanzania among a group of female long-distance runners. Her research examined the ways in which sport is increasingly being incorporated into international development programmes, with the aim of empowering marginalised groups.

Acknowledgements

This book is dedicated to all who campaigned for the decriminalisation of sex work in New Zealand, including sex workers, supporters, academics, organisations, politicians and others.

We would also like to acknowledge the Health Research Council of New Zealand as well as the Ministry of Justice, which funded much of the research drawn on in this book.

ONE

Introduction

Gillian Abel and Lisa Fitzgerald

Prior to 2003, although sex work in New Zealand was not illegal, all associated activities, such as soliciting, brothel keeping, living on the earnings of prostitution and procuring, were criminalised. This created an environment in which violence, exploitation and coercion could flourish (Lowman, 2000; WHO, 2005). Sustained social action over nearly two decades, which involved advocacy and lobbying by the New Zealand Prostitutes' Collective (NZPC), politicians across the political spectrum, women's rights activists, academics and other volunteers, was effective in bringing about legislative change. In June 2003, New Zealand became the first country to decriminalise sex work when the 2003 Prostitution Reform Act (PRA[1]) was voted on and passed by a majority of one vote in Parliament[2]. This legislative approach differs to other international approaches as it represents a shift from regulating sex work from a moral perspective to acknowledging the human rights of this section of the population. Decriminalisation meant that prostitution was acknowledged as service work and sex workers in New Zealand were able to operate under the same employment and legal rights accorded to any other occupational group.

The particular historical, social and cultural context within New Zealand was influential in legislating for the decriminalisation of sex work. New Zealand is a young society and has less strict gendered, class and ethnic social structures than countries such as the United Kingdom. The dominant political ideology of New Zealand from the days of early colonisation has been liberalism and this has shaped the laws of this country (Duncan, 2007). New Zealand women in the 19th century had more freedom socially and physically and, in 1893, were the first to be enfranchised. New Zealand was also at the forefront of a raft of other social reforms such as the 1898 Old Age Pensions Act, which led some commentators to state that New Zealand was the 'sociological experiment station of the world' (Le Rossignol and Stewart, 1910, cited in Duncan, 2007, p 18). The principles of liberalism, such as respect for diversity, freedom of choice and human rights, continue to dominate the policy environment in New Zealand in the 21st century.

---

[1] www.legislation.govt.nz/act/public/2003/0028/latest/DLM197815.html

[2] New South Wales, Australia decriminalised non-street sex work in 1995, but some street-based workers remained criminalised. Other states of Australia have legalised sex work. New Zealand, as a nation, was the first to decriminalise all sectors of the sex industry.

The particularities of the history of prostitution in New Zealand, how it evolved and its acceptance in the new colony also set the scene for decriminalisation.

Regulation of sex work

Several approaches have been taken to regulate the sex industry, with most countries seeking to regulate rather than totally eliminate prostitution (Jordan, 2005). Legislation has taken the form of criminalisation, criminalisation of the client, legalisation or decriminalisation. There has been much confusion with the terms legalisation and decriminalisation and in some literature it is incorrectly claimed that countries such as Germany and the Netherlands have decriminalised sex work (for example, Harcourt et al, 2005). Currently, however, only the state of New South Wales in Australia and New Zealand have gone down the road of decriminalisation.

Moral perspectives have historically been drawn on in the regulation of sex work in countries where the activities associated with sex work are criminalised, but in recent decades other perspectives have been gaining ground. Radical feminist perspectives of sex work as violence against women are instrumental in legislation that criminalises the client, a situation currently in practice in Sweden. However, in some countries, liberal feminist, sex workers' rights and public health perspectives are being taken on board.

Criminalisation of the sex worker

Criminalisation may take the form of prohibition, where sex work is illegal, or, as is more often the case, of a modified form of abolition that allows for the sale of sex but bans all related activities. It is a legislative approach that draws heavily on 'public nuisance' and moral order discourses (Kantola and Squires, 2004) and this is evident in policy debates in many western countries, including the United Kingdom and Canada. The public nuisance discourse depicts sex workers as dirty, disease-ridden, having no morals and associated with a criminal underworld, a stereotype often fuelled by media reporting. Sex workers are constructed as a threat to public morality and hygiene with an emphasis on the need for measures of control to contain this threat (Kantola and Squires, 2004). They are framed as vectors of disease and hubs for dangerous activities such as drugs and crime, placing 'good' citizens in the community at risk.

In contrast to the public nuisance discourse, the moral order discourse constructs sex workers as innocent victims, requiring protection and relocation (Kantola and Squires, 2004). This discourse has arisen following an emerging debate about trafficking in people, particularly children, for sexual exploitation. It draws on elements of traditional morality, child welfare concerns, international human rights agendas and feminist perspectives of sexual domination (Kantola and Squires, 2004). There are overlapping elements of these discourses despite other areas of contention (Kantola and Squires, 2004), yet they all share a preoccupation with the protection of innocent victims of trafficking and tend to ignore the voluntary sex worker. The trafficking rhetoric has gained momentum since the mid-1990s with reports worldwide of the millions of children and women trafficked both within and between countries (Sanghera, 2005). Women who migrate voluntarily, with the full knowledge that they will be working in the sex industry, are conflated with helpless women and children, forced against their will to a life of slavery and sex work, both acquiring the label of trafficked victims. The trafficking debate, as Weitzer (2007, p 467) contends, bears 'all the hallmarks of a moral crusade'.

Criminalised sex workers have none of the rights accorded to workers in other occupations and therefore they are open to coercion and exploitation by managers, pimps and clients. No health and safety guidelines govern working conditions and adverse experiences such as being physically assaulted, threatened with physical assault, being held against their will, being forced to have unprotected sex, having clients refuse to pay for their service and having money stolen are common occurrences in the lives of many sex workers, especially those working on the streets (Plumridge and Abel, 2001). There are also psychological consequences to criminalisation, as the arrest process itself is humiliating and degrading, the sex worker's occupation may have previously been unknown to family and friends and the stigma given to sex work can often have harmful psychological effects. The consequences of having a criminal record are also far reaching. It may make it even more difficult for sex workers to leave the industry, as they may not be able to find other employment. They also may have limitations put on travel and the ability to get home mortgages or other loans (Davis and Shaffer, 1994).

In the UK, sex work itself is not illegal but many offences associated with it are, including soliciting, brothel keeping, living on the earnings of prostitution, procuring sexual intercourse and non-licensing of massage parlours, bawdy houses or brothels. In most cases, the laws regulating these activities are invocated through old laws (Hancock, 1991). Some of these laws seek to protect sex workers from third parties and some are meant to protect the public from the 'nuisance' effects of prostitution (Lowman in Davis and Shaffer, 1994). These laws make it impossible for sex workers to provide commercial sex without committing a number of offences. The regulations tend to increase the vulnerability of sex workers by driving them underground, where fear of detection and arrest override concerns for health and safety (Davis and Shaffer, 1994; Jordan, 2005).

Prior to 2000, the UK was principally concerned with the public nuisance effect of sex work. Persistent soliciting in a street or public place was penalised through a fine of up to £1,000. Then in 2002, kerb crawling was made an arrestable offence, and in 2004 further stringent steps were taken by making it possible to disqualify a kerb crawler from driving (Westmarland, 2006). In this way, government sought to 'disrupt the market' by focusing on the demand side of sex work (Westmarland, 2006).

More recently, the trafficking debate has also been influential in amendments to the regulation of sex work in the UK. In December 2000, the UK signed the United Nations Convention against Transnational Organized Crime and in

2001 became a signatory to the European Union draft framework decision on combating trafficking in human beings (Kantola and Squires, 2004). Whereas kerb-crawling and soliciting legislation was brought about through community activism, trafficking then emerged as an issue through international and European influence (Kantola and Squires, 2004). Although the Home Office has made unsubstantiated claims of between 140 and 1,400 women and children per year being trafficked into the UK to work in the off-street sector of the sex industry, few victims of trafficking have been identified by police, vice squad and immigration service visits to massage parlours (O'Connell Davidson, 2006). In 2003, although 295 women were found to be immigrants working illegally in the sex industry, only five were found to be victims of trafficking (O'Connell Davidson, 2006). In their critique of the strategy adopted by the Home Office, Boynton and Cusick (2006) commented on the lack of understanding shown concerning risk and the implications the laws would have on health outcomes for sex workers and their ability to access healthcare. They highlighted the negative consequences the policing of kerb crawling would have, most notably that displacing workers would increase the prevalence of acquisitive crime and that there would be a reduction in sex workers' negotiation powers leading to increased violence, unsafe sex practices and increased public disorder.

Criminalisation of the client

Criminalisation of the client seeks to reduce the demand for sex work and in the process either reduce or eliminate the sex industry altogether (Jordan, 2005). Radical feminists' claim that prostitution is an institutionalised form of male violence towards all women has been influential in policy debate in Sweden, where legislative changes have ensured that clients and not sex workers are criminalised (Hunter, 1991). Inequality and subordination of women are seen as the underpinnings of 'prostitution'. Radical feminists do not recognise 'prostitution' as work and resist more liberal calls to define 'prostitution' as 'sex work' (MacKinnon, 2001; Sullivan, 2007). In viewing sex work as violence, radical feminists never see this as a 'choice', but a violation of human rights (Sullivan, 2007).

Barry (1995) asserts that whether or not there is consent, when a human body is objectified to sexually service another, violation has occurred. She contends that sex work is 'structured to invoke women's consent', given the condition of class domination that promotes oppression (1995, p 24). She leaves no place for individual agency or choice for women to consent to sex work, arguing that although agreeing to go with a client and exchange sex for money appears to be a choice, it is in fact merely an 'appearance of choice' as an act of survival (1995, p 33). Sex workers are thus seen as passive victims with no control over the commercial sexual transaction and any arguments that are presented by sex workers to the contrary are met with claims of a 'false consciousness' or 'false sense of control' (Barry, 1995; Jeffreys, 1997; Farley, 2004).

Radical feminists argue for abolition of the sex industry to counter the victimisation of 'prostitutes' in a patriarchal society through decriminalisation of sex workers and criminalisation of the clients, while strengthening laws that repress the procurement and pimping of sex workers. It is believed that if there were no customers there would be no market for the victims of the trade, i.e. the sex workers, and thus sex work will ultimately be eliminated (Farley and Barkan, 1998; Svanstrom, 2006).

Sweden has been unique in prohibiting the buying of sex and supporters of this stance have heralded Sweden as signalling to the world that sex work is not acceptable in a gender-equal society (Gould, 2001). The fact that legislation to this effect was passed in 1998 is due to a particularly strong women's movement in Sweden (Kulick, 2003; Svanstrom, 2006). Although a Commission set up in 1993 to investigate options for regulation had recommended both the criminalisation of the client and the sex worker, this stance was criticised by some experts and taken up by the media. It was claimed that such legislation would obscure the fact that sex work was about men's power over women and that punishing the sex workers would mean punishing the victims of sex work (Gould, 2001; Svanstrom, 2006). The idea that sex work was voluntarily chosen as a profession was totally rejected as an argument, with claims made that 'nobody willingly sells their body for money' and that women enter the industry either because of poverty, dependence on drugs or because they are trafficked (Gould, 2001). No input from sex workers or sex work organisations was sought in any of the debates informing the legislation (Gould, 2001; Kulick, 2003; Ostergren, 2006).

A 'fear of the foreign' added impetus to legislative change when it was apparent that Sweden was about to join the European Union (EU). Media reports at this time sensationalised the invasion of foreign sex workers from Eastern Europe into western cities (Gould, 2001; Kulick, 2003). Although Sweden's sex worker population was low[3], there were fears that this influx would greatly increase the number of workers in Sweden.

Although many groups in Sweden opposed to criminalisation[4] put forward arguments that such legislation would drive the sex industry underground, leading to an increase in violence, unsafe sex practices and exploitation of sex workers, proponents claimed that much of the industry was already underground and the law would decrease the demand for paid sexual services. There were also arguments that there would be complications in implementing the law. As sex with a sex worker was not illegal but the purchasing or attempt to purchase a 'temporary sexual relation' was, it would be a difficult action to prove if both parties denied

---

[3] Estimates of the number of sex workers in Sweden prior to the enactment of the 1999 law were about 2,500 workers in a population of 8.5 million (0.3 per 1,000) with an estimated 1,000 working on the street (Kilvington et al, 2001; Kulick, 2003; Svanstrom, 2006).

[4] Groups opposing the criminalisation of the client were the National Board of Police, the National Social Welfare Board, the Attorney General and the National Courts Administration (Kulick, 2003).

it (Kulick, 2003). Indeed, since the law has been in force, very few offences have reached the courts (Kulick, 2003).

The legislation had the immediate effect of reducing the number of workers on the streets of Stockholm and Gothenburg, but numbers have since started to increase (Kilvington et al, 2001). Government reports evaluating the law have all concluded that there has been no significant drop in numbers (Kulick, 2003). Commentators have proposed that the initial reduction in the number of workers seen on the street did not mean that the number of sex workers had decreased but that they had chosen less visible ways of making contact with clients (Kilvington et al, 2001; Ostergren, 2006). This posed a number of threats to sex workers' health and safety by driving the industry underground where sex workers were vulnerable to exploitation and abuse and less easily accessed by health and social workers.

The limited research coming out of Sweden that is available in English highlights that sex workers are finding it difficult to adequately assess clients prior to going with them as clients are more nervous and wish to conduct business in a more rapid manner (Ostergren, 2006). Sex workers are also reporting more emotional stress under the current legal system. The implications of criminalising people living on the earnings of sex work means that some workers are reluctant to reveal what they are doing to landlords or alternatively, are exploited by landlords and having to pay exorbitant rents (Ostergren, 2006). This clause also means that it is illegal to work indoors under a system of management or work with others, environments that are safer than working on the streets. Non-Swedish workers are deported immediately if found with a client (Kulick, 2003). Proponents of the law, however, defend the stance that has been taken, saying that it sends a message to society that sex work is unacceptable and does not belong in Sweden (Kulick, 2003).

Legalisation

Reducing harm to sex workers is not necessarily the reason why legalisation of the sex industry is often advocated; rather, drawing on moral rhetoric, it can be an attempt to control the industry by keeping it limited to certain areas where it will not offend the wider population (Davis and Shaffer, 1994; English Collective of Prostitutes, 1997; Arnot, 2002). Some European countries, such as the Netherlands and Germany, and some states of Australia, including Victoria, Queensland and South Australia, have legalised sex work. Legalisation permits sex work in certain forms, but it is usually heavily regulated through the licensing of sex workers and sex work establishments within zoned areas (English Collective of Prostitutes, 1997; Jordan, 2005). Municipalities have complete control over the granting or refusing of licenses and thus the number of legal brothels and sex workers has generally been greatly limited (Lewis and Maticka-Tyndale, 2000; Jordan, 2005). Many sex workers are unwilling to work in the legal brothels where brothel owners are often exploitative (Scambler and Scambler, 1997). Instead, they elect to work illegally, which creates a two-tier system. Illegal workers are vulnerable to exploitation and violence and are less visible to health and social worker (Scambler and Scambler, 1997).

Brothels were allowed to operate in Victoria, Australia from 1986 with the passing of the Prostitution Regulation Act provided that they had special planning permits (Sullivan, 1999; Perkins and Lovejoy, 2007). Not only did this Act make it possible to be legally employed in a brothel, but it was also theoretically possible for private sex workers to work from their homes. In reality, however, few licenses were granted by local councils, which failed to treat sex work like any other business, and this meant that most sex workers continued to work illegally (Sullivan, 1999). In addition, the Act increased penalties for sex workers who worked illegally and so most sex workers in Victoria were vulnerable to exploitation (Sullivan, 1999).

In 1995, the Prostitution Control Act was passed in Victoria. This Act requires escort and brothel operators to obtain a license to operate a legal business (Sullivan, 1999). All other forms of sex work, such as working from unlicensed premises and on the street, continues to be criminalised. The Business Licensing Authority oversees the licensing of brothels. Regulations require that applicants (and associates of applicants) have no criminal record. Licenses are expensive and have been limited to certain non-residential areas and to a very few businesses in these areas, resulting in a shortage of legal employment for sex workers (Sullivan, 1999; Arnot, 2002). This has forced many sex workers to operate illegally. Because of the shortage of legal work, some brothel owners have been able to exploit their workers and this has resulted in poor working conditions for those sex workers who wish to work legally (Arnot, 2002). Other legal brothels have been attentive to the health and safety of sex workers on their premises, although mostly sex workers are paid as sub-contractors and not employees and thus do not have the benefits of being employed, such as being eligible for annual and sick leave (Sullivan, 1999).

Brothel operators must provide their employees with condoms as well as safe-sex education material for employees and clients. Sex workers are legally required to undergo sexual health checks with monthly swabs and three-monthly blood tests and it is a criminal offence for a sex worker to work with a sexually transmitted infection (STI) (Metzenrath, 1999). Certificates showing that someone has not got an STI are only valid until the next occasion of sexual intercourse and thus it is argued that the requirement of compulsory testing is futile (Metzenrath, 1999). It instead provides clients with more incentive to pressurise sex workers into unprotected sex, as they believe that they are 'clean'.

Street-based sex workers tend to be exposed to greater risk than brothel workers, in large part due to their criminalised status. The absence of legal protection and the lack of peer and community support contribute to the difficulties they experience in negotiating safe sex (Pyett and Warr, 1997). Many are reluctant to report violent crimes, such as rape and assault, to the police because of perceptions of disconnection from the justice system due to their illegal status (Pyett and Warr, 1997, 1999).

Decriminalisation

Decriminalisation aims to remove the social exclusion that makes sex workers subject to exploitation (West, 2000). It encompasses the complete removal of the laws governing sex work and sex work-related offences. The sex work industry then becomes subject to the same controls and regulations as those under which other businesses operate (Jordan, 2005). Decriminalisation is seen by liberal feminists, sex workers' rights activists and public health professionals as the only way to protect the human rights of sex workers and minimise the amount of harm incurred by their occupation.

In contrast to radical feminists' claims that sex workers are passive recipients of male domination, Chapkis (1997) and Sullivan (2004a) maintain that many sex workers actively resist men's power and control within sexual interactions by charging a fee for what is normally given freely. In so doing, they are taking control of the sexual interaction and dictating what they are willing to provide for that fee. Denying freedom of consent to work as a sex worker is problematic as it means that no distinction can be made between sex work and rape (Sullivan, 2004a). This would mean that it would be difficult for sex workers to pursue charges of rape against a client, as the police and the court system may not take such charges seriously. Sullivan (2004a, p 138) maintains that instead of taking punitive measures against sex workers and/or their clients, sex workers' freedom and consensual capacity will be maximised when sex workers have 'safe and legal working conditions, access to other employment options …, access to the criminal justice system and a politico-legal system that encourages the development of new rights as workers for prostitutes'.

Liberal feminists therefore argue that the abolition of prostitution is an act of repression (Jenness, 1993) and that decriminalisation of sex work would be a pre-condition for improvements in working conditions, which would include empowering workers in their interactions with clients and managers (Sullivan, 1991; 2004a). It is the denial of sex workers' human, civil and employment rights that leads to the abuse and exploitation prevalent in the sex industry (O'Connell Davidson, 2006).

As Frances and Gray (2007) and Sullivan (2004b) argue, the impetus for amendment to the law regulating sex work in New South Wales (NSW), Australia in 1979 came about through the concerted efforts of Australian feminists and sex workers. Prior to 1979, most of the activities associated with sex work in NSW were criminalised and as a consequence, the exploitation of sex workers was common, even by police who took bribes from sex workers in return for not arresting them (Donovan and Harcourt, 1996; Frances and Gray, 2007; Perkins and Lovejoy, 2007). In 1979, NSW decriminalised soliciting, thus enabling sex workers to legally work on the street, privately or in a brothel. However, other activities, such as living on the earnings and owning or operating a business in which commercial sexual exchanges occurred, were still deemed a crime. When street-based sex work began to expand from the Kings Cross area of Sydney into surrounding suburbs, partly as a response to the continuing restrictions on brothel operation, the Labour government amended legislation in 1983 to restrict legal soliciting zones to areas that were not 'near' a dwelling, school, church or hospital (Frances and Gray, 2007; Perkins and Lovejoy, 2007). This law was further amended in 1988 to state that soliciting was not permitted 'within view from' any of these locations. In 1995, through amendments to the 1943 Disorderly Houses Act and the 1988 Summary Offences Act, brothel keeping was decriminalised and owners, managers and other brothel staff were allowed to legally live on the earnings of sex work (Scott, 2003; Perkins and Lovejoy, 2007).

NSW achieved recognition for having the least oppressive regulations on sex work but there are still arguments that some continuing restrictions have prevented all sex workers in NSW from achieving their full human rights. While much of the sex industry in NSW is decriminalised, there are still restrictions on where street-based sex workers may operate (Donovan and Harcourt, 1996; Scott, 2003). In this way, the NSW government has sought to erase the more visible sectors of the sex industry that it characterises as constituting a danger to the community and a public nuisance. The private sector is also not unregulated and licensing of brothels by local councils is required. Planning laws have frequently been interpreted too rigidly and applications for licensing outside of designated zones have been successfully blocked by local councils (SWOP, 2003; Harcourt et al, 2005). The definition of brothel has also not been clarified and premises where one or two workers operate fall under the definition of brothel. This has meant that many private workers work illegally as they find it difficult to comply with council requirements to operate within designated areas (Harcourt et al, 2005). Non-resident sex workers are also marginalized, as legally they are not entitled to work as a sex worker in NSW (Donovan and Harcourt, 1996). Such a two-tiered system has necessarily resulted in a legal and an illegal sector to the sex industry. Although to date there is little research on the health and safety of sex workers in NSW and the impact of decriminalisation, there are claims that police corruption in relation to sex work has diminished (Donovan and Harcourt, 1996) and in terms of sexual health, the prevalence and incidence of STIs among female sex workers in NSW is extremely low (Donovan et al, 2008).

A segmented industry

Sex workers are not a homogenous population. Sex workers may work under a system of management, either in a brothel or for an escort agency. They may also work alone or with other workers from their own home or rented premises. Alternatively, they could work on the street. There are a number of reasons why people decide to work in the sex industry and also different motivations behind selecting which sector to work in within the industry. These motivations change as sex workers navigate through different sectors of the industry. Sex workers are intersectorally mobile; many work in more than one sector and some start work in one sector and move to another after a period of time. When movement between sectors is discussed, it is usually in relation to economics – a downturn in business may require sex workers to diversify and move to working in another sector to supplement their income (Lewis et al, 2005). Some findings have shown that people who start working on the street are the most intersectorally mobile (Day, 2007). Winter temperatures and high-intensity policing may prompt street-based workers to move indoors (Lewis et al, 2005). In New Zealand, however, there appears to have been a movement from the managed to the private sector following decriminalisation (Abel et al, 2009).

Location plays an influential role in constructing people's experience of work and their exposure to risk, and each sector has different occupational risks (Whittaker and Hart, 1996). Most research studies focus on street-based workers, who represent a very small segment of the sex worker population, constituting only around 10-20% of sex workers in all developed countries (Scambler, 1997; Vanwesenbeeck, 2001, 2005; Weitzer, 2005). However, they constitute a particularly vulnerable segment of the industry (Lowman, 2000; Kinnell, 2006). They are the sector of the industry that do experience more violence, are more likely to be involved in drug use and are less likely than their 'indoor' counterparts to use condoms in every commercial transaction (Benoit and Millar, 2001; Plumridge and Abel, 2001; Vanwesenbeeck, 2001; Sanders, 2004). Street-based workers are also likely to be less educated, of lower socioeconomic status, more likely to report behaviour disorders in childhood and adolescence and more likely to have been sexually abused prior to entering the industry than 'indoor' workers (Vanwesenbeeck, 2001). The media, like many researchers, also tends to focus on street-based workers, perhaps because they are the most visible sector of the sex industry. Thus, stereotypes of what a sex worker is are perpetuated, conflating all sex workers under the rubric of 'deviant' fallen women or 'victims'. Yet, the majority of sex workers do not fit the popular stereotype of the drug-addicted, immoral, pimped, street-based worker who works in an environment of violence, crime and hopelessness. Many are autonomous and able to 'evade public and (even) self-labelling as outsiders or outcasts' (Scambler, 1997, p 118). There are different environmental influences on sex workers that affect their health and safety and it is important to look at all sectors of the industry.

As well as being an industry segmented by location of work, sex work is segmented by gender and ethnicity. Although the majority of sex workers are female, there are also male and transgender/transsexual workers who work in the industry. In research, male and transgender sex workers are often ignored, but gender, too, plays an important part in people's experience of the sex industry. Indigenous populations in colonised countries are also most often over-represented in the sex worker population (Abel et al., 2007; Benoit and Millar, 2001). In New Zealand, almost two thirds of street-based sex workers identify as Maori, and Maori and Pacific are more likely than other ethnic groups to identify as transgender (Abel et al, 2007).

In New Zealand, all sectors of the sex industry have been decriminalised and the research detailed in this book as well as elsewhere (Abel et al, 2007, 2009; Mossman and Mayhew, 2007; Weir, 2007; PLRC, 2008) provides the evidence to make an assessment of whether this has been a success. The experience of decriminalisation is documented over the following 14 chapters, with contributions from people from diverse backgrounds who provide their unique perspectives. Two of the editors of this book, Gillian Abel and Lisa Fitzgerald, as well as some of the other authors, Cheryl Brunton, Elaine Mossman and Dean Knight, were involved in research that contributed to the evidence drawn on in evaluating the PRA. Catherine Healy, Calum Bennachie and Anna Reed work at the NZPC and they played a key role in lobbying for decriminalisation. Tim Barnett was the Member of Parliament who introduced the Prostitution Reform Bill to Parliament as a Private Member's Bill. Jan Jordan and Catherine Healy were members of the Prostitution Law Review Committee and Paul Fitzharris, a retired policeman, chaired this committee. Alison Laurie has provided a perspective as a feminist who actively campaigned for the decriminalisation of sex work. The variety of perspectives drawn on adds value to this book. In addition, the research presented in many of the chapters gives voice to the sex workers in New Zealand, who provide their perspective on the impact of decriminalisation.

Outline of the book

Chapters Two to Six provide a lead-up to the passing of the PRA in 2003. In Chapter Two, Jan Jordan, a leading criminologist in New Zealand who has previously published in the field of sex work (Jordan, 1991a, 1991b, 2005), details the history of the sex industry in New Zealand from the time of the arrival of early explorers in the late 17th century, through colonisation in the 19th century, to the latter part of the 20th century. The chapter both describes the organisation of commercial prostitution services and analyses the contested terrain surrounding their existence. The role played by prostitution in New Zealand society is discussed from diverse perspectives: the ways it existed as an option for economic survival for women; the role it performed in meeting men's sexual demands and fantasies; and the ways in which it provided an impetus and mobilising device for social and moral campaigners. How New Zealand legislation reflected double standards of morality is critiqued from a feminist perspective, illustrating the inequities existing prior to the PRA and the necessity for positive intervention. Through reference to historical ideas and movements, this chapter explores why New Zealand became the first country to decriminalise sex work and how such legislative change is consistent with this particular social and cultural context.

Since the 1970s and 1980s, sex workers' rights organisations have been established in most developed countries and since the 1990s in many developing countries. The discourses of such organisations have had a variable influence on law reform worldwide and in many cases have played a part in the implementation of health and occupational initiatives (West, 2000). Sex worker organisations in the United States and the United Kingdom, for example, have had little influence in informing law reform, but have had an important role to play in developing health initiatives (West, 2000). However, in New Zealand, the Netherlands and some Australian states, effective advocacy of sex workers' rights groups has led to significant gains in the deregulation of the sex industry (West, 2000). Chapter Three discusses the formation of NZPC in 1987 and tracks the efforts of this organisation since then to confront social stigma and overturn legislation that has had a negative impact on the lives of sex workers.

The key issue for sex workers' rights groups like NZPC is the notion that sex work is a work issue; that it is service work that should be respected and protected like work in any other service occupation (Jenness, 1993; Alexander, 1997; Simmons, 1999). It is argued that most sex workers choose to work in the sex industry and the rights and ability of these individuals to exercise this agency should be supported along with the right not to be subjected to public harassment, such as stigmatisation, rape, violence, denial of healthcare, denial of protection by and under the law and denial of alternative opportunities. This is seen as a human rights issue. Lack of legal protection and occupational rights increases sex workers' vulnerability to STIs and leaves them lacking in the information, materials and authority to adequately protect themselves (Alexander, 1997; Bindman, 1998; Cabezas, 1998). The primary goal, therefore, of sex workers' rights groups is the elimination of all laws regulating sex work so that sex workers can lead less victimised lives. Laws prohibiting sex for sale ensure that sex workers remain open to abuse and have no legal recourse to action against the perpetrators of the abuse (Jenness, 1993; Overs and Druce, 1994; Alexander, 1997; Simmons, 1999). Thus, sex workers' rights groups advocate for the decriminalisation of the sex industry and the regulation of the industry in line with other service industries.

Chapter Three describes the leading role NZPC played in building support for decriminalisation through simultaneously engaging a broad spectrum of politicians and a diverse range of community groups, which contributed significantly to changes in policy at government level. The relationship NZPC has with sex workers as a service provider and as an advocate for the rights of sex workers, then and now, is examined.

The process of lobbying and the passing of the PRA are documented in Chapter Four. Perspectives from both Tim Barnett and the NZPC are provided on the networking, conceptualisation and drafting of the Bill, as well as the campaign building and finally the process of the Bill through parliament. The purposes and content of the PRA and a description of the sections and clauses within the Act are described in Chapter Five. The Act reflects a public health and human rights approach, aiming to: safeguard the human rights of sex workers and protect them from exploitation; promote the welfare and occupational health and safety of sex workers; be conducive to public health; prohibit the use in prostitution of persons under 18 years of age; and implement certain other related reforms. This chapter examines how these aims are addressed in a section-by-section discussion of the Act.

Different feminist debates have influenced the regulation of sex work internationally. As argued already in this chapter, feminists hold polarised views on sexuality. Some feminists have criticised restrictions on women's sexual behaviour and called for a sexual liberation that would work for both men and women, while others consider sexual liberalisation as an extension of male privilege (Rubin, 1984). The latter are more radical in their views and understand sex work as sexual exploitation and violence against women, equating 'prostitution' with rape, sexual harassment, domestic violence, incest and child sexual abuse (Barry, 1995; Jeffreys, 1997; Farley and Barkan, 1998; Sullivan, 2007). In contrast to radical feminists, from a liberal feminist perspective, women have the right to self-determination, especially with regard to their bodies and sexuality.

Alison Laurie argues, in Chapter Six, that groups opposing and supporting the Prostitution Reform Bill (PRB) drew on both radical and liberal feminist perspectives in submissions to the Select Committee. She provides an overview of the main arguments presented in feminist submissions for the PRB, the majority of which drew on liberal feminists' ideas of equality and fair treatment for women, both as individuals and as members of occupational or other groups within New Zealand society.

The chapters in Section Two of this book examine what has happened since the enactment of the PRA. Chapter Seven outlines the statutory authority for the Prostitution Law Review Committee, and its membership and role, as written by the chair of the committee, Paul Fitzharris. The committee was required to produce two reports on the review of the operation of the Act. Its first report (PLRC, 2005), tabled in the New Zealand parliament on 18 April 2005, described the nature and extent of the sex industry in New Zealand prior to decriminalisation in 2003 and is summarised in this chapter. A second report was completed in June 2008. This report reviewed the operation of the Act, assessed the numbers of persons working as sex workers, assessed the nature and adequacy of the means to cease working as sex workers, and considered whether any amendments to the legislation were required (PLRC, 2008). The review was underpinned by the 'purpose' of the legislation, which focused on human rights, welfare, health and safety of sex workers and the prohibition of young persons in the sex industry. This chapter outlines the approach the committee adopted to complete its work. This included consultation with government agencies and local authorities, inviting submissions from interested organisations and the public, and research by Victoria University's Crime and Justice Research Centre and the University of Otago, Christchurch School of Medicine (CSoM) to inform its report. This chapter outlines the findings of the committee and its recommendations to the Minister of Justice.

The material presented in Chapter Eight is from a Victoria University of Wellington research project commissioned by the Ministry of Justice for the review of the PRA. It examines perspectives on the PRA of those who have been able to observe first hand the impact of the PRA on sex workers and the sex industry. This includes brothel owners and operators and the non-government organisations most active in providing support, advocacy, education and health services to sex workers. Interviews with these groups ascertained their level of support for the PRA both before and after its implementation. Their views and observations on the effectiveness of the Act in meeting its stated objectives were also noted. With a few notable exceptions, the majority view was that they were happy with what had been provided for by the PRA. They felt the PRA had 'set the scene' and that the intentions of the Act could be fully realised with more time and an increase in monitoring and enforcement of its provisions.

The PRA gave local government a number of powers to regulate aspects of the sex industry, including the location of brothels. Some of the local councils, influenced by moralistic arguments, attempted to limit the locations where sex work could happen. Sex workers are often depicted as the 'embodiment of vulgar and conspicuous sex' (Hubbard, 1998b, p 66) – predatory sexual actors who pose a threat to traditional community values anchored in marriage and the family (Bondi, 1998). Sex workers' presence in public, like any other 'deviant' population group, is seen as compromising normal family space. This difference causes anxieties, as it is seen as polluting and threatening, not normal and therefore 'other', creating a distancing in both social and spatial relationships (Sibley, 1998). Moral panics arise over contested spaces, where communities are intent on excluding the offending 'other' who are a threat to core values and by this exclusion, eliminating difference (Sibley, 1995). It has been argued that the exclusion of deviant groups such as sex workers from public spaces has created social boundaries that have enabled dominant groups, often comprising white, middle-class heterosexuals, to marginalise and control groups who do not conform to the 'normative' way of behaving (Sibley, 1995; Hubbard, 1998a). Chapter Nine looks at the response of local government, addressing the various regulatory models adopted by local authorities to regulate the location of brothels (including bylaws and district plan controls), along with some proposed attempts to continue to regulate street prostitution. It also discusses the courts' supervision of these regulatory responses, including the challenges, successful and unsuccessful, to bylaws regulating the location of brothels.

Research done by the CSoM drawn on in the PRA review is detailed in Chapters Ten to Fourteen. Chapter Ten gives details of the methodological approach and the methods used in carrying out this large multi-methods project. The research took a community-based participatory approach, with researchers working in partnership with NZPC. The quantitative phase of the study collected data through a questionnaire with 772 sex workers in five locations of New Zealand. The qualitative phase consisted of in-depth interviews with 58 sex workers and nine regulatory officers and a document analysis was done of 11 submissions made by medical officers of health to local authorities. In addition, a content analysis was carried out of newsprint reporting of the PRA. Some of the findings of this study are presented in Chapters Ten to Thirteen.

Public health authorities' experiences in implementing the requirements of the PRA are discussed in Chapter Eleven. The PRA makes Medical Officers of Health, who are designated officers under the 1956 Health Act, inspectors of brothels and gives them powers in relation to that function, including the appointment of other inspectors. Medical Officers of Health, and the public health services in which they work, have also made submissions to local authorities on proposed bylaws under the PRA. This chapter discusses the views of Medical Officers of Health and other public health workers about their new role under the PRA. It also analyses the content of public health submissions on proposed bylaws under the PRA and discusses the effect these submissions had (or in some cases, failed to have) on subsequent bylaws.

The media plays a key role in identifying sex workers as 'deviant' and 'other' and as such is instrumental in fuelling moral panics that increase public anxiety around sex work (Hubbard, 1998b, 2000, 2002; O'Neill et al, 2008). Such moral panics are often followed by reactive government policies that try to diffuse the moral panic (Hubbard, 2002; O'Neill et al, 2008). The role and impact of the print media in its reporting on the PRA is examined in Chapter Twelve. Using content analysis, it looks at the messages communicated in and by the print media in New Zealand between 2003 and 2006. It highlights how the debate in the print media has been moralistic in nature, rather than focusing on an evidence-based public health approach to the issue. There has been repetition of assumptions, opinions and associations regarding increased crime and nuisance associated with sex work, and claims of increased numbers of under-age sex workers. Sex workers have been represented as the immoral 'other' and sex work as a threat to dominant morality. The implications of these messages are discussed, as well as the perceptions of sex workers to the media reporting.

Decriminalisation of the sex industry has been advocated by public health workers in New Zealand and elsewhere as a strategy for harm minimisation. It has been proposed that by repealing the laws that criminalise all activities associated with sex work, sex workers' autonomy would increase as well as their capacity to protect themselves. Chapter Thirteen discusses sex workers' understandings and experiences of decriminalisation, including their perceived rights following decriminalisation of the sex industry. These rights include employment, occupational safety and health and legal rights. Sex workers discussed three main risks to working in the sex industry relating to sexual health, experiences of violence and exploitation, and emotional health. While gains were identified in negotiating safe sex and managing violence and exploitation, the emotional risks attached to sex work have not lessened to the same extent as these other risks in a decriminalised environment.

Chapter Fourteen presents ongoing perceptions of stigma as discussed by sex workers in the CSoM study. Stigma has been identified as an important contributor to sex workers' poor mental health and this chapter provides a comprehensive examination of stigma. Goffman's (1990) writings on stigma are critiqued in light of the growing literature that problematises his lack of accounting for structural conditions that lead to the reproduction of inequality and exclusion (Riessman, 2000; Link and Phelan, 2001; Parker and Aggleton, 2003; Scambler, 2007; Scambler and Paoli, 2008). Participants argued how they actively resisted stigma rather than, as Goffman suggested, internalising their shame. They also discussed the different roles they played in the private and public domains and how they endeavoured to maintain a separation of these roles. The stress of keeping the roles separate was also a risk to their mental health.

The concluding chapter brings together the material covered in the book, summarising the effects of decriminalisation of the sex industry in New Zealand. It draws conclusions about the extent to which the evidence from the New Zealand experience supports or refutes the claims for and against decriminalisation.

References

Abel, G., Fitzgerald, L. and Brunton, C. (2007) *The impact of the Prostitution Reform Act on the health and safety practices of sex workers: Report to the Prostitution Law Review Committee*, Christchurch: University of Otago, www.justice.govt.nz/prostitution-law-review-committee/publications/impact-health-safety/index.html

Abel, G., Fitzgerald, L. and Brunton, C. (2009) 'The impact of decriminalisation on the number of sex workers in New Zealand', *Journal of Social Policy*, vol 38, no 3, pp 515-31.

Alexander, P. (1997) 'Feminism, sex workers, and human rights', in J. Nagle (ed) *Whores and other feminists*, New York, NY: Routledge.

Arnot, A. (2002) *Legalisation of the sex industry in the state of Victoria, Australia: The impact of prostitution law reform on the working and private lives of women in the legal Victorian sex industry*, Melbourne: Department of Criminology, University of Melbourne.

Barry, K. (1995) *The prostitution of sexuality: The global exploitation of women*, New York, NY/London: New York University Press.

Benoit, C. and Millar, A. (2001) *Dispelling myths and understanding realities: Working conditions, health status, and exiting experiences of sex workers*, British Columbia: University of Victoria.

Bindman, J. (1998) 'An international perspective on slavery in the sex industry', in K. Kempadoo and J. Doezema (eds) *Global sex workers: Rights, resistance, and redefinition*, New York, NY: Routledge.

Bondi, L. (1998) 'Sexing the city', in R. Fincher and J. Jacobs (eds) *Cities of difference*, New York, NY: Guilford Press.

Boynton, P. and Cusick, L. (2006) 'Sex workers to pay the price: UK plans to cut street prostitution will threaten sex workers' health', *British Medical Journal*, vol 332, pp 190-1.

Cabezas, A. (1998) 'Discourses of prostitution: the case of Cuba', in K. Kempadoo and J. Doezema (eds) *Global sex workers: Rights, resistance, and redefinition*, New York, NY: Routledge.

Chapkis, W. (1997) *Live sex acts: Women performing erotic labor*, New York, NY: Routledge.

Davis, S. and Shaffer, M. (1994) *Prostitution in Canada: The invisible menace or the menace of invisibility?*, Vancouver: Commercial Sex Information Service, www.walnet.org/csis/papers/sdavis.html

Day, S. (2007) *On the game: Women and sex work*, London: Pluto Press.

Donovan, B. and Harcourt, C. (1996) 'Prostitution: to decriminalise or to legalise', *The Lancet*, vol 348, no 9032, p 962.

Donovan, B., Harcourt, C., O'Connor, J., Wand, H., Lu, H. and McNulty, A. (2008) 'Sex work in a decriminalised and unlicensed environment: a 15-year study in Sydney', Paper presented at Sexual Health Congress, Perth, Australia, 16 September 2008.

Duncan, G. (2007) *Society and politics: New Zealand social policy*, Auckland: Pearson Education New Zealand.

English Collective of Prostitutes (1997) 'Campaigning for legal change', in G. Scambler and A. Scambler (eds) *Rethinking prostitution: Purchasing sex in the 1990s*, London/New York, NY: Routledge.

Farley, M. (2004) '"Bad for the body, bad for the heart": prostitution harms women even if legalized or decriminalized', *Violence Against Women*, vol 10, no 10, pp 1087-125.

Farley, M. and Barkan, H. (1998) 'Prostitution, violence, and posttraumatic stress disorder', *Women and Health*, vol 27, no 3, pp 37-49.

Frances, R. and Gray, A. (2007) 'Unsatisfactory, discriminatory, unjust and inviting corruption: feminists and the decriminalisation of street prostitution in New South Wales', *Australian Feminist Studies*, vol 22, no 53, pp 307-24.

Gould, A. (2001) 'The criminalisation of buying sex: the politics of prostitution in Sweden', *Journal of Social Policy*, vol 30, no 3, pp 437-56.

Hancock, L. (1991) 'Legal regulation of prostitution: what or who is being controlled?', in S.-A. Gerull and B. Halstead (eds) *Sex Industry and Public Policy Conference*, Canberra: Australian Institute of Criminology.

Harcourt, C., Egger, S. and Donovan, B. (2005) 'Sex work and the law', *Sexual Health*, vol 2, no 3, pp 121-8.

Hubbard, P. (1998a) 'Community action and the displacement of street prostitution: evidence from British cities', *Geoforum*, vol 29, no 3, pp 269-86.

Hubbard, P. (1998b) 'Sexuality, immorality and the city: red-light districts and the marginalisation of female street prostitutes', *Gender, Place and Culture*, vol 5, no 1, pp 55-72.

Hubbard, P. (2000) 'Desire/disgust: mapping the moral contours of heterosexuality', *Progress in Human Geography*, vol 24, no 2, pp 191-217.

Hubbard, P. (2002) 'Maintaining family values? Cleansing the streets of sex advertising', *Area*, vol 34, no 4, pp 353-60.

Hunter, A. (1991) 'The development of theoretical approaches to sex work in Australian sex-worker rights groups', in S.-A. Gerull and B. Halstead, B (eds) *Sex Industry and Public Policy Conference*, Canberra: Australian Institute of Criminology.

Jeffreys, S. (1997) *The idea of prostitution*, Melbourne: Spinifex Press.

Jenness, V. (1993) *Making it work: The prostitutes' rights movement in perspective*, New York, NY: Aldine de Gruyter.

Jordan, J. (1991a) 'Sex, law and social control: the sex industry in New Zealand today', in S.-A. Gerull and B. Halstead (eds) *Sex Industry and Public Policy Conference*, Canberra: Australian Institute of Criminology.

Jordan, J. (1991b) *Working girls: Women in the New Zealand sex industry talk to Jan Jordan*, Auckland: Penguin Books.

Jordan, J. (2005) *The sex industry in New Zealand: a literature review*, Wellington: Ministry of Justice, www.justice.govt.nz/pubs/reports/2005/sex-industry-in-nz-literature-review/index.html

Kantola, J. and Squires, J. (2004) 'Discourses surrounding prostitution policies in the UK', *European Journal of Women's Studies*, vol 11, no 1, pp 77-101.

Kilvington, J., Day, S. and Ward, H. (2001) 'Prostitution policy in Europe: a time of change?', *Feminist Review*, no 67, Spring, pp 78-93.

Kinnell, H. (2006) 'Murder made easy: the final solution to prostitution?', in R. Campbell and M. O'Neill (eds), *Sex work now*, Cullompton: Willan.

Kulick, D. (2003) 'Sex in the new Europe: the criminalization of clients and Swedish fear of penetration', *Anthropological Theory*, vol 3, no 2, pp 199-218.

Lewis, J. and Maticka-Tyndale, E. (2000) 'Licensing sex work: public policy and women's lives', *Canadian Public Policy - Analyse de Politiques*, vol 26, no 4, pp 437-49.

Lewis, J., Maticka-Tyndale, E., Shaver, F. and Schramm, H. (2005) 'Managing risk and safety on the job', *Journal of Psychology and Human Sexuality*, vol 17, no 1, pp 147-67.

Link, B. and Phelan, J. (2001) 'Conceptualizing stigma', *Annual Review of Sociology*, vol 27, pp 363-85.

Lowman, J. (2000) 'Violence and the outlaw status of (street) prostitution in Canada', *Violence Against Women*, vol 6, no 9, pp 987-1011.

MacKinnon, C. (2001) *Sex inequality*, New York, NY: Foundation Press.

Metzenrath, S. (1999) 'To test or not to test?', *Social Alternatives*, vol 18, no 3, pp 25-30.

Mossman, E. and Mayhew, P. (2007) *Key informant interviews: Review of the Prostitution Reform Act 2003*, Wellington: Crime and Justice Research Centre, www.justice.govt.nz/prostitution-law-review-committee/publications/key-informant-interviews/report.pdf

O'Connell Davidson, J. (2006) 'Will the real sex slave please stand up?', *Feminist Review*, no 83, pp 4-22.

O'Neill, M., Campbell, R., Hubbard, P., Pitcher, J. and Scoular, J. (2008) 'Living with the other: street sex work, contingent communities and degrees of tolerance', *Crime, Media, Culture*, vol 4, no 1, pp 73-93.

Ostergren, P. (2006) 'Sex workers' critique of Swedish prostitution policy', www.petraostergren.com/content/view/44/38/

Overs, C. and Druce, N. (1994) 'Sex work, HIV and the state: an interview with Nel Druce', *Feminist Review*, no 48, pp 114-21.

Parker, R. and Aggleton, P. (2003) 'HIV and AIDS-related stigma and discrimination: a conceptual framework and implications for action', *Social Science and Medicine*, vol 57, no 1, pp 13-24.

Perkins, R. and Lovejoy, F. (2007) *Call girls: Private sex workers in Australia*, Crawley: University of Western Australia Press.

PLRC (Prostitution Law Review Committee) (2005) *The nature and extent of the sex industry in New Zealand: An estimation*, Wellington: Ministry of Justice, www.justice.govt.nz/pubs/reports/2005/nature-extent-sex-industry-in-nz-estimation/index.html

PLRC (2008) *Report of the Prostitution Law Review Committee on the operation of the Prostitution Reform Act 2003*, Wellington: Ministry of Justice, www.justice.govt.nz/prostitution-law-review-committee/publications/plrc-report/index.html

Plumridge, L. and Abel, G. (2001) 'A "segmented" sex industry in New Zealand: sexual and personal safety of female sex workers', *Australian and New Zealand Journal of Public Health*, vol 25, no 1, pp 78-83.

Pyett, P. and Warr, D. (1997) 'Vulnerability on the streets: female sex workers and HIV risk', *AIDS Care*, vol 9, no 5, pp 539-47.

Pyett, P. and Warr, D. (1999) 'Women at risk in sex work: strategies for survival', *Journal of Sociology*, vol 35, no 2, pp 183-97.

Riessman, C. (2000) 'Stigma and everyday resistance practices: childless women in South India', *Gender and Society*, vol 14, no 1, pp 111-35.

Rubin, G. (1984) 'Thinking sex: notes for a radical theory of the politics of sexuality', in C. Vance (ed) *Pleasure and danger: Exploring female sexuality*, Boston/London/ Melbourne/Henley: Routledge and Kegan Paul.

Sanders, T. (2004) 'The risks of street prostitution: punters, police and protesters', *Urban Studies*, vol 41, no 9, pp 1703-17.

Sanghera, J. (2005) 'Unpacking the trafficking discourse', in K. Kempadoo, J. Sanghera and B. Pattanaik (eds) *Trafficking and prostitution reconsidered: New perspectives on migration, sex work, and human rights*, London: Paradigm Publishers.

Scambler, G. (1997) 'Conspicuous and inconspicuous sex work: the neglect of the ordinary and mundane', in G. Scambler and A. Scambler (eds) *Rethinking prostitution: Purchasing sex in the 1990s*, London/New York, NY: Routledge.

Scambler, G. (2007) 'Sex work stigma: opportunist migrants in London', *Sociology*, vol 41, no 6, pp 1079-96.

Scambler, G. and Paoli, F. (2008) 'Health work, female sex workers and HIV/AIDS: global and local dimensions of stigma and deviance as barriers to effective interventions', *Social Science and Medicine*, vol 66, no 8, pp 1848-62.

Scambler, G. and Scambler, A. (1997) 'Afterword', in G. Scambler. and A. Scambler (eds) *Rethinking prostitution: Purchasing sex in the 1990s*, London/New York, NY: Routledge.

Scott, J. (2003) 'Prostitution and public health in New South Wales', *Culture, Health and Sexuality*, vol 5, no 3, pp 277-93.

Sibley, D. (1995) *Geographies of exclusion: Society and difference in the west*, London: Routledge.

Sibley, D. (1998) 'The problematic nature of exclusion', *Geoforum*, vol 29, no 2, pp 119-21.

Simmons, M. (1999) 'Theorizing prostitution: the question of agency', in B. Dank and R. Refinetti (eds) *Sex work and sex workers: Sexuality and Culture vol 2*, London: Transaction Publishers, pp 125-48.

Sullivan, B. (1991) 'Feminist approaches to the sex industry', in S.-A. Gerull and B. Halstead (eds) *Sex Industry and Public Policy*, Canberra: Australian Institute of Criminology.

Sullivan, B. (1999), 'Prostitution law reform in Australia: a preliminary evaluation', *Social Alternatives*, vol 18, no 3, pp 9-14.

Sullivan, B. (2004a) 'Prostitution and consent: beyond the liberal dichotomy of "free or forced"', in M. Cowling and P. Reynolds (eds) *Making sense of sexual consent*, Aldershot: Ashgate.

Sullivan, B. (2004b) 'The women's movement and prostitution politics in Australia', in J. Outshoorn (ed) *The politics of prostitution: Women's movements, democratic states and the globalisation of sex commerce*, Cambridge: Cambridge University Press.

Sullivan, M. (2007) *Making sex work: A failed experiment with legalised prostitution*, Melbourne: Spinifex.

Svanstrom, Y. (2006) 'Prostitution in Sweden: debates and policies 1980-2004', in G. Gangoli and N. Westmarland (eds) *International approaches to prostitution: Law and policy in Europe and Asia*, Bristol: The Policy Press.

SWOP (Sex Workers Outreach Project) (2003) *Unfinished business: Achieving effective regulation of the NSW sex industry*, Chippendale: Sex Workers Outreach Project.

Vanwesenbeeck, I. (2001) 'Another decade of social scientific work on sex work: a review of research 1990-2000', *Annual Review of Sex Research*, vol 12, pp 242-89.

Vanwesenbeeck, I. (2005) 'Burnout among female indoor sex workers', *Archives of Sexual Behavior*, vol 34, no 6, pp 627-39.

Weir, T. (2007) The implementation of occupational health and safety in the New Zealand brothel sector since decriminalisation, *Public Health and General Practice*, Christchurch: University of Otago.

Weitzer, R. (2005) 'Flawed theory and method in studies of prostitution', *Violence Against Women*, vol 11, no 7, pp 934-49.

Weitzer, R. (2007) 'The social construction of sex trafficking: ideology and institutionalization of a moral crusade', *Politics and Society*, vol 35, no 3, pp 447-75.

West, J. (2000) 'Prostitution: collectives and the politics of regulation', *Gender, Work and Organization*, vol 7, no 2, pp 106-18.

Westmarland, N. (2006), 'From the personal to the political: shifting perspectives on street prostitution in England and Wales', in Gangoli, G. and Westmarland, N. (eds.), *International approaches to prostitution: Law and policy in Europe and Asia*, Bristol: The Policy Press.

Whittaker, D. and Hart, G. (1996) 'Research note: managing risks: the social organisation of indoor sex work', *Sociology of Health and Illness*, vol 18, no 3, pp 399-414.

WHO (World Health Organization) (2005) *Violence against women and HIV/ AIDS: Critical intersections*, Information Bulletin Series, No 3, Geneva: WHO.

Part One

Lead-up to the passing of the 2003
Prostitution Reform Act

Of whalers, diggers and 'soiled doves': a history of the sex industry in New Zealand

Jan Jordan[1]

Introduction

While often debated as if it were a contemporary problem reflecting growing social and moral decay, prostitution has a history stretching back to antiquity. Evidence from early Greek and Roman societies suggests that not only was prostitution commonplace but it was also socially and legally accepted for men to buy sex (Bullough and Bullough, 1987; Philip, 1991; Roberts, 1992; Brooks-Gordon and Gelsthorpe, 2003). One of the first examples of the widespread selling of sexual intercourse developed in ancient Athens, in approximately 600 BC, when government-run prostitution businesses were established as a means of financing the expansion of the Greek military (Wells, 1982).

Tolerance for the purchaser, however, has seldom been matched by equal acceptance of those expected to provide commercial sexual services. Instead, the history of prostitution is largely characterised by condemnation and vilification of the 'whore', contrasted with a knowing wink and a nod at her/his clients. The primary legal stance adopted by governments reflected a desire to control and regulate the sex industry rather than seek its eradication (Robinson, 1984; Bullough and Bullough, 1987; Jordan, 2005). This attitude reflected that embraced by many in the early Christian church, who accepted prostitution as a necessary social evil (Tong, 1984). The justification for this view emanated from a belief in men's uncontrollable sexual appetites – driven by lust, it was virtually impossible for all but the most saintly men to remain virgins until marriage, or faithful after it. Individuals were required to provide prostitution services in such a way that men's ability to acquire or maintain wives to be the mothers of their children would not be disrupted. The result was the madonna/whore dichotomy, whereby women were divided and polarised against each other – the good and virtuous women fit to be dutiful wives versus the depraved prostitute (Robinson, 1984; Tong, 1984).

---

[1] The author wishes to thank Stevan Eldred-Grigg for comments on an earlier draft of this paper.

This chapter examines key aspects characterising the history of sex work in New Zealand prior to the passing of the 2003 Prostitution Reform Act (PRA). New Zealand as a country shares many similarities with other settler societies such as Australia and Canada, all of which had established indigenous populations when colonised by British and European nations (Tinker, 1995). Settler development in New Zealand differed in part due to the much smaller physical size of the country, and the nature and levels of contact between early settlers and the Maori population. The colonisation process occurred slightly later and was influenced by the vision held by many for the country to become a 'little Britain', but without the poverty and problems besetting 19th- century England (Tinker, 1995). While Australia became a preferred destination for the transportation of convicts, immigration agents sought to ensure, not always successfully, that the ships headed for New Zealand were filled with immigrants of good character (Macdonald, 1986).

The chapter begins by discussing the impact of colonisation and the attitudes towards prostitution that emerged in the 19th century, using these as a backdrop to consider the more recent influences culminating in the 2003 law change. The focus of this chapter is on women working in the sex industry, while also acknowledging some clients' preferences for male prostitutes. The aim of this chapter is to suggest, through reference to historical ideas and movements, why New Zealand became the first country to decriminalise sex work and how such legislative change is consistent with this particular social and cultural context.

Explorers, whalers and early colonisation

Reference to prostitution as 'the oldest profession' has fuelled an assumption that it has existed in all societies at all times. Such claims to universality have been refuted by evidence suggesting this not to be the case. Writing within the Australian context, for example, Raelene Frances asserts: 'As far as we know, prostitution, in the sense of the exchange of sexual services for goods or money, did not exist in traditional Aboriginal society' (Frances, 1994, p 29).

Activities resembling prostitution did not appear until after the 1670s when Macassar fishermen, who began visiting the shores of northern Australia, demanded access to sexual services and then later became an integral part of the convict colony. A similar pattern was observed in New Zealand, where prostitution was considered unnecessary in pre-colonial Maori society, since men had sexual access to female slaves (Kehoe, 1992) and also because pre-marital sex was accepted among young Maori (Eldred-Grigg, 1984).

From the time of Captain Cook's voyages to New Zealand in 1769, commentators observed the considerable interaction that occurred between Pacific Island women with the sailors who charted Pacific and New Zealand waters (Chappell, 1992). Some commentators remarked that ships' crews had to learn that in New Zealand 'married' Maori women were not sexually available and restrict their approaches to younger or captive women (cited in Kehoe, 1992).

When the French ship, *La Coquille*, visited the Bay of Islands in the 1820s, the naval doctor penned this account of the local prostitution industry:

> Canoes arrived crammed (the word is not too strong) full of women, and our bridge was overrun with swarms of girls; for the seventy-man crew, more than a hundred and fifty samples of this unorthodox merchandise came like a flock of ewes in search of buyers. The captain tried to get rid of this lascivious livestock, but to no avail. (Lesson, cited in Kehoe, 1992, p 109, quoting Sharp, 1971, p 54)

The whalers, sealers and traders who flocked to New Zealand regularly exchanged muskets and other goods for sexual access to Maori women (Donne, 1927; Belich, 1996), with some preferring male partners. One of the most notorious in such exchanges was clergyman William Yate, who allegedly had sexual liaisons with 50-100 Maori boys and men during his mission, including paying one lad, Pehi, a pound of tobacco in exchange for fellatio (Binney, 1975; Eldred-Grigg, 1984).

Trade was particularly brisk in Kororareka (Russell) in the Bay of Islands, which by the 1830s had become the largest whaling port in the southern hemisphere. Edward Markham described in 1834 how 30-35 whaling vessels would:

> … come in for three weeks to the Bay and 400 [to] 500 Sailors requires as many Women, and they have been out [at sea] one year.… These young ladies go off to the Ships, and three weeks on board are spent much to their satisfaction, as they get from the Sailors a Fowling piece [shotgun] for the Father or Brother, Blankets, Gowns etc. (Cited in Belich, 1996, p 152)

The three-week marriages frequently negotiated between these whalers and local women often resulted in the latter bearing tattoos associated with their itinerant lovers. While the sailors would sometimes live ashore, on other occasions the women might stay on the ship for the duration of its stay in New Zealand waters (Belich, 1996). Records from 1840 show over 700 vessels visiting that year alone, each with an average of 30 crewmen seeking rest, recreation and provisioning (Kororareka, New Zealand History online). On shore they met up with Kororareka's other residents, principally men described as 'adventurers, deserters and escaped convicts from Australia' (Kororareka, New Zealand History online) and the town gained a reputation as the 'hell-hole of the Pacific' (King, 2004). Alcohol was plentiful, drunkenness rife, and exotic 'native' women abundant in what have been termed these 'islands of sex in a vast sexless ocean' (Belich, 1996, p 154).

It soon became commonplace in New Zealand seaports for Maori women to provide sexual services to Pakeha[2] men (Eldred-Grigg, 1984; King, 2004) and

---

[2] Pakeha refers to non-indigenous New Zealanders.

some chiefs began organising this practice 'to provide an income for the tribe rather than a bonus for the prostitute' (Eldred-Grigg, 1984, p 30). Chief Pomare, for instance, in the Bay of Islands, was reported to have up to one hundred girls available for this purpose (Donne, 1927). The 'normal price' was reportedly a gun for the tribe plus possibly a dress for the woman (Belich, 1996). These mutual benefits may have been enjoyed by some, but as one historian has pointed out:

> … there was also a grimmer form of the sex industry, which could involve greater male control, multiple partners rather than temporary marriage, a single price (which went to Maori men), 'very little girls' and, increasingly, slavery. (Belich, 1996, p 153)

New Zealand's history of Pakeha interaction with Maori included exploitative and coercive colonising practices along with some elements of respect for diverse social and cultural norms. The Treaty of Waitangi signalled in part a willingness to establish a bicultural national identity. While the subsequent course of Maori/ Pakeha interactions often failed to live up to its principles, both populations had to find ways of living alongside each other, given the lack of land available for indigenous population to retreat or be moved to, as in some other colonies, such as Australia for example.

After 1840, the systematic organisation and enslavement of Maori prostitution ceased (Eldred-Grigg, 1984), but by no means did the demand for prostitution services. In the wake of the sailors and whalers came soldiers and settlers, and prostitution flourished during the early years of colonisation. Edward Gibbon Wakefield, a key developer in colonial New Zealand, had predicted that the unbalanced sex ratio would create a market for prostitution (Jordan, 2005) and the men of the new colony worked hard to prove him right. As towns grew so did the presence of bars and brothels. While some Maori women worked voluntarily and casually as sex workers (Eldred-Grigg, 1984), they were soon outnumbered by the numbers of white immigrant women within the industry, and few accounts of Maori involvement exist beyond this point.

Gold diggers and soiled doves

Considerable debate arose during the 1860s regarding perceptions of the moral quality of the women attracted to New Zealand's shores. Fears were expressed that what the women learned, and earned, on the long ship voyages persuaded some to view prostitution as more appealing than domestic service (Eldred-Grigg, 1984; Macdonald, 1986).

Demand for prostitution services was particularly high on the goldfields when the 'rush' years of the 1850s and 1860s saw an abundance of men, money and alcohol, accompanied by what has been termed their 'travelling "support cast"' (Belich, 1996, p 347). Women followed the gold rushes from California and Canada to Australia and then New Zealand (Eldred-Grigg, 2008), knowing that where there was gold, there were men, and where there were men, there was the equivalent of gold for the prostitutes. The influx of young men to the Otago goldfields during the 1860s, for example, was accompanied by a growing demand for prostitution services, followed by moves to outlaw 'dancing girls' in hotels (Olssen, 1999). By 1864, it was claimed that Dunedin could boast 200 full-time prostitutes (Olssen, 1999), with many brothels congregated in an area called the 'Devil's Half Acre' (Mead, 2001, p 35). Its streets 'thronged with more whores than any other city in the colony. Two hundred were still working its streets full-time even three years after the first strike at Gabriel's Gully' (Eldred-Grigg, 2008, p 388). Some brothel owners obtained liquor licences, while other prostitutes gathered in public bars, and were sometimes provided by publicans with rooms to use with their clients (Eldred-Grigg, 1984). Other brothels existed behind shop-fronts – in Christchurch, for example, brothels were found in the back rooms behind a vegetable shop, an oyster saloon and a lolly shop (Eldred-Grigg, 1984). In Dunedin, the City Buffet was supposedly a coffee shop, but when police called one night they found 'Blanche, a French whore, dancing the cancan' (Eldred-Grigg, 2008, p 390). When they returned a few nights later, they discovered musicians playing while around 25 men were dancing merrily with five sex workers. The brothels were typically run by madams but on the streets many women worked independently, taking clients to alleys, parks and backyards (Eldred-Grigg, 2008).

Towns located near the goldfields also attracted large numbers of sex workers. A parson describing the streets of Hokitika lamented the number of 'gin palaces' and other low establishments, despairing at 'so much ungodliness, to hear oaths and curses on every hand, and to witness so many fallen women pacing the streets' (Haslam, cited in Eldred-Grigg, 2008, p 149).

Such women were paid well and fared considerably better than most servant girls. As one digger wrote: 'We work in wet, cold and misery. All our hard-earned gold goes away to pay for bad grog and finery for the soiled doves' (cited in Eldred-Grigg, 2008, p 388). While some of the women dressed very finely indeed and worked from lavishly decorated establishments, many were attired more shabbily and worked out of 'shanties'. In 1878, a Dunedin newspaper described 'fifty or sixty hovels, or what might better be described as dog kennels', housing 'the lowest class of prostitutes and thieves' (cited in Eldred-Grigg, 2008, p 390).

The tolerance of prostitution was not unique to colonies with unequal sex ratios, but instead reflected more widely held attitudes that viewed it as a complement to marriage (Eldred-Grigg, 1984). Respectable women in Victorian society were told to consider sex disgraceful and distasteful, a duty to be entered into reluctantly and submitted to passively. It has been argued that such an attitude also encouraged married men to visit prostitutes:

> Prostitution was the business partner of marriage throughout the western world in the nineteenth century. Wedded men, together with men not yet wedded, paid for sexual services so willingly that every town had its brothels and nearly every poor or working class household

sent some of its daughters, sisters, nieces or cousins onto the streets to make money by renting out the body. (Eldred-Grigg, 2008, p 387)

Concern about the 'social evil'

As the 19th century progressed, fluctuating waves of settlers made the long journey of emigration to New Zealand and small towns developed. The numbers of European women grew and replicated in part the class structure of the land they left behind. A few married well, living gentrified lives, with many others obtaining employment as their domestic servants. Most sizeable towns throughout the colony had a 'red-light' district by the 1860s (Eldred-Grigg, 1984; Olssen, 1999), with even smaller towns like Invercargill having several known brothels (Belich, 1996).

In Christchurch, Kilmore Sreet was described as 'the headquarters of the most depraved of our female population' (Eldred-Grigg, 1984, p 36), with more discreet brothels operating elsewhere in the city. A police register in 1869 recorded 28 known brothels in Christchurch, while an official survey in Dunedin that same year identified 26 'houses of ill-fame' (Eldred-Grigg, 1984, p 36). Farther north, Te Aro became the centre for Wellington's red-light district, as did Upper Queen Street in Auckland.

The relationship in New Zealand between female immigration and sex work was somewhat paradoxical in that young single women were sought as immigrants to reduce the sex imbalance and improve the men's behaviour, yet were simultaneously blamed for providing prostitution services when they arrived (Eldred-Grigg, 1984; Macdonald, 1986, 1990; Robinson, 1987). Men's indulgence in prostitution was excused through reference to the shortage of women, with this argument turned against the sex workers, who, it was perceived, had abundant options for marriage and respectable employment (Macdonald, 1990). The proliferation of street prostitutes and 'houses of ill-fame' was accompanied by growing anxiety regarding the 'quality' of female immigrants entering the colony. As historian Erik Olssen has observed: 'For many colonists, prostitution and syphilis represented the most degraded Old World ills from which they had fled' (Olssen, 1999, p 47).

By the 1860s, views were often polarised regarding how widespread the 'social evil' had become and what should be done about it (Macdonald, 1986; Robinson, 1983). This polarisation seems to have been influenced more by social class and religious denomination than gender. Maria Rye, the founder of the Female Middle Class Emigration Society, declared the upper attics of the Otago immigration barracks to be 'occupied by a body of women known only to night and evil deeds, women who never have and never intend to go out into service' (cited in Macdonald, 1990, p 175). She had herself become agitated seeing a young woman 'counting out paper money, gold and silver, and there was no moral proof that she had obtained it properly' (cited in Macdonald, 1990, p 175).

By 1867, the newspapers in Christchurch carried a barrage of letters deploring the levels of degradation evident on the streets of the settlement. One writer lamented: 'Almost every shipload of immigrants adds to the number of unfortunate women on our streets; evil example and evil influence are daily doing their deadly work; we have no time to lose' (cited in Macdonald, 1990, p 179).

Local residents sometimes advocated fierce punishments as deterrents – a letter to the newspaper urged:

> If pimps, panders, and prostitutes were informed before landing on these shores that a severe horsewhipping at the cat's tail, and a term of imprisonment with hard labour awaited them if discovered plying their abominable trade, they would give the colony a wide berth, and we should be rid of the social pest. (The Christchurch *Press*, 21 February, 1868)

A public meeting was called in Christchurch to discuss the strong increase in prostitution, 'both as regarded the numbers of women, and the boldness, openness, and defiance of law and decency with which their iniquitous trade was carried on' (Dean Jacobs, 1867, cited in Macdonald, 1990, p 179). Ridding the nation of the social pest did not seem to be the primary goal of this meeting, as most of the men attending accepted the existence of prostitution as inevitable and favoured using legislative means of controlling it. Support was high for a proposal that would require sex workers to be registered and subjected to police supervision and regular medical examination (Macdonald, 1990).

The Contagious Diseases Acts were passed first in Britain in 1864 and later its colonies, including New Zealand, Australia and Canada (Robinson, 1983; Macdonald, 1986; Knight, 1987; Frances, 1994; Lichtenstein, 1997). The impetus for this legislation allegedly arose from growing concerns that Britain's military stature risked being compromised by venereal disease, with the solution being seen as ensuring that prostitutes in the English ports and garrison towns were disease-free (Frances, 1994). Similar legislation was advocated for ports regularly visited by British troopships, although unlike the British legislation, the colonial versions were not restricted to port and military towns.

In New Zealand, however, there was little evidence to suggest that venereal disease was prevalent among imperial troops stationed here, nor even among the European population overall (Eldred-Grigg, 1984). Analysis of the introduction and operation of the Contagious Diseases Act here in 1869 suggests that the motivation arose from a desire by those concerned about high levels of prostitution in the colony to adopt such legislation as a means of introducing an official licensing system. Under this legislation, any girl or woman 'deemed to be a prostitute' risked being subjected to compulsory medical examination and to forcible detention if found to be suffering from a venereal disease (Robinson, 1983; Eldred-Grigg, 1984; Knight, 1987; Macdonald, 1986; Lichtenstein, 1997). It was left to police discretion to ascertain who was a 'common prostitute', with the onus then being placed on the woman to prove she was not, if she objected to being so treated and classified. The legislation also made it an offence for house-owners to let rooms to women known to be common prostitutes who were also suffering from any venereal disease.

Initially in New Zealand, the Act was enforced only in Canterbury, and later for a short time in Auckland (Macdonald, 1990). Unlike in Britain, there were no lock hospitals specifically housing venereal disease patients; instead, patients were housed in prisons – in Christchurch, Addington Prison served as a Female Reformatory under the Contagious Diseases Act until 1886 when such provisions were no longer enforced (Sutch, 1973). The Contagious Diseases Acts came to be identified by many as not only a health measure but also a means of controlling women's, and especially prostitutes', behaviour more generally. The discriminatory nature of the legislation was overlooked by most politicians, with few acknowledging the illogicality of ignoring the health status of the men who presumably infected the sex workers initially (Frances, 1994).

Concern regarding the 'social evil' of prostitution in Canterbury also led to the first of a number of female refuges being established there (Tennant, 1986). Prominent citizens established institutions not only to accommodate burgeoning numbers of illegitimate and unwanted children, but also to provide homes for the rehabilitation of prostitutes (Eldred-Grigg, 1984). To middle-class, Christian idealists, prostitution was considered embarrassing and 'inexcusable' in the new land: 'Because of the lateness of colonisation, New Zealand was supposed to have learnt from the mistakes of other British territories' (Tennant, 1986, p 492).

Control and regulation

The Contagious Diseases Acts were only one of the measures introduced in an attempt to regulate the sex industry. Other New Zealand laws addressing prostitution were also imported from England and reflected a tolerant stance as long as it was conducted in an orderly and well-regulated manner (Robinson, 1983; Eldred-Grigg, 1984). Prostitution itself was not illegal and the offences prostitutes were most likely to risk being arrested for involved vagrancy or drunk and disorderly offences. The earliest legislation derived from the 1824 English Vagrancy Act, which could be invoked against a 'prostitute wandering in the public street or in any place of public resort and behaving in a riotous or indecent manner' (Eldred-Grigg, 1984, p 31). This Act remained in force until New Zealand passed its own 1866 Vagrant Act, which specified that any 'common prostitute' who acted in a 'riotous or disorderly manner' in a public place could be deemed an 'idle and disorderly person' and imprisoned for up to three months (Eldred-Grigg, 1984, p 31). Local governments were responsible for the control of brothels, as in England, where this responsibility fell to municipal and county authorities. Some towns opted for framing their own bylaws, but there was great variability – Auckland, for instance, outlawed brothels in 1854, Timaru acted similarly but not until 1875, and Nelson passed no bylaws at all (Eldred-Grigg, 1984, p 31).

Enforcement of legislation against prostitutes was rigorous at times, particularly from the mid-1860s onwards. In Dunedin, for example, the 1866 Vagrant Act was enforced so strictly that streetwalkers virtually disappeared from city streets completely for a time (Eldred-Grigg, 1984). During the 1870s, more than 3,000 women throughout the colony, most of them prostitutes, were convicted under the Vagrant Act, while some prostitutes were charged with other offences that could result in confinement in prisons or lunatic asylums (Eldred-Grigg, 1984). The predominant aim, however, was not to eradicate prostitution but to keep it orderly, and those operating quietly and discreetly were generally tolerated. The police tended to refrain from arresting those involved in the prostitution industry unless they were operating in a disorderly manner. It has been suggested that such tolerance may have derived from the fact that many officers themselves were clients, with some even running brothels, such as Martin Cash in Christchurch and Sergeant McMyn in Hokitika (Eldred-Grigg, 1984). The Vagrant Act was repealed with the introduction of the 1884 Police Offences Act, which contained provisions relating to 'common prostitutes' soliciting or importuning passers-by.

The dominant state response from the 19th century to today has ambivalently reflected tolerance of prostitution as 'a necessary evil' alongside fears that its existence would corrupt and deprave social mores. The principal way in which states have sought to resolve this tension has been through the politics of control and regulation, with a particular emphasis on minimising the public visibility of prostitutes (Robinson, 1984; Frances, 1994). This resulted in the increasing use of existing laws, such as vagrancy and drunkenness statutes, being applied to prostitutes, as well as the enactment of specific prostitution-related offences. It was primarily working-class prostitutes who attracted police attention and risked such interventions in their lives (Robinson, 1983). In Canterbury, Police Registers of Prostitutes were compiled and submitted to the Commissioner of Police in Wellington. The 1893 register listed the names of 142 prostitutes. Most (n=109) were described as 'quiet' and attracted little attention while the 33 designated as 'rowdy' women typically had numerous convictions for criminal offences (Robinson, 1983, 1984).

By the late 19th century, attitudes towards prostitution began changing. While during the early years of colonial settlement there had been almost complete acceptance that men would seek 'carnal solace in the arms of prostitutes' (Frances, 1994, p 37), such tolerance began to abate, as increasing dissent was voiced regarding the numbers of streetwalkers and bawdy houses plying their trade. Early forms of tourist prostitution were also becoming evident, as increasing numbers of travellers went to see the sights in towns such as Rotorua, a resort condemned for its 'shocking debauchery and reckless expenditure', not to mention its 'gross and shameless immorality' (Spencer, 1892, cited in Eldred-Grigg, 1984, p 31). The involvement of young women in sex work was also of concern in the 1890s, attracting public correspondence and debate. During this debate, for example, a letter writer to a Christchurch newspaper condemned the way in which young girls could be seen 'scampering up and down "the beat", jostling the men, giggling and grossly misbehaving', but declared most of these girls:

> … are not bad girls, are not larrikin girls of the lowest type, are not children of disreputable parents; they are the daughters of respectable parents who, in nine cases out of ten, believe their girls are quietly attending their church or chapel evening service! (*Lyttelton Times*, 6 February, 1892)

Reasons advanced to explain the decreased tolerance reflect the growing social reform emphasis in Protestant societies internationally. The expansion of the middle class and the transformation of urban spaces resulted in increasing numbers of leisured wives and daughters visiting towns to shop and promenade (Frances, 1994). It was not deemed 'proper' for these respectable women to risk being accosted by such downtown 'nuisances' as beggars, drunks and prostitutes, and it was especially unacceptable for 'good women' to be mistakenly perceived and propositioned as whores (Robinson, 1983; Frances, 1994). It was considered shocking that men's earnings were enabling some prostitutes to indulge in the 'high life' – a clergyman in Auckland observed that some of its most 'magnificent houses' were now owned by whores (Eldred-Grigg, 2008). Similarly, in 1885, a Christchurch citizen described encountering loud and lively groups of women at the theatre, 'flaunting their colours with shameless audacity', exciting the curiosity of 'the young of both sexes' and tossing 'their feathers, their paint, their gaudy robes'. He concluded: 'Surely the wages of sin is – prosperity' (cited in Eldred-Grigg, 1984, pp 40-1).

Until now men had dominated debates about prostitution as well as controlling law making and its enforcement. Towards the end of the 19th century, such control was increasingly resisted as the first wave of feminism washed across the land.

Feminist campaigns and women's rights

New Zealand's early colonial status, as we have seen, saw it being strongly influenced in its legislation and attitudes by Britain. The gendered division of labour resulted in men dominating law making and enforcement, while women predominated in the 'social work' domains of refuges and rescue homes (Tennant, 1986). Street prostitutes were identified by reformers and charity workers as women in clear need of 'rescuing', although most failed to recognise this fact in ways synonymous with sex workers' frequent rejection of the 'victim' label today.

While several thousand women in the late 19th century became active in charities and temperance groups, such as the Women's Christian Temperance Union, they realised their opportunities for impact were limited (Dalziel, 1977; Bunkle, 1980). This is in part why the campaign for women's suffrage was fought so rigorously: 'Unable to make headway through their own woman–centred initiatives, they were forced to negotiate access to existing, male-dominated structures' (Tennant, 1986, p 500).

Groups such as the Women's Christian Temperance Union and the National Council of Women condemned prostitutes and barmaids for being the two female groups identified as posing the largest threats to the family unit (Grigg, 1983). A campaign began in earnest to enhance the nation's 'moral purity', one of the goals associated with the women's suffrage movement (Brookes, 1993).

When fears were raised in Britain regarding a white slave traffic, New Zealand feminists were unsure as to the extent to which such a problem existed here, but used the rhetoric of white slavery to support arguments advocating greater social freedom for women (Dalley, 2000). This was evident in feminist efforts to raise the age of consent to 16 years, with supporters maintaining that the current age of 12 linked it to juvenile prostitution and compromised female sexual safety (Brookes, 1993).

Arguments were increasingly made regarding the important role played by women as the moral 'civilisers' of society, a role made even more critical in New Zealand where women were a minority (Dalziel, 1977; Tennant, 1986). One of the arguments advanced in support of women's suffrage revolved around the need to 'civilise' parliament and the moral need for women's representation (Dalziel, 1977). This campaign succeeded in 1893, with New Zealand becoming the first country to enfranchise women. Such success did not, however, bring the substantive shifts desired. While claims based around women's moral and civilising worth may have contributed to their obtaining the right to vote, women's suffrage had little perceptible influence in an environment still reluctant to accept that women belonged in institutions such as the police or parliament (Tennant, 1986). Instead, such claims were turned against an expansion of their roles in favour of relegating them to a moralising influence within the home, breeding and socialising the future Empire.

Prostitution, meanwhile, continued unabated. In 1899, the police in Auckland estimated there to be about 800 prostitutes working 'not merely in the slums of the city, but in the respectable streets too' (cited in Eldred-Grigg, 1984, p 163). Fears were expressed that Queen Street resembled little more than 'a parade for immoral characters'. Pressure was placed, unsuccessfully, on Auckland City Council to introduce a curfew prohibiting standing on the streets, with the Women's Christian Temperance Union hoping this might curb soliciting by young girls.

New Zealand's early history provides an essential back-drop to appreciating the later context leading to the decriminalisation of prostitution in 2003. Key themes evident by the end of the 19th century included a widespread acceptance of prostitution existing as long as this was not blatantly flaunted, with a corresponding justification of enforcement efforts to target its more visible, 'rowdy' face. Health concerns were accepted as a means to legitimate intervention, reflecting historical stereotypes of prostitutes as disease carriers, and some women's groups were expressing growing concerns about the double standards that worked to men's advantage, but at women's expense. Since these attitudes were also apparent in

Australia and Canada, they cannot be argued to be 'unique' or the only factors influencing the New Zealand context. One possibility is that the difference in relationships between the colonisers and the colonised here, as evidenced by the Treaty of Waitangi, contributed to the development of a stronger human rights focus, although this should not be over-stated, given the multiple ways in which Maori were subsequently discriminated against and exploited.

The sex industry in the 20th century

Throughout much of the 20th century, there was a pretence regarding the availability and use of commercial sexual services. No longer did there seem to be an acceptable reason for their existence, the exceptions being during times of war. Indeed, anxieties concerning prostitution became pronounced during the First World War, with New Zealand health campaigner Ettie Rout becoming well known for her efforts to combat venereal disease in Kiwi soldiers serving in Africa and Europe (O'Connor, 1967; Tolerton, 1992). By 1922, however, sex work seems to have dwindled; the police claimed they knew of only 104 professional prostitutes within the entire country and a Board of Health committee said there remained 'little evidence of a definite prostitute class in New Zealand' (Eldred-Grigg, 1984, p 164). The 'invasion' of American servicemen during World War Two, however, saw anxieties rise again as the troops eagerly included New Zealand women in their 'rest and recuperation' activities, and concerns about venereal disease and the morality of 'good time girls' resurfaced (Jordan, 2005).

From the 1920s to the 1960s, the social veneer was dominated by smiling, suburban happy families, with scant recognition that a prostitution industry even existed, although the high-profile Auckland parlour run by Flora McKenzie seems to have flourished during this period (Jordan, 2000). Considerable concern was expressed at times regarding 'youth' immorality, manifest in the controversial Mazengarb Report (Jordan, 2005), with the primary focus of this being the presumed sexual activity of young women. Awareness of the 'ship girls' phenomenon also attracted moral condemnation in port cities, where sailors were only too willing to entertain female visitors on board ship, establish temporary relationships with them on land, or provide 'free passage' in exchange for sexual favours (Jordan, 1994). In the 1950s and 1960s, in particular, many young women, particularly young Maori women, were sent to borstal institutions in the hopes of reforming them (Templeton, 1981; Jordan, 1994).

During these debates, the clients remained virtually invisible. Little attention was given to the demand side of prostitution, and what social condemnation there was largely centred on the providers of such services. This was consistent with a view of men as weak when it came to sexual matters, easily tempted by lust and vulnerable to seductive female charms. Corseting the women seemed the best strategy.

The sex industry continued to be characterised by class dimensions, both in terms of the majority of those entering prostitution being drawn from poorer socioeconomic groups as well as these groups being the ones to bear the brunt of legislative interventions and controls. Women from the middle classes have often been able to work in more discreet settings, from more exclusive brothels or as higher-class escorts and call-girls. The public face of prostitution continued to be the street scene, which became increasingly dominated in the 1960s and 1970s by transgender sex workers, most notable of whom was Carmen (Carmen, 1988). Sex work was viewed as one of the few occupations available to transgender persons at the time, many of whom identified as Maori takataapui (referring to intimate friends of the same sex) or fa'afafine, a Samoan word meaning 'way of women' (Worth, 2003).

Rising concerns regarding drugs as a social problem ignited fears of crime being rampant behind the closed doors of brothels, and was a key factor underlying the 1978 Massage Parlours Act (Robinson, 1987). Under this legislation, a massage parlour (the euphemism for a brothel) was deemed a public place, meaning that undercover police could pose as clients and arrest a sex worker for soliciting in a public place. A conviction was grounds for preventing her from working in a massage parlour for 10 years, yet also meant she now had a criminal record for prostitution that would detrimentally affect her ability to obtain other employment. For some, this meant that the only option was to work on the streets, an environment where the risk of violence and exploitation was even greater.

The women's rights and gay liberation movements of the 1970s began drawing public attention to the prevailing double standard of morality and to abuses of human rights, but as support for these issues grew, a new spectre appeared on the horizon – HIV/AIDS. Sex workers and gay males found themselves at the centre of another moral panic, blamed and scapegoated once more as disease carriers threatening society's health and stability (Robinson and Kehoe, 1989; McKeganey and Barnard, 1994; Janssen, 1997). In New Zealand, few cases of HIV transmission were linked to sex workers. What became significant here, however, was that public health fears were effectively transformed into a campaign supporting sex workers' rights. This illustrates well an observation made in the Australian context that not all changes in prostitution can be attributed to state intervention, since 'the State does not simply apply its policies to a passive prostitution industry' (Frances, 1994, pp 47-8).

To ensure their economic and social survival, sex workers have often resisted or found ways of managing the attempts to control their lives. This occurred more at the individual or informal level until the relatively recent proliferation of sex workers' collectives and alliances, including the New Zealand Prostitutes' Collective (Jordan, 1993). Its formation in 1987 at the height of the AIDS scare helped to secure Ministry of Health recognition and funding. The collective quickly built a strong national profile and attracted a broad base of support for law reform measures aimed at reducing the stigmatisation and penalising of sex workers. Feminist analyses of the oppression of women highlighted the double standard that existed regarding the sex industry (Robinson, 1987; Jordan, 1992; Sullivan, 1994). Outrage grew over the fact that prostitution was regarded as an immoral female activity, not an immoral male activity, even though the women existed as service providers to meet men's sexual demands. The campaign for decriminalisation garnered support from a diverse range of groups, including some with relatively conservative credentials, such as the National Council of Women, the Business and Professional Women's Federation and the Young Women's Christian Association (YWCA). In explaining the group's stance, the YWCAs Executive Director asserted:

> The law is structured so that it acknowledges that the act of prostitution occurs, but ensures that it occurs only on the clients' terms. It labels sex workers as the criminals and their customers as victims.... Allowing women to work without fear of prosecution would at least help provide a safer working environment. (Keenan, 1996)

Another factor that may have aided the campaign was that sex workers in New Zealand were generally not a highly criminalised group. The arrests of sex workers in New Zealand were low in number, with few being imprisoned for prostitution-related offences. Nor did New Zealand have the kerb-crawling legislation that brought the street sector under such stringent scrutiny in countries such as England. The relative tolerance evident here may have been extended by a growing awareness of the social and economic factors underlying women's involvement in the sex industry. There was a willingness, in some sectors at least, to acknowledge and understand those aspects of society seen as less desirable. When the book *Working girls* was published in 1991 (Jordan, 1991), invitations came from all over the country, even the deep conservative south, to have public talks to raise awareness – even if these were occasionally accompanied by protests. Similarly, Lions and Rotary groups frequently requested breakfast and after-dinner talks on prostitution that provided a consciousness-raising platform regarding the desirability of law reform.

   Changes in public attitudes and practices have become evident in other ways also. In the 19th century, prostitutes existed to provide sexual services that men could not obtain easily elsewhere. When few women were available to a large population of single men, the demand for straightforward sexual access was strong. This was especially so given social mores among many groups condemning premarital sex, and at a time when women, both married and unmarried, feared pregnancy. More recently, better contraceptive devices and more relaxed sexual mores have enabled many men to find willing sexual partners outside of prostitution, with some turning to the sex industry only when temporarily away from home – for example, miners, oil riggers and servicemen, or men on sports or business trips. Others may approach sex workers seeking more 'kinky' or bizarre forms of sex, informed on occasion by ideas fuelled by pornography. Such changes can potentially place unwelcome pressures on some sex workers to engage in ever more extreme behaviours (Frances, 1994), although interestingly most still maintain a certain boring familiarity to the practices requested (Jordan, 1991).

As early as 1996 it was reported that:

> The mood within Parliament appears to be shifting in favour of full legalisation of prostitution [with] Justice Minister Doug Graham, one of the more socially conservative National ministers [saying] it was time to consider making soliciting legal … 'I don't think it's terribly satisfactory to have a law where a man who offers money commits no offence, while a woman who offers her services does commit an offence.' (Laugesen, 1996)

What all of this suggests is a growing acceptance in New Zealand of the inevitability of prostitution, combined with a pragmatic human rights-based approach to its existence. This underlying stance was brought into the public domain by a diverse range of groups and individuals intent on legislative reform. Included among these were feminists and other women's organisations, politicians and academics, all of whom helped to bolster the arguments for change advanced by the New Zealand Prostitutes' Collective.

Why the PRA? Why here? Why now?

What this chapter is suggesting is that there are links between the early development of prostitution and the acceptance of its role in the new colony with later attitudes that enabled a more human rights-based approach to its legislative status. Many New Zealand women in the 19th century were not as corseted as their Victorian counterparts in England, physically or socially. Pioneer women had to work alongside men to establish homes, gardens and farms in what must often have felt like a hostile landscape.

The ways in which prostitution developed here may also have promoted a greater tolerance of its existence, since evidence of some of the most feared aspects seen overseas have been largely absent from the local context. For example, large-scale pimping has not been a feature of the New Zealand sex industry, nor has much evidence been uncovered of extensive police corruption, links with organised crime rings or widespread trafficking (PLRC, 2008).

The country's small population size saw the sex industry located primarily in a few key centres and lacking the extremes of coercion and exploitation evidenced in many Western metropolitan locations. While most countries tolerated prostitution, New Zealand's early history saw its widespread acceptance, with even the later debates surrounding it not resulting in legislation or steps to suppress its existence entirely. Although concerns were raised at times regarding the visibility of those working on the streets, the numbers involved throughout the 20th century were small and relatively discreet compared with the large street sectors often apparent elsewhere.

International moves supporting women's rights had strong uptake in New Zealand, where second-wave feminists sought to build on their 19th-century sisters' earlier achievements. The women's movement in New Zealand was particularly effective in securing greater recognition for the worth and value of women's work, as well as fundamentally challenging what was viewed as 'women's work'. Recent years have seen women occupying the roles of Prime Minister, Governor General and Chief Justice as well as an increasing number of chief executive roles and Cabinet positions. One of the first politicians to support prostitution law reform was the woman MP, Katherine O'Regan (Tyler, 1997), and the campaign drew support from a diverse range of women's and community groups. Much of the campaign centred around the need to end the double standard that discriminated against sex workers, as well as the desirability of adopting a harm-minimisation approach. During the debates preceding the law change, Labour MP Tim Barnett, the sponsor of the Bill, argued in an article entitled 'Outmoded ethics let evil thrive':

> The Prostitution Reform Bill is unashamedly a decriminalisation measure. It removes the blanket bans on activities around prostitution that are not of themselves harmful (brothel-keeping, procuring), and replaces them with clearer and tougher law concerning the real evils (sex with an under-age prostitute, coercion of a sex worker). (Barnett, 2003)

One effect of the broadening tolerance and recognition of human diversity in 1990s New Zealand was a reduction in the use and power of the 'deviance' label. Sex workers, though still stigmatised, were increasingly viewed as normal women even if they were doing what may still have been seen as a deviant job. Their clients also came to be viewed less censoriously. Interviews with sex workers, and accounts published documenting their lives, have revealed varying and often understandable reasons for their entry into sex work (Jordan, 1991; Perkins, 1991; Hanson, 1996; Langdon, 2001). These have also suggested that the women themselves come from diverse backgrounds and hold divergent attitudes towards their work, in ways that make it impossible to sustain any narrow representations of sex workers only being viewable as pitiful, coerced victims. This is not to suggest an absence of coercion and exploitation within the sex industry, but does indicate a respect for the ways in which sex workers themselves articulate their own employment context and develop their own ways of surviving within it. This perception of sex work has undoubtedly been strengthened by the high-profile and measured stance consistently advanced by the New Zealand Prostitutes' Collective.

Increasing concern was expressed during the 1990s regarding the ways in which the existing legal situation exacerbated the risks of violence. The law's negative attitudes reinforced the stigma of prostitution while also reducing the likelihood of sex workers informing the police about victimising incidents or individuals. Soon after it was reported that in the month of October 1996 three Auckland sex workers had been murdered and three Christchurch sex workers raped, there were calls for prostitution to be decriminalised in order to improve the safety of their working environment (Keenan, 1996). Arguments regarding alternative legal responses, such as criminalising the clients, gathered relatively little traction here, where the dominant message articulated by those seeking reform was to ensure that any measures introduced reduced sex worker vulnerability and recognised their rights to respect and safety.

Where most objections to the pre-PRA system lay was in relation to how it discriminated against the sex worker while simultaneously protecting men's access to commercial sexual services. She bore all of the blame and penalties, and these were penalties that worked often to entrench and consolidate her in a life of prostitution. A prostitution-related conviction could bring in its wake devastating impacts on future employment, travel and financial options. Accordingly, much of the feminist argument supporting decriminalisation was linked to a desire to reduce the pressures on women to stay working in prostitution and increase their options for exiting the sex industry – if they wanted to. Also of concern was a desire to end the pretence and acknowledge the existence of the industry in ways that would make it more open and transparent – bringing the sex industry out of hiding was seen as a means of enabling more open discussion, for example, around health initiatives and promoting sex workers' safety. The hypocrisy of seizing condoms to use against sex workers as evidence of their involvement in prostitution was recognised by many (Keenan, 1996), along with the dangers of retaining police powers of arrest against women at risk of violence.

A sex worker articulated well her vision for a decriminalised sex industry when she passionately argued to the Select Committee considering law reform:

> I want to be a sex worker, I don't want to be a criminal, and I don't deserve to be. I work in a demand driven industry. Without clients there would be no workers. We are not predators. I sit in a secured building and clients choose to come and see me. When you are thinking about the industry, it's not something 'over there', to do with a whole sector of society cut off from everyone else. What we are talking about is my life, and the lives of a whole lot of women and men in this society. It's often hard enough dealing with the social stigma of being a sex worker, please don't leave us to be criminals any longer. I'm not asking any of you to condone sex work, or believe that what I do is OK, I'm just asking for the full human rights that this Bill would give us. (PRB 107A, 2001, p 6)

The backdrop of social attitudes supporting human and women's rights was in place, the stage was set for greater appreciation of diversity and recognition of difference and key actors took their positions on cue, pressing for the necessary changes to be made. The coming together of all these factors enabled the relatively brave step of decriminalisation to be taken – and the rest, as they say, is history.

References

Barnett, T. (2003) 'Outmoded ethics let evil thrive', *New Zealand Herald*, 25 June.

Belich, J. (1996) *Making peoples: A history of the New Zealanders. From Polynesian settlement to the end of the nineteenth century*, Auckland: Allen Lane/Penguin Books.

Binney, J. (1975) 'Whatever happened to poor Mr Yate? An exercise in voyeurism', *New Zealand Journal of History*, vol 9, no 2, pp 111-25.

Brookes, B. (1993) 'A weakness for strong subjects: the women's movement and sexuality', *New Zealand Journal of History*, vol 27, no 2, pp 140-56.

Brooks-Gordon, B. and Gelsthorpe, L. (2003) 'Prostitutes' clients, Ken Livingstone and a new Trojan horse', *The Howard Journal*, vol 42, no 5, pp 437-51.

Bullough, V. and B. Bullough (1987) *Women and prostitution: A social history*, New York, NY: Prometheus Books.

Bunkle, P. (1980) 'The origins of the women's movement in New Zealand: the Women's Christian Temperance Union in 1885 and 1895', in P. Bunkle and B.

Hughes (eds) *Women in New Zealand Society*, Sydney: George Allen and Unwin, pp 54-62.

Carmen (1988) *My life (as told to Paul Martin)*, Auckland: Benton Ross.

Chappell, D.A. (1992) 'Shipboard relations between Pacific Island women and Euroamerican man 1767-1887', *Journal of Pacific History*, vol 27, no 2, pp 131-49.

Dalley, B. (2000) '"Fresh attractions": White slavery and feminism in New Zealand, 1885-1918', *Women's History Review*, vol 9, no 3, pp 585-606.

Dalziel, R. (1977) 'The colonial helpmeet: women's role and the vote in nineteenth-century New Zealand', *New Zealand Journal of History*, vol 11, no 2, pp 112-23.

Donne, T.E. (1927) *The Maori, past and present*, London: Sealey Service.

Eldred-Grigg, S. (1984) *Pleasures of the flesh: Sex and drugs in colonial New Zealand 1840-1915*, Wellington: A.H. and A.W. Reed.

Eldred-Grigg, S. (2008) *Diggers, hatters and whores: The story of the New Zealand gold rushes*, Auckland: Random House New Zealand.

Frances, R. (1994) 'The history of female prostitution in Australia', in R. Perkins et al (eds) *Sex work and sex workers in Australia*, Sydney: University of New South Wales Press, pp 27-52.

Grigg, A.R. (1983) 'Prohibition and women: the preservation of an ideal and a myth', *New Zealand Journal of History*, vol 17, no 2, pp 144-65.

Hanson, J. (1996) 'Learning to be a prostitute: education and training in the New Zealand sex industry', *Women's Studies Journal*, vol 12, no 2, pp 77-85.

Janssen, K. (1997) 'In it for the money: the social stereotype versus the reality of sex work in New Zealand', BA Thesis, Dunedin: University of Otago.

Jordan, J. (1991) *Working girls: Women in the New Zealand sex industry*, Auckland: Penguin Books.

Jordan, J. (1992) 'Feminism and sex work: connections and contradictions', in R.D. Plessis (ed) *Feminist voices: Women's studies texts for Aotearoa/New Zealand*, Auckland: Oxford University Press, pp 180-96.

Jordan, J. (1993) 'New Zealand Prostitutes' Collective', in A. Else (ed) *Women together: A history of women's organisations in New Zealand*, Wellington: Daphne Brassell Press.

Jordan, J. (1994) *Ship girls: The invisible women of the sea*, Institute of Criminology Occasional Paper Series no 2, Wellington: Institute of Criminology, Victoria University of Wellington.

Jordan, J. (2000) 'Flora McKenzie', in C. Orange (ed) *The Dictionary of New Zealand Biography, Volume Five, 1941-1960*, Auckland: Auckland University Press.

Jordan, J. (2005) *The sex industry in New Zealand: A literature review*, Wellington: Ministry of Justice.

Keenan, D. (1996) 'YWCA backs Prostitutes' Collective', *The Press*, 31 October (2nd edn), p 4.

Kehoe, J.M. (1992) 'Medicine, sexuality and imperialism: British medical discourses surrounding venereal disease in New Zealand and Japan: a socio-historical and comparative study', PhD Thesis, Wellington: Victoria University of Wellington.

King, M. (2004) *The Penguin history of New Zealand*, Auckland: Viking.

Knight, A. (1987) 'Prostitution and the law', *Race, Gender, Class*, vol 5, pp 57-70.

Kororareka, New Zealand History online, New Zealand Ministry for Culture and Heritage, www.nzhistory.net.nz/culture/missionaries/kororareka

Langdon, C. (2001) 'Sex, guys and law reform', *The Dominion*, 5 May (2nd edn), p 2.

Laugesen, R. (1996) 'Mood favours change in prostitution laws', *The Dominion*, 28 June (2nd edn), p 2.

Lichtenstein, B. (1997) 'Tradition and experiment in New Zealand AIDS policy', *AIDS and Public Policy Journal*, vol 12, no 2, pp 79-88.

Macdonald, C. (1986) 'The "social evil": prostitution and the passage of the Contagious Diseases Act (1869)', in C. Macdonald, M. Tennant and B. Brookes (eds) *Women in history: Essays on European women in New Zealand*, Wellington: Allen and Unwin/Port Nicholson Press.

Macdonald, C. (1990) *A woman of good character: Single women as immigrant settlers in nineteenth-century New Zealand*, Wellington: Allen and Unwin/Historical Branch.

McKeganey, N. and Barnard, M. (1994) *Sex work on the streets: Prostitutes and their clients*, Philadelphia, PA: Open University Press.

Mead, K. (2001) 'Sex workers challenging stereotypes: a case study in Dunedin, New Zealand', MA Thesis, Dunedin, University of Otago.

O'Connor, P.S. (1967) 'Venus and the lonely Kiwi: the war effort of Miss Ettie A. Rout', *New Zealand Journal of History*, vol 1, no 1, pp 1-32.

Olssen, E. (1999) 'Families and the gendering of European New Zealand in the colonial period, 1840-80', in C. Daley and D. Montgomery (eds) *The gendered Kiwi*, Auckland: Auckland University Press.

Perkins, R. (1991) *Working girls: Prostitutes, their life and social control*, Canberra: Australian Institute of Criminology.

Philip, N. (1991) *Working girls: An illustrated history of the oldest profession*, London: Bloomsbury.

PLRC (Prostitution Law Review Committee) (2008) *Report of the Prostitution Law Review Committee on the operation of the Prostitution Reform Act 2003*, Wellington: Ministry of Justice, www.justice.govt.nz/prostitution-law-review-committee/publications/plrc-report/index.html

Roberts, N. (1992) *Whores in history: Prostitution in western society*, London: Harper Collins.

Robinson, J. (1983) '"Of diverse persons, men and women and whores": women and Crime in nineteenth century Canterbury', MA Thesis, Christchurch: University of Canterbury.

Robinson, J. (1984) 'Canterbury's rowdy women: whores, madonnas and female criminality', *Women's Studies Journal*, vol 1, no 1, pp 6-25.

Robinson, J. (1987) 'The oldest profession', in S. Cox (ed) *Public and private worlds: Women in contemporary New Zealand*, Wellington: Allen and Unwin/Port Nicholson Press, pp 177-191.

Robinson, J. and Kehoe, J. (1989) *Regulation and resistance: Disease, sexuality and social control*, paper presented at Women's Studies Association Conference, Wellington: Women's Studies Association.

Sullivan, B. (1994) 'Feminism and female prostitution', in R. Perkins, G. Prestage, R. Sharp and F. Lovejoy (eds) *Sex work and sex workers in Australia*, Sydney: University of New South Wales Press.

Sutch, W.B. (1973) *Women with a cause*, Wellington: New Zealand University Press.

Templeton, C. (1981) *Pillpopper: Live and die*, Martinborough: Alister Taylor.

Tennant, M. (1986) '"Magdalens and moral imbeciles": women's homes in nineteenth-century New Zealand', *Women's Studies International Forum*, vol 9, no 5, pp 491-502.

Tinker, H. (1995) 'The British colonies of settlement', in R. Cohen (ed) *The Cambridge Survey of World Migration*, Cambridge: Cambridge University Press.

Tolerton, J. (1992) *Ettie: A life of Ettie Rout*, Auckland: Penguin Books.

Tong, R. (1984) *Women, sex and the law*, Savage, MD: Rowman and Littlefield Publishers.

Tyler, V. (1997) 'Sex for sale – legally', *Sunday News*, 20 April (1st edn), p 8.

Wells, J. (1982) *A herstory of prostitution in western Europe*, Berkeley, CA: Shameless Hussy Press.

Worth, H. (2003) *Gay men, sex and HIV in New Zealand*, Palmerston North: Dunmore Press.

Submissions to Justice and Electoral Select Committee on 2001 Prostitution Reform Bill

PRB/107A Private submission

THREE

History of the New Zealand Prostitutes' Collective

Catherine Healy, Calum Bennachie and Anna Reed

Introduction

This chapter describes the history of the New Zealand Prostitutes' Collective (NZPC), tracking the collective's efforts, since its formation, to confront social stigma and overturn legislation that had a negative impact on the lives of sex workers in New Zealand. The chapter begins with a brief outline of the socio-political context in which the NZPC emerged in the late 1980s, before describing the ways in which the collective built support for decriminalising sex work in New Zealand.

Background

Most activities related to sex work at the time of NZPC's inception were illegal and most female sex workers worked disguised as 'masseuses' in massage parlours. In 1978, the Massage Parlours Act (MPA) was introduced to regulate the operation of licensed massage parlours. Under the MPA, massage parlour operators were required to hold licenses and were prohibited from employing individuals with drug- or prostitution-related convictions. The MPA also required that all employees' details be recorded and available for inspection by police at any time. The police visited massage parlours regularly to uplift the names of 'masseuses' working there and check that they had no drug or prostitution convictions that would prevent them from working in a parlour.

Smaller numbers of sex workers worked for themselves, either on the street, from home, on the ports through known bars, or as escorts in escort agencies. Undercover police regularly masqueraded as clients in massage parlours and on the street, typically encouraging sex workers to offer sex for money, as a strategy to arrest them for soliciting. The police would also record the names and other personal information of sex workers, which would be held on a police database of 'Known Prostitutes'. While police claimed they did this to teach a lesson to massage parlour licence holders who were 'too soft' and did not keep 'their girls' in line, this had a big impact on not only the lives of those sex workers who were arrested, but also on the lives of those who were working with them.

The police would also round up sex workers on the streets and process them through the courts where they would be convicted of 'soliciting for the purposes of prostitution in a public place' under section 26 of the 1981 Summary Offences Act. Such a conviction would lead to a $200 fine, which the police considered insignificant. Those working in massage parlours lost their jobs and were prohibited from operating from these venues for 10 years. They couldn't stop working completely, as they still had their fines to pay, but, overnight, their options were reduced and they had to find other areas in which to work as sex workers. Some were forced to work in areas where they were not as confident, as escorts, for example, or on unfamiliar streets away from their usual area. Such arrests and court appearances would usually attract media attention and names would be well reported in the daily newspapers. A conviction would therefore have a major effect on the lives of those prosecuted. It would sit on their record, acting as a barrier to some types of employment outside sex work, and for those who did succeed in finding alternative employment, it would be like a sword of Damocles hanging over their heads, which if discovered, could result in dismissal.

In 1987, a group of nine Wellington women working in massage parlours met to discuss forming an organisation to represent sex workers in New Zealand. Soon after, they connected with other sex workers, including those working on the streets and as escorts. Women, transgendered and male sex workers were all part of the mix. There was outrage over the laws prohibiting most sex work-related activities, which usually targeted people because they were sex workers. At this time, sex workers were frustrated with the negative perceptions people held of them and the frequent misrepresentations of their lives, depicting them as a homogenous group and portraying them as a reservoir of disease, out of control of their lives and irresponsible. There were also concerns that managers of some massage parlours and escort agencies were treating their staff unfairly through arbitrary and unfair management practices and that, as sex workers, they had no legal rights to protect them in their work. In addition, the founding members of NZPC were keen to organise themselves to prevent the spread of HIV and AIDS in the sex industry. They wanted sex workers' voices to be heard and for them to inform the discourses that framed their work and lives. In October of 1988, the group received funding from the New Zealand Minister of Health and opened a drop-in centre in Wellington for all sex workers. The New Zealand Prostitutes' Collective (NZPC) was officially under way.

Becoming a government-funded organisation

In the beginning, NZPC resisted the formality of things such as group registration and membership lists because it wanted to create a more fluid movement that people could move in and out of easily. These kinds of formalities were seen as barriers to becoming part of a move for change, as many sex workers were reluctant to be formally identified as such. A flat structure was preferred where everyone would have a part to play and the idea of having formal meetings did not initially appeal to the group. It utilised everyday social events – in people's homes, on the beach or in the pub – as fora in which to discuss its actions and ideas (Jordan, 1991, pp 271-4).

At the time of NZPC's formation, the term 'sex worker' was only just beginning to gain some currency, and the word 'prostitute' was heavily stigmatised. Although it seemed many people were uncomfortable with the word 'prostitute', the group deliberately chose to call itself the New Zealand Prostitutes' Collective in order to confront the stigma attached to it. It wanted to avoid an acronym that glossed over people's identity as sex workers. Another reason for using the word 'prostitute' in the title was to express solidarity with other sex worker collectives around the world, such as the Prostitutes' Collective of Victoria (PCV) in Australia and the English Collective of Prostitutes. The PCV was particularly valuable in providing cultural clues on how best to go about forming a similar collective in New Zealand.

Shortly after the group had started meeting in 1987, an official from the Department of Health – who had heard about it via personal connections – contacted it and asked to meet up. The group agreed because it was curious about officials' response to sex workers. There was a feeling that the health department was a more benign government agency than the ones sex workers were used to, that is, the police and the justice system. Meeting with the health officials enabled the group to talk very frankly about the issues and realities sex workers faced in the course of their sex work. The sex workers felt that they would have been unable to do this with other government agencies at that time and would normally have kept silent about these issues as they feared repercussions, such as being arrested or having their children removed from their care.

The Department of Health wanted NZPC to run an HIV prevention programme in the sex industry and invited the group to submit a proposal outlining how it planned to undertake this. The group was pleased, yet challenged, when this request was made, although there was a debate within the organisation about receiving government funding at the risk of losing its autonomy to express its thoughts. However, it also realised that this was a good opportunity for it to make its case for change, and to demonstrate sex workers' responsibility and role as participants in society. It was very important for sex workers to run these programmes in their own way and to ensure that they remained relevant and were sex worker-driven. The group was keen to avoid an overly rigid approach and being controlled by a government agency. It wanted sex worker cultures to complement these prevention programmes.

Around this time, NZPC also started producing a magazine entitled *Sex Industry Rights Education Network (SIREN)*, which was distributed to sex workers everywhere. The first edition contained an introductory letter that urged sex workers to contribute (Healy, 1988). It was important to bring a voice to sex workers in all sectors of the sex industry, as many were quite isolated and did not encounter each other. In an editorial in *SIREN*, the national co-ordinator noted:

> The government is following trends in funding groups like ours and has come to us for assistance. The Collective is run on voluntary labour from within the industry. Therefore it has an immediate advantage over the salaried social workers who would be working from the outside. (Healy, 1988)

NZPC agreed that it would be a good idea to work with the Department of Health towards preventing HIV in the sex industry. While the collective knew of no cases of HIV affecting sex workers or their clients, it had heard of cases among the general population in New Zealand and felt this was an issue that needed to be addressed. The collective also felt that, as sex workers, their practical knowledge of safe-sex strategies was superior to that of other sexually active people and that they could, therefore, help educate people about this.

A lot of things started to happen around this time. The group expanded by involving other sex workers around the country, visiting them in their places of work – in massage parlours, on the street, in strip clubs, and in bars where sex workers would meet after work. They also informed the vice police in Wellington that they were 'coming out' as sex workers and forming an organisation and explained the importance of doing so in the context of HIV prevention. These local vice officers were immediately supportive, although subsequent squads were not.

When the funding came through in 1988, the collective's contract with the Ministry of Health enabled it, initially for the sum of NZ$50,000 per annum, to provide a national programme with the following components:

• to form community drop-in centres in which sex workers could meet away from their workplaces to support each other and exchange ideas, including ideas about strategies for safe sex;
• to produce and disseminate a regular magazine in which safe sex issues were included, as well as other issues of importance to sex workers;
• to strengthen the social networks between sex workers throughout New Zealand, in order to connect sex workers to each other to build peer support; and
• to operate a condom distribution programme nationwide (Chetwynd, 1991, p 3).

The collective's first community base opened in Wellington and the group organised a meeting with the New Zealand AIDS Foundation (a solid ally), the vice police and parlour owners, to voice its ideas about HIV prevention within the sex industry. It realised that it needed to work through these gatekeepers to facilitate contact with sex workers and to realise its prevention message. It was possibly the first time that police, parlour owners and sex workers had sat in the one room and discussed sex work openly and without legal conflict. As one of the founding members recently reflected about this time: "At last, as sex workers, we felt we had the strength to take any system on". It is important to note that at this time that the Department of Health had not discussed the role of NZPC and its peer education HIV prevention programme with the police at any level and had left it to the collective to manage these relationships.

Expansion

Shortly after opening its first community base in Wellington, NZPC opened a branch in Auckland, initially sharing premises with an existing needle exchange but later moving to its own autonomous premises. In the development of subsequent community bases, NZPC implemented its own needle exchange programmes. These community bases were where sex workers could come and meet with each other, exchange ideas and information and receive peer support. While some members of the group encountered some negative discrimination, there was also a lot of support from across the board (*Bay of Plenty Times*, 1995, p 3).

NZPC soon encompassed a variety of sex workers and a number of groups began to emerge with their own identities. For example, the Maori Action Group was formed, comprising sex workers from all genders who were Maori. Transgendered sex workers formed a group called Ongoing Network Transgender Outreach Project (ONTOP), and there was an attempt to establish this as an autonomous group from NZPC. Another premise was opened for this group to be self-managing, although police soon requested that this be shut down, as it was thought to be a brothel in which street-based sex workers took their clients. This attempt to be autonomous was thus short-lived, and today ONTOP is again part of the NZPC.

Pride and Unity for Male Prostitutes (PUMP) was formed for male sex workers. Male sex workers generally worked privately and were stigmatised, both for being homosexual and, within the gay community, for being sex workers. As a result, male sex workers were often very isolated from each other, and there were few networks connecting the male sex worker community. Furthermore, much of the information for male sex workers was gay-focused, which excluded those who were not 'out', those who were marginalised by the gay community, such as gay sex workers, and those who did not identify as being gay and did not have any other affiliation with gay organisations.

Groups of male sex workers who were already part of the NZPC decided to start contacting other men they knew were working, to provide support and education, particularly to men who were working privately and who did not necessarily know other men who were working. People met predominantly via word of mouth and through talking to people involved with the New Zealand AIDS Foundation and gay organisations. The New Zealand AIDS Foundation was very focused on gay men at this time. PUMP wanted to deal with issues that were specific to male sex workers, the vast majority of whom worked with male clients, even if they identified as heterosexual.

The lack of formality with which the NZPC operated meant that sex workers were comfortable bringing friends and other sex workers in to the drop-in centres. Thus, groups grew quickly by word of mouth and there was a lot of overlap between the different sex worker networks. PUMP and all other separate groups were always a part of NZPC and no additional funding was obtained to run them because the NZPC's mandate was to engage sex workers of all genders and ethnicities. Having a diversity of identities under a unified organisation strengthens the NZPC. NZPC is therefore a collective of collectives.

Reactions from within the industry

There were initial pockets of resistance to *SIREN* magazine and also to NZPC as a whole. Some parlour owners banned their staff from reading *SIREN*, commenting that they did not need to 'worry their pretty little heads' about things like that. Some controlling and coercive operators forbade their staff to have contact with the NZPC because they did not want their mistreatment of staff to be challenged. Other parlour owners and operators were cautious about being associated with sex work out of fear of being prosecuted for brothel keeping.

Many parlour owners were also wary of sex workers organising themselves into a force that could be reckoned with and gaining more control in their work environment, although others would claim that the NZPC was their representative too and would encourage the collective's advocacy for their legal rights as well. All of this in fact encouraged sex workers to come to the NZPC community bases to seek out information. NZPC did not call itself a union, but recognised that some of its beliefs and actions were very similar to that of a union.

The reaction from sex workers themselves was generally very favourable. Sex workers were well connected with each other within the sector in which they worked, and the sense of community within the industry meant that the workers involved in organising NZPC and those involved as peer educators were mostly known and trusted within the respective peer groups. Particularly good responses came from within Maori street-based worker networks, whereas some opposition was faced from sex workers who did not want to be identified as such. Affected by the stigma associated with sex work, some workers preferred to be thought of in other ways, retaining the old labels of masseuse, escort, or even courtesan.

The media

Right from the outset, NZPC's aim was to create opportunities for sex workers from all sectors to express their ideas and be heard. This included having a voice and being heard by the media. Prior to NZPC, most media reports were written by people not otherwise involved in the sex industry and, as argued by a founding member of NZPC, there was:

'... a lot of talk about prostitution but seldom talk with prostitutes. There is an image, but there are never real people whose opinions are asked for.' (NZPC, 1989a)

To ensure that sex workers' voices were heard, NZPC engaged with media and did not shy away from tackling any issue they raised, if anything turning the media attention to its advantage. One such issue was HIV prevalence within the sex industry. Although some journalists ignored the facts and were quick to scapegoat sex workers for HIV transmission within New Zealand, other media such as *North and South* (van Wetering, 1989) used NZPC's input to report on research showing how sex workers often had lower exposure to HIV and other sexually transmitted infections than people outside the industry.

The media was particularly useful in raising the issue of law reform. This provided NZPC with many opportunities to raise awareness of the need for the decriminalisation of activities related to sex work. NZPC aimed to bring all types of sex worker – not just one particular group – into the discussions that were taking place in order to inform the public of the reality of sex work. Ironically, as some spokespeople did not fit the stereotypical media image of a sex worker, some journalists would ask if they could 'talk to a real sex worker'.

Composition of NZPC

NZPC's board and staff are comprised of past and present sex workers, but individuals with specialised knowledge are also contracted as required. NZPC engages with sex workers from all sectors of the sex industry throughout the country and involves them at all levels of its operation, but does not have a formal membership. To date, the organisation has a mix of people, including founding members as well as people who are relatively new. Although some people leave NZPC, they often come back, which indicates a high level of commitment, with many new faces appearing on a regular basis. Any sex worker can become involved.

NZPC is contracted to the Ministry of Health, but also has a small independent source of income from the sale of water-based lubricants to non-sex workers. Some parts of the organisation operate on a purely service delivery model, while others are focused on ensuring that sex workers have the means through which they can advocate for change. NZPC has long-standing relationships with other non-governmental organisations and collaborates with some organisations in areas of service provision and advocacy, such as sexual and reproductive health clinics, counselling services and human rights organisations.

The push for law reform

In 1989, the formal move for decriminalisation began with NZPC making a submission to the Justice and Law Reform Select Committee on the Crimes Amendment Bill. There were attempts being made at this time to further extend powers to arrest sex workers on charges of solicitation in escort agencies and outcall services. NZPC had concerns that the intent of the Bill, if enacted, was to further criminalise sex work activities (NZPC, 1989b, pp 10-11). NZPC cautioned that changes in the law should not unintentionally encourage a class of pimps who would exploit sex workers and who would not have the same interest in limiting the spread of HIV/AIDS that sex workers had. The ideas NZPC expressed were related to decriminalising sex work rather than adding another layer of punishments (NZPC, 1989b, pp 12-13).

There were few submitters who supported NZPC's viewpoint. Most notably, the National Council of Women submitted that clients should also be criminalised. However, a politician on the Select Committee picked up NZPC's ideas and wrote an opinion piece in favour of amending the law to decriminalise sex work:

> No criminal law will ever succeed in abolishing the sex industry. How much better would it be, rather than pushing the sex industry further underground, to decriminalise it entirely.... That would be better for the worker and the client. (de Cleene, 1989)

At this stage, NZPC realised that it was important to build on its earlier work and to begin networking with other government and non-government organisations to achieve its goals of improving conditions for sex workers and decriminalising sex work. In April of 1988, Catherine Healy – one of the founding members of the NZPC – had been appointed by the Minister of Health to the National Council on AIDS. This National Council encompassed 22 people from diverse backgrounds whose task was to make recommendations to the Minister of Health on ways to prevent and control the transmission of HIV. The appointment of a representative of a sex worker organisation at this level not only gave sex workers a voice, but also a certain amount of credibility.

In 1991, police posing as clients moved to enforce soliciting legislation and conducted a series of operations against massage parlours and street-based sex workers. Some founding members were caught in these operations and felt deliberately targeted. Despite the strong reputation NZPC had built in the public health arena, and its high profile in the media, it became difficult for outreach workers and peer educators, most of whom were voluntary, to feel they could fulfil the public health contract with the Department of Health.

NZPC wrote a letter to the Associate Minister of Health explaining that the laws made it increasingly difficult for the collective to effectively perform its task of promoting safe-sex practices within the sex industry. The police sometimes seized condoms and NZPC's safe-sex literature as part of the evidence to arrest sex workers or people they suspected of brothel keeping in massage parlours. NZPC argued that sex workers were increasingly reluctant to identify themselves as such, because doing so made them vulnerable to laws that could potentially criminalise them. This not only made it more difficult for NZPC to build networks within the sex worker community, but also made sex workers more reluctant to step forward and act as peer educators and leaders in safe-sex promotion programmes.

NZPC was also adamant that to ensure that sex workers had the means to prevent the transmission of HIV, they needed to be supported to continue the practice of educating each other, and their clients, about the importance of safe-sex practices to protect their health and livelihoods. NZPC stated that it would hand its funding back unless there was an interdepartmental committee established to review the legislation, and its threat was taken seriously. Such a committee was established, and included the Ministry of Women's Affairs, the police, the Department of Health and the Ministry of Justice. The Associate Minister of Health called for a report on the effects of the current legislation and it felt like NZPC was getting somewhere by raising awareness inside these government agencies. The Ministry of Women's Affairs announced at this time that its interests lay with sex workers, not clients or the sex industry itself (Ministry of Women's Affairs, 1991, p 8). It also stated:

> It (the law) is discriminatory because it criminalises prostitutes but not their clients, and operates to perpetuate poor working conditions and trap workers within the industry. (Ministry of Women's Affairs, 1991, p 7)

Nevertheless, the Ministry of Women's Affairs did not want to prosecute clients (Ministry of Women's Affairs, 1991). Its discussion paper reflected many of the ideals that NZPC had expressed in its submission to the Justice and Law Reform Select Committee two years previously. It was, therefore, a significant indication that decriminalisation of prostitution was going to be taken seriously in the New Zealand context.

Throughout the 1990s, NZPC continued to make an impact on government agencies and their policies. In 1993, after discussions with NZPC, the police created a policy directive around the non-seizure of safe-sex products, including condoms and safe-sex literature, in cases related to sex workers who were arrested for soliciting (Doone, 1993).

During this period, NZPC continued to build support for decriminalisation from non-governmental agencies beyond those who were concerned with public health and HIV. By the mid-1990s, major women's organisations were responding to NZPC's call for change. NZPC was frequently invited to present its case at conferences and other fora. The Business and Professional Women's Federation, followed by the Young Women's Christian Association and the National Council of Women, all came out publicly in support of law reform.

Opposition to decriminalisation was, at this time, contained to a few prominent New Zealanders, expressing their opinion in editorials in newspapers (McLeod, 1996; Roger, 1996; Stringer, 1997). Sandra Coney, of the Women's Health Collective, stated that:

> Decriminalisation would put society's seal of approval on a squalid side of male sexual behaviour. If anything, consorting with a prostitute should be a criminal offence. This would at least get rid of the double standard in the sex trade. (Coney, 1996)

In the sex industry, some massage parlour operators had been proactive in advocating change, but usually with a heavily regulated approach, running contrary to NZPC's vision for an inclusive industry that would enable sex workers to have many options about where they could work.

> I think it is appalling that escort services can be set up by anyone at any time.... I believe that the conduct of escort services should be controlled and the only way to do this is to have parliament pass legislation similar to the Massage Parlour Act. (Wood, 1992, p 1)

Conclusion

By the latter part of the 1990s, NZPC had created solid support for the decriminalisation of sex work, not only with a cross-section of non-governmental organisations, but also with politicians. It drafted a Bill in 1994, although this underwent many changes over the following years as its understanding of the reality of decriminalisation expanded. Its vision for decriminalisation was about to be realised.

References

Bay of Plenty Times (1995) 'Collective keeps new base secret', 20 September, p 3.

Chetwynd, J. (1991) *The New Zealand Prostitutes' Collective: A process evaluation of its formation and operation*, Christchurch: University of Otago, Christchurch School of Medicine.

Coney, S. (1996) 'Sex and violence old bedfellows', *Sunday Star Times*, 3 November.

de Cleene, T. (1989) 'The case for a legalised sex industry', Opinion, *Evening Post*, 5 September, p 6.

Doone, P.E.C. (1993) 'Policy Circular 1993/13: seizure of safe-sex materials when policing prostitution, brothel-keeping or allied offences', *Ten-One*, no 43, 4 June.

Healy, C. (1988) *SIREN* introductory letter, insert, *SIREN*, no 1, November.

Jordan, J. (1991) *Working girls: Women in the New Zealand sex industry talk to Jan Jordan*, Auckland: Penguin Books.

Mcleod, R. (1996) 'Modern whores scrub up well, but it's the same job', *The Dominion*, 5 December.

Ministry of Women's Affairs (1991) *Prostitution: A background paper*, Wellington: Ministry of Women's Affairs.

NZPC (New Zealand Prostitutes' Collective) (1989a) 'Prostitutes', *Broadsheet*, no 166, pp 7-8.

Roger, W. (1996) 'No place for prostitution in decent society', *The Evening Post*, 11 November.

Stringer, J. (1997) 'Legalised soliciting would be grave error', *The Evening Post*, 4 January.

van Wetering, V. (1989) 'Four corners: the new face of prostitution', *North and South*, March issue, pp 16-17.

Wood, R.G.W. (1992) Unpublished covering letter accompanying a petition to MPs requesting greater control of escort agencies, 9 February.

Submission to Justice and Electoral Select Committee on the 1989 Crimes Bill
NZPC (1989b)

FOUR

Lobbying for decriminalisation

Tim Barnett, Catherine Healy, Anna Reed and Calum Bennachie

Introduction

The successful campaign for the reform of New Zealand's sex work laws took nearly two decades. Inevitably for a law reform campaign in a vigorous parliamentary democracy, the process of law reform went through a series of largely predictable stages. Early on, the people who stood to gain most from law reform became aware of the injustices of the old laws and began networking to build the New Zealand Prostitutes' Collective (NZPC), a nationwide sex worker organisation. Through the NZPC, sex workers began building awareness and support for their cause, creating a space to look to the long term.

Flowing from that, a decision-making and conceptualisation process was carried out to decide which model of law reform was best suited to New Zealand, based on the impact it would have on sex workers. Following this conceptualisation phase was the pragmatic process of drafting law, which involved moulding the decriminalisation model into something meaningful and politically feasible for the New Zealand parliamentary process. The Prostitution Reform Bill (PRB) was written and submitted to parliament at the end of this drafting period.

There was a great deal of overlap between the networking, conceptualisation and drafting stages and, throughout all of these stages, campaign building was also taking place. Campaign building was critical to raising awareness and understanding, not only within the sex industry, but also outside it, with government and non-governmental organisations (NGOs), political parties, politicians, the media and others.

The parliamentary process eventually brought all of these various stages together in what became the most public and memorable element of the process of law reform. As the PRB began its long journey through parliament, the thinking behind it needed to be communicated and explained publicly. This chapter follows the networking, conceptualisation, drafting and campaign-building stages of the law reform, before describing the process of further explanation of the law to the public and outlining the parliamentary process through which the law passed. The chapter ends with reflections on the campaign and its outcome from the perspective of Tim Barnett, the Member of Parliament (MP) who sponsored and introduced the Bill in parliament, as well as the perspective of members of NZPC.

Before entering into this discussion, it is important to understand the political context in which decriminalisation occurred. It can be argued that the parliamentary system operating in New Zealand at the time of decriminalisation played an important role in achieving legislative change. In November 1993, 100 years after becoming the first nation to enfranchise women, New Zealand again made electoral reform history by replacing its first-past-the-post (FPP) method of electing legislators with a new, mixed-member proportional (MMP) system (Nagel, 1994). The MMP system was derived from that operating in Germany, although it was adapted in various ways, and New Zealand was the first English-speaking democracy to adopt proportional representation based on party lists (Vowles, 1995).

Under the MMP system, voters could cast two ballots; one for a local constituency representative elected by FPP and one for a national party list. Under MMP, seats were allocated so that the overall representation in parliament was proportional to party votes cast. This meant that, while New Zealand had been accustomed to parliament dominated by two major parties – Labour and National – the MMP system made institutionalised multiparty politics possible, as well as the formation of coalition and minority governments as a matter of course (Vowles, 1995).

The success of the radical electoral reform that brought about change from FPP to MMP stemmed from widespread public discontent with the electoral process in New Zealand. New Zealand is distinctive in its lack of constitutional restraints on government, and a succession of governments throughout the 1980s and 1990s had thus been relatively unconstrained in putting through controversial economic reforms in the face of public opposition (Vowles, 1995). New Zealand's political institutions effectively facilitated 'elective dictatorship' under the FPP system (Mulgan, 1990).

Support for proportional representation thus increased throughout the 1980s and intensified following the 1990 general election, in which the National Party obtained 69% of the seats with only 48% of the votes, leaving Labour with only 29 seats (Vowles, 1995). In the immediate aftermath of the 1990 election, public support for proportional representation reached 65% with only 18% supporting the status quo (Vowles, 1995).

New Zealand has experienced five elections since the introduction of MMP, resulting in three left-leaning and two right-leaning coalitions. With a few exceptions, the electorate (constituency) race remains between Labour and National; people are more adventurous with their party vote, meaning that no single party has held a majority of seats after any election. The tradition has emerged that during an election campaign (or sometimes in the period preceding that) the smaller parties make it clear which of the large parties they could and could not work with in government, and which policies they regard as their own 'bottom line'. This has meant that the skills of flexibility, negotiation and policy analysis (including the ability to see one issue from many different viewpoints) are crucial to the working of government.

By the mid–1990s, the debate on prostitution reform was particularly heated in New Zealand when Christian fundamentalist and some feminist groups galvanised against the idea of law reform. Indeed, the challenging of the arguments raised by these groups was crucial to achieving decriminalisation of sex work in New Zealand.

Creating awareness and building support for law reform

New Zealand was the first country in the world to introduce women's suffrage nationwide, and was also a pioneer on the world stage from the early 20th century in changing laws that affected women's reproductive rights. As a result, New Zealand has since been considered a socially liberal country. A powerful NGO sector and strong public health and human rights ethos grew in New Zealand, as did a world-leading policy platform on women's rights and, from the 1970s, human rights.

The emergence of HIV/AIDS created global concern in the 1980s and strategies were developed to minimise the spread of this disease. The response of the New Zealand government to the advent of HIV/AIDS was in the form of legislation, not only to minimise the spread of disease, but to safeguard the human rights of certain population groups (Paterson, 1996). Some population groups were identified as being more likely than others to be responsible for the spread of this disease to the general public. In 1986, the Homosexual Law Reform Bill decriminalised consensual homosexual acts between males aged 16 years and over (Davis and Lichtenstein, 1996). In May 1987, the Department of Health introduced the needle and syringe exchange scheme (Needle Exchange Programme), which allowed for the sale of needles and syringes through approved pharmacies to injecting drug users (Kemp, 1996). During this time, the government also funded the NZPC, as discussed in the previous chapter, to create a supportive social environment for sex workers and to prevent the transmission of HIV. At this stage, the decriminalisation of sex work was being discussed, but no Bill to decriminalise sex work had yet been drafted.

The government funding of the NZPC was significant because it indicated that politicians saw a sex worker-driven organisation as a valid holder of public funds and it also enabled isolated sex workers and their local advocates to form a loose national network. Tensions soon emerged, however, because of inconsistencies between government policies and the services the NZPC was expected to provide. One example of this was that, on the one hand, the NZPC was expected to provide condoms to sex workers as part of their HIV prevention programme. On the other hand, police sometimes seized these condoms as evidence that sex work was taking place, resulting in sex workers and massage parlour operators being convicted of prostitution-related offences. Consequently, many parlour owners were reluctant to have condoms, used and unused, on their premises that could be linked to them. There was also a reluctance to display safe-sex posters in parlours and for sex workers to disclose the nature of their work to health professionals.

NZPC articulated the tensions publicly to raise awareness of the contradictions of the law, which essentially allowed for sex workers to exist, provided they did not practice. In 1989, NZPC presented its first arguments for decriminalisation in parliament to a Select Committee on Justice and Law Reform (NZPC, 1989). This submission was widely reported in the media and a Labour MP, Trevor de Cleene, supported NZPC by submitting an opinion piece to the *Evening Post* (de Cleene, 1989). This was the first example of collaboration between sex workers, politicians and the media in explaining the consequences of the existing legislation and the need for reform.

In anticipation of criticisms and possible accusations of opponents that they were merely embellishing on the problems of the existing laws, NZPC was keen to develop relationships with academics to provide evidence-based research to back up their concerns about the realities sex workers were facing. A relationship was established with the Department of Public Health and General Practice, University of Otago, Christchurch School of Medicine (CSoM) in the early 1990s and this relationship is still continuing. In addition to a study looking at sex workers' perspectives on their health and safety and a client study, the CSoM conducted a process evaluation of NZPC and produced a number of publications from this early research (Chetwynd, 1992, 1996; Chetwynd and Plumridge, 1993, 1994; Plumridge and Abel, 2000; Plumridge and Chetwynd, 1994; Plumridge et al, 1996, 1997a, 1997b; Plumridge, 2001; Plumridge and Abel, 2001). Later, other researchers also collaborated with NZPC, which added to the growing body of evidence on the reality of sex work in New Zealand.

Conceptualising a model of law reform

Whichever particular model of law was to be adopted in New Zealand, prostitution law reform necessarily implied a move towards an acceptance of the reality of sex work. NZPC was stimulated by ideas from the Prostitutes' Collective Victoria, Australia and the English Collective of Prostitutes. Between 1990 and 1996, the debate around reforming laws governing sex work gained focus and shape, and a range of agencies began engaging in discussions and forming their own policies on how sex work should be regulated. Many of these agencies were influenced by NZPC.

An interesting aspect of the law reform in New Zealand was that it contained elements that attracted politicians from opposing political ideologies. Ironically, it was a male MP from the more conservative National Party[1], Hon Maurice Williamson, who in 1991, after meeting with the NZPC, was the first to speak out frequently and passionately about the injustice of the laws. He was joined by his colleague, Hon Katherine O'Regan, who had previously supported the Homosexual Reform Bill and later proposed an amendment to the Human Rights

---

[1] The National Party was seen as more conservative than the Labour Party, which was viewed as more socially liberal.

Bill to end discrimination against the lesbian, gay and bisexual communities. These politicians became the most consistent advocates for law reform in parliament in the early 1990s. As the two Associate Ministers of Health, they advocated for decriminalisation of soliciting, but were met with opposition from their mainly morally conservative ministerial colleagues.

Meanwhile, as highlighted in the previous chapter, NZPC was becoming increasingly frustrated with police actions in enforcing the law and the impact this had on the work they were contracted to do in running community prevention programmes for HIV and AIDS. It threatened to refuse funding from the Department of Health and go back underground unless there was a review of the law and the establishment of an inter-departmental committee to address inconsistencies in the law. Maurice Williamson commissioned a report from a committee comprising representatives from health, justice, women's affairs and the police to inform Cabinet of options for law reform (Ministry of Women's Affairs, 1991).

In 1993, the Commerce Commission began looking at industries for which to design occupational safety and health legislation. In consulting the massage industry, it encountered the difficulties of developing legislation for what was on the face of things a massage industry, but in practice also included a significant number of people who were involved in commercial sex. NZPC developed a submission to this commission, outlining the problems with the existing law for the occupational safety and health of sex workers (NZPC, 1990).

Increasingly, government agencies and subsets of political parties were becoming aware of the contradictions in the law. Organisations like the Business and Professional Women's Federation publicly called for the decriminalisation of prostitution and other women's organisations were encouraged by NZPC to join this movement. This provided the impetus for a coalition of organisations with diverse interests, such as the Young Women's Christian Association, Venereological Society, the NZ AIDS Foundation, the Public Health Association, the Massage Institute, the National Council of Women, Maori Women's Welfare League and the Council of Trade Unions, as well as individual Catholic nuns and churches, who joined the call for the decriminalisation of sex work. The meaning of decriminalisation within the New Zealand context started to be clarified.

The rationale for decriminalisation was explained initially in the context of public health and the prevention of STIs and HIV. This expanded to include other concerns expressed by sex workers, including human rights, encompassing concerns about the double standard that existed between sex workers and clients (see Chapter Two), unfair employment practices and protection of youth. By 1993, the New Zealand Labour Party had agreed a General Election manifesto commitment to decriminalise soliciting, which was repeated in the 1996 manifesto.

Drafting the Prostitution Reform Bill

NZPC worked with lawyers, academics, students and others in drafting a model law in 1994 to meet the needs of sex workers. This underwent several changes, but many of the concepts from the original text were eventually incorporated in the PRB. Hon Katherine O'Regan used the drafting process to gather an initial campaign team, which comprised one other MP, Labour MP for Christchurch Central Tim Barnett[2], and representatives of NZPC, as well as progressive Christian and women's networks.

The final draft of the PRB was written by Bill Hastings, who had been a Professor of Law at Victoria University of Wellington and later became Chief Censor. The Bill was brief and brought all sex work–related law together while suggesting the repeal of numerous pieces of legislation contained in many different statutes. In 1998, Hon O'Regan, Catherine Healy and Tim Barnett visited New South Wales, Australia, where most forms of sex work had been decriminalised in 1995. State and local politicians, public health experts and sex worker organisations also emphasised the importance of putting the interests of sex workers first and urged law makers to avoid zoning of brothels or street-based sex work and to ensure that sex workers who worked from home would not be excluded by the new law.

Campaign building

In successful law reform processes, crucial things tend to happen simultaneously. Once the Bill started to progress, the campaign began to take shape. From this point through the next four years, the campaign had four main features:

- *frequently highlighted in the media:* the media was in general supportive in its reporting of the idea of decriminalisation of sex work prior to 2003. However, opponents of law reform were becoming more vocal and utilised the media to deliver their messages. For example, the Maxim Institute paid for a billboard to be erected near the capital city's airport claiming there would be 'more child prostitution' and referencing a Save the Children report (Save the Children,

---

[2] Tim Barnett had involvement with the sex workers' movement through membership of the New Zealand AIDS Foundation Board at the same time as Catherine Healy of NZPC. He also had engagement with Anna Reed from the local branch of the NZPC in Christchurch and both were also involved with the local New Zealand AIDS Foundation centre and activities and the Christchurch campaign for human rights law reform in 1992-93. In 1996, when Tim Barnett was elected to parliament, his Christchurch Central electorate contained New Zealand's largest concentration of brothels and street-based sex workers outside central Auckland, so he had political reason and justification to be engaged in the debate.

1999)[3]. Opponents said the law reform would lead to 'more, more, more' of everything – more sex workers, more brothels, more violence, more coercion and more child abuse (for example, *New Zealand Herald*, 2003);

- *small, non-hierarchical and centralised:* the campaign was not highly structured and it relied on many opportunistic events to build strategies. It focused on delivering outcomes, in particular a majority of MPs voting for a model of law reform acceptable to the campaign. It was not a funded campaign and did not have a dedicated headquarters or staff. Activity took place in the NZPC headquarters and regional offices and in Tim Barnett's parliamentary office;

- *tightly focused on parliament:* The approach was necessarily and wisely targeted, with key tools being databases of MPs' interests and voting intentions, written arguments and identified networks out in the community, keen to lobby local MPs. The existence of the parliamentary media gallery meant that the passport to high-profile coverage was literally only a few steps away for those at the heart of the campaign. The initiative attracted cross-party support, which enabled and necessitated it being explained in a variety of ways to politicians with contrasting values;

- *comprised of NGOs and activists:* the Bill was sponsored by an individual MP (a 'Member's Bill') and was not a government initiative. Having an MP behind the campaign whose party was in power was crucial if any emergent legislation was to pass, because it would rely on a conscience vote which would in turn rely on significant Labour support, with backing from some MPs from other parties. The attitude to the Bill of officials, departments and ministers in their official capacity was broadly neutral. Rather, active support came from sex workers, public health experts, human rights groups, students, progressive religious/rationalist groups and women's organisations. It would be wrong to suggest that there was mass mobilisation of public support of the Bill, and it was difficult, partly because of the complexity of the arguments and the stigma associated with sex work, to get large numbers of the general public to actively lobby for reform. It was an intellectual rather than muscular campaign, which did not involve street protests or demonstrations.

Facing an increasingly obsessive and effective opposition

Initially, the opposition was disparate and weak. As the campaign and Bill progressed, and particularly after the 2002 General Election, which saw a lurching of parliament to the right and the arrival of a small and dedicated group of Christian fundamentalist MPs, its impact increased. By the end of the campaign period, the opponents' messages were more focused, but still not evidence-based. Supported by the religious right and radical anti-sex feminists, a very small number

---

[3] However, the Save the Children report states: '(i) it has been difficult to determine whether the number has been increasing or decreasing' and that any increase was anecdotal rather than evidence-based (Save the Children, 1999, pp 98-9).

of ex-sex workers were even prepared to publicly oppose the law reform, with a consequently powerful media impact.

Residents and business owners claiming that they would be affected by the presence of brothels in their neighbourhood also had definite views. Opposition from those who might be thought to benefit from law reform is a constant presence in such debates. Several massage parlour/brothel operators gave submissions to the Parliamentary Select Committee opposing the Bill and occasionally argued in the media and elsewhere against the law reform (Cooper, 2000, pp 1–2; Wall and Garner, 2000; Auckland Commercial Massage Operators and Adult Entertainment Owners, 2001, pp 4–7; Miller, 2001, pp 1–2). An intended long-term outcome of decriminalisation was to provide sex workers with a range of choices from which to work safely. For example, brothel workers could move from being managed in brothels (some of which had a reputation for abusive work conditions) into situations where they could work with small numbers of other sex workers from shared apartments. This was regarded by massage parlour/brothel operators as a threat to the near monopoly that had existed, de facto, under the current law.

Some members of the United Future Party were so opposed to the law reform that they argued in parliament that the issues at stake were of such a level of constitutional importance that they should be put to a referendum (Hansard, 2003). However, New Zealand is near unique in having no single written constitution and no great tradition of referenda. In addition, there is a Citizens Initiated Referenda arrangement that needs one in 10 registered voters to sign a petition to force a referendum. After the law reform was enacted, some members of an opposing political party sought to have a Citizens Initiated Referendum. However, they failed to achieve enough support to force it to happen.

Explaining the proposed law

Prostitution law reform became one of the more complex matters for New Zealand politicians to address, because many who were being asked to make decisions on it had little or no exposure to sex work. Reforming sex work laws was a Member's Bill, and the resources of government were therefore not available to explain and defend its contents. Other than those MPs who spoke personally to lobbying sex workers, the concepts underpinning the law reform – that sex work per se was not necessarily a problem and that making sex work illegal was no guarantee that it would stop – were not widely understood and so failed to make the necessary political impact. There were also the two concepts of 'decriminalisation' and 'legalisation', which were explained endlessly (and not necessarily entirely consistently) by all involved in the campaign for law reform.

Harm minimisation was at the heart of the Bill for public health officials and some politicians, and it was a concept that was helpful for many one-to-one lobbying conversations. The concept of harm minimisation did enable those with a strong personal antipathy towards sex work to accept that the driving need was for law to focus on minimising harm. For other politicians, sex workers and other organisations, human rights were at its heart.

The parliamentary process

New Zealand has a single chamber parliament, operating in the Westminster system. The parliamentary process involves four key processes in the Chamber. A Bill undergoes three readings with a vote taken after each. In each case, a simple majority vote of parliament is required. The only exception, not relevant in this case, is that where there is existing legislation of constitutional standing, it can be 'entrenched' and only directly amended if two thirds of MPs voting support that. If a Bill passes the vote after the First Reading, it goes to the Select Committee stage, which has representation from a number of political parties. Submissions are heard and the Bill is amended and then comes back into parliament for its Second Reading. Changes can then be made again after this reading. The Third Reading is preceded by votes on each part or even clause of the Bill in a stage called the Committee of the Whole House. There is an inter-party mechanism – the Business Committee – that meets weekly while parliament is meeting to oversee the progress of legislation and the future agenda of the House. Members' Bills are controlled by individual MPs; in the case of the Prostitution Reform Bill, this was Tim Barnett.

Tim Barnett MP placed the PRB in the Members' ballot in September 2000. It was (most unusually and very luckily) drawn out of the old biscuit tin used for the ballot the very next day – one of only three Bills drawn out of approximately 40 in the tin. The parliamentary process was slow progressing through five stages – three readings interspersed with a Select Committee and Committee of the Whole House.

In October 2000, the Bill received its First Reading, and was passed by 87 votes to 21. It took two years to pass through the Justice and Electoral Select Committee, including many days of hearing dozens of public submissions. The committee made numerous amendments to make the Bill more workable[4]. The Second Reading, held after the 2002 General Election, passed by only 64 votes to 56, reflecting both the strengthening opposition lobby and a more conservative balance of parliament. This tightening of the gap necessitated further amendments at the Committee of the Whole House stage to satisfy the concerns of some

---

[4] This is unusual for a Member's Bill, which traditionally goes through committee with minimal amendment, maximising the opportunity for all MPs to amend it later.

interest blocs[5]. Three examples were: the introduction of a certification system for 'operators of businesses of prostitution', a ban on sex work being a skills ground for those seeking to immigrate under the skills category, and the insertion of a Review Committee to report back to the Minister of Justice between three to five years after the law passed. Prime Minister Helen Clark endorsed and voted for the law reform drawing on her past ministerial work on public health and human rights matters. Comment from her on these matters came with a depth of knowledge, and many MPs had conversations with her as the crucial votes approached. The last few weeks of the parliamentary campaign were noisy and confused, with the media attempting to undertake its own number-counting exercises but in the process neglecting to interrogate a handful of MPs who had opposed the legislation but were prepared to vote for (or even, in one case, abstain) at the Third (and final) Reading, or would prove sufficiently strong to resist intense and personal opposition lobbies targeted at them. Personal approaches by individual sex workers to some politicians who were initially opposed to the Bill were effective in convincing them to support the proposed changes to the law.

The Prostitution Reform Act (PRA) was eventually passed on 25 June 2003 by 60 votes to 59, with one abstention, and largely came into effect three days after that. New Zealand thus became the first country in the world to decriminalise indoor and outdoor sex work nationally.

Reflection on the campaign and its outcome – Tim Barnett

There was a widespread perception that the Labour-led government had introduced 'unpopular' legislation such as the PRA, despite the fact that it was a Private Member's Bill. With justification, some commentators believed that prostitution law reform became the launch pad for a fundamentalist lobby that came close to significant victories later in the period of that Labour-led government, and whose presence seemed to act as a veto to government or parliamentary progress on such matters as same-sex adoption, cannabis law reform and euthanasia. Certainly, the core of opposition to this law reform came from people and groups who believed that sex work was in opposition to biblical teaching and that the creation of laws that 'normalised' such activity was wrong. If the PRB had been defeated (which, just looking at the arithmetic of the final vote, was clearly a real possibility), it would have been a strong endorsement of the power and potential of the fundamentalist lobby. The close nature of the June 2003 vote thus takes on historic importance – those risking their local political

[5] Opponents, whose core was Christian fundamentalists, but also included a strand of feminists who regarded any attempt to address prostitution neutrally as state-sponsored abuse of women, attempted a series of wrecking amendments at the Committee of the Whole House stage. These included, most notably, one that aimed completely to reverse the design of the law to criminalise the client, not the sex worker (the Swedish model – it was defeated 19 to 96) and another that moved to criminalise both the client and the worker, which was defeated 12 to 103.

lives in supporting this law reform (and a number believed that they were), were effectively, by voting for the Bill, endorsing a continuation of a mini-wave of liberal law reform, of which civil union was a significant element.

The three factors in relation to parliament that were crucial to the passing of the PRA were:

- a strong and politically supportive and diverse majority at First Reading, which survived in admittedly reduced form right through;
- a sponsor who was reasonably popular within the parliament, perceived as non-ideological and genuine in relation to the issue of prostitution; and
- the near universal support of a strong group of women MPs, including the Prime Minister at the time.

The existence of MMP helped in relation to all these factors. In general, in relation to MMP, there has been a neutral impact with regard to visionary law reform. The advocates of such reforms are more likely to be in parliament than before, since there is a greater diversity of people and parties there. The development of the Select Committee system has opened doors to lobbying civil society. However, the length of time that legislation now takes to go through – which has been increased by the introduction of MMP – means that proposals are subject to great scrutiny and vulnerable to sustained attack.

Would prostitution law reform have got through parliament without MMP? That is very hard to say. Certainly, the debates on it would have been more sterile in the old politics; the diversity and structures of the contemporary New Zealand parliament, so transformed for the better by MMP, have encouraged a more sophisticated understanding of the issues involved. The more complex and diverse party political composition of parliament generated by MMP has changed the whole lobby process from a matter of purely personal contact within a broadly predictable party political split to one that needs to take the particular philosophy of the MP's party into account. Conscience, free or personal votes were not unknown in the old pre-MMP parliament. The pattern MPs tended to fall into when voting on many of the iconic liberal issues was predictable. Among the old parties, this split has survived in the new MMP age. 'Old Labour' voted with the bulk of National MPs for the status quo. 'Liberal National' voted with the bulk of Labour for a progressive outcome. The small parties, present in parliament thanks to MMP, tended to split internally along those lines. Only the Greens were reliably on the liberal side, as a bloc. The Progressives, the conservative side of the Alliance Party that split in 2002, opposed prostitution law reform; ACT split down the middle (having a purely liberal and morally conservative wing in parliament at that stage); and New Zealand First was solidly against. Some politicians see such personal votes as a chance to make up their own mind, influenced by ideology; others see them as a chance to gauge the public mood in their electorate or sector and vote along those lines. Some try to please all sides and end up looking a little silly.

Maybe the greatest benefit provided by MMP to the law reform was its enervating impact on the power and energy of the parliamentary institutions, notably Select Committees and the Committee of the Whole House. The Select Committee stage of this Bill was more energised and extensive than in the past, offering essential validation that the proposed law had been through significant public exposure and enabling sex workers themselves to appear in private, making a powerful impression. The Committee of the Whole House (the penultimate stage) was rigorous, and became the forum and stage for necessary, last-minute bartering. The multi-party system made inter-party communication easier; MPs in MMP have become more used to working across the barriers. One other political spin-off from the measures was the positive experience of the political coalitions forged in the process, notably between Green and Labour MPs and also between a small group of liberal National MPs and mainstream Labour ones. The Green–Labour organising axis is a natural political entry point for many NGOs. A further impact was on NGOs. The lobby experience around this Bill politicised many of them, since they had ample opportunity to engage in very public ways, especially at Select Committee.

Conversely, there was some political fallout involved in the measure. Agreement to a law that gave rights to sex workers was always going to annoy some people who were not active in the campaign but were persuaded by the subsequent arguments. Labour canvassers in the 2002 General Election (and in 2005) faced difficult times with some voters who were traditional Labour supporters but were vehemently opposed to the reform Bill. Although the threats were many, organised opposition to the law reform after it passed into law did not inspire the creation of new political movements, and National's majority opposition to the reform did not seem to last through to the 2008 General Election. Public opinion at the time of the law reform, as polled, was marginally supportive of the measure. Of course, what is said and done at the time of such a reform, and in the short period afterwards, is not so important. It is the public view a few years on that is much more vital and relevant. By the 2008 General Election, there was a sense across the political divide that public and political support had cemented in favour of the law reform, with the only active debate being around street prostitution. The very detailed and deep review of prostitution law reform, built into the original law and delivered on time in mid-2008, helped people to rationalise a change of mind from opposition to support.

Prostitution reform was barely an election issue in the 2008 General Election beyond media attempts to label the Labour government as being out of touch with the public, citing this legislation as one of a number of examples. The issue registered minimally on the doorstep and in public meetings. Of more interest was whether the new conservative administration would attempt wholesale reform. Since two of its three key partners in government – the Maori Party and ACT – were essentially (as parties or as individual MPs in other parties at the time) supportive of the law reform, and since there is a cross-party fear of raising issues for debate when there is a range of powerful and polarised lobbies just waiting to pounce (abortion is the perfect example), the status quo may be protected for some time yet.

The continued difficulty faced by most countries in trying to develop a rational approach to prostitution law is an indication of the height of the barriers that New Zealand overcame through this law reform. It took time for the true extent of the achievement to be recognised, but leading up to and after the production of the review report on it in June 2008 (PLRC, 2008), a series of media stories worldwide – enhanced by the New Zealand law being repeatedly cited by academics, sex worker organisations, programme managers and others as the world model – constituted evidence that there was real interest in a law that was workable, liberal and capable of being monitored.

Reflection on the campaign and its outcome – NZPC

Following law reform, sex workers became more open and frank in their discussions with NZPC outreach workers, and among themselves inside brothels. New workers were conscious of the right to work and told NZPC educators that they 'wanted to do it all properly'. As a result, the work of NZPC in exchanging ideas with sex workers and brothel operators about sexual health issues and occupational safety and health has become easier because conversations about sex work can be conducted more frankly.

While brothel/parlour operators had been saying for years that they wanted to 'do things' legally, they were frustrated by the old laws. Now they had to 'front up' to a law that gave sex workers rights to lay official complaints against them to judicial bodies. NZPC has supported sex workers through the Disputes Tribunal, and there are indications that the officials are mindful of the rights of sex workers and seem to be taking these into consideration in their judgements.

Many organisations have responded to the change in the law and have wanted to engage with NZPC and the sex industry now that its activities have been decriminalised. Caregivers who look after people with disabilities have contacted NZPC to establish links between their clients and sex workers. Financial institutions promote their willingness to work with sex workers to NZPC. The dominant telephone provider in New Zealand has cooperated with NZPC to enhance the safety of street-based sex workers by developing a network for rapid text messaging of descriptions of dangerous clients to all workers on the database. It approached NZPC after the murders of two street-based workers in Christchurch. Some sex workers are more likely to approach moteliers and landlords and openly negotiate rooms from which to operate. However, discrimination can still occur and some motels and body corporates in apartment complexes specifically exclude sex work in rental contracts.

There has been continuing support for a decriminalised sex industry from health professionals to the police, and relationships that previously would not have been possible have developed and flourished. In particular, the police in Christchurch, where violence has occurred against sex workers, have been outstanding. This has resulted in a greater flow of information between workers, NZPC and the police, always with an emphasis on protecting the health and safety of sex workers, rather than treating them as criminals. On more than one occasion, street-based workers have negotiated with police in patrol cars so that they do not interfere with their ability to attract clients through parking their cars directly in front of the sex workers' spot on the street. Many police officers have demonstrated extreme courtesy to ensure that they do not scare potential clients away. However, in some areas of New Zealand, we occasionally do hear of situations where police are returning to practices that they used before law reform, such as taking photographs and details of people working on the street. In such cases, complaints to the police have quickly stopped these practices.

Meanwhile, the media has been determined to criticise the law, but is having difficulty in doing so without having to rely on incorrect information from opponents. These opponents continue to spread misinformation – more brothels, more sex workers, more youth involved – although they are unable to produce any evidence-based research to support their claims. This does not deter the media from reiterating these stories despite contradictory evidence from the Prostitution Law Review Committee (PLRC, 2008) and the University of Otago, Christchurch School of Medicine (CSoM) (Abel et al, 2007). Some of the main political opponents of the law reform were initially behind most of the adverse media releases. There was a move by a minor political party inside parliament to gain support to overturn the Act. However, this opposition has not achieved any success to date. Occasionally, individual local and central government politicians do speak out in opposition of decriminalisation of sex work, especially in relation to street-based sex workers, youth in sex work and suburban brothels. There appears to be widespread acceptance among these opponents that sex workers should be protected by the law but contained within brothels and not "on the street for all to see" (Curtis, Radio New Zealand, 12 September 2006).

Some local councils opted to utilise their powers to regulate the location of brothels (see Chapter Nine). They introduced bylaws that made it difficult for individual sex workers to operate legally if they wished to work from their home outside of the central business district (CBD). In addition, they reduced options for these sex workers to work with two or three others as a safety strategy. These councils essentially strengthened the hand of the bigger brothels and their management. In order to be able to operate legally, these sex workers would have to rent more expensive and sometimes unaffordable premises within the CBD. Often within the CBD, landlords expect to have longer leases on rental properties than in normal residential areas, which adds another layer of concern to sex workers if they wish to stop sex work before their lease has expired. Understandably, many in this situation opted to work in breach of these bylaws. These sex workers were unable financially to take these councils to court and felt most disempowered. Some big brothels whose operation was also affected by the introduction of bylaws took the councils to court. NZPC was called as an expert witness and was able to draw attention to the harmful effect these bylaws had on individual sex workers and small owner operated brothels. NZPC was offered counsel from sympathetic legal experts who were concerned about the injustice of the bylaws. Some bylaws were overturned and the councils had to pay huge legal fees. There was then a perception, which was actively encouraged by NZPC, that these councils had overreacted and wasted ratepayers' money and this was widely reported in the media (Scanlon, 2006).

NZPC is now concerned about the legal situation of people who have come to New Zealand either to be sex workers or decide once they arrive to go into sex work. Under the PRA, they do not have the right to work as sex workers; they can have their visas revoked and be returned to their country of origin. One such group includes international students who find that sex work fits in their study schedules, but fear having their study terminated if they are found to be sex workers.

Another of NZPC's concerns relates to claims that the PRA will lead to greater trafficking of people. Often people from other countries who are working illegally are defined as trafficked sex workers even though there is no evidence of coercion. NZPC has contact with sex workers who are working illegally on a regular basis. In its experience, sex workers and clients operating in a decriminalised environment are more aware of, and more empowered to speak out about, other sex workers who may be exploited, including migrant sex workers. Since the change in law, Immigration Services has stated that there have been no instances where sex workers have been found to be trafficked (PLRC, 2008, p 167).

NZPC has a steady stream of enquiries and visits from people from other countries, including sex worker organisations, high-ranking police, politicians, academics, media and other individuals who look to this legislation as being the best model to date. People across the board are recognising that the PRA has improved conditions for sex workers. However, attitudes are slow to change and there is still some way to go before sex workers realise their full rights. Commitment to human rights for all citizens is of great importance in New Zealand. The country has fought hard for human rights and now it works to keep them.

References

Abel, G., Fitzgerald, L. and Brunton, C. (2007) *The impact of the Prostitution Reform Act on the health and safety practices of sex workers: Report to the Prostitution Law Review Committee*, Christchurch: University of Otago, www.justice.govt.nz/prostitution-law-review-committee/publications/impact-health-safety/index.html

Chetwynd, J. (1992) 'HIV/AIDS and sex workers', *New Zealand Medical Journal*, vol 105, p 227.

Chetwynd, J. (1996) 'The Prostitutes' Collective: a uniquely New Zealand institution', in P. Davis (ed) *Intimate details and vital statistics: AIDS, sexuality and the social order in New Zealand*, Auckland: Auckland University Press.

Chetwynd, J. and Plumridge, E. (1993) *Clients of female sex workers: A pilot study*, Christchurch: University of Otago, Christchurch School of Medicine.

Chetwynd, J. and Plumridge, E. (1994) 'Knowledge, attitudes and activities of male clients of female sex workers: risk factors for HIV', *New Zealand Medical Journal*, vol 107, pp 351-3.

Davis, P. and Lichtenstein, B. (1996) 'Introduction: AIDS, sexuality and the social order in New Zealand', in P. Davis (ed) *Intimate details and vital statistics: AIDS, sexuality and social order in New Zealand*, Auckland: Auckland University Press.

de Cleene, T. (1989) 'The case for a legalised sex industry', Opinion, *Evening Post*, 5 September, p 6.

Hansard (2003) Marc Alexander, Speech to the House on the Prostitution Reform Bill, Committee of the Whole House, *Parliamentary Debates*, 26 March, www.parliament.nz/enNZ/PB/Debates/Debates/1/8/0/47HansD_20030326_00001231-Prostitution-Reform-Bill-Instruction-to.htm

Kemp, R. (1996) 'From a bang to a whimper: policy responses to injecting drug use and viral infection', in P. Davis (ed) *Intimate details and vital statistics: AIDS, sexuality and the social order in New Zealand*, Auckland: Auckland University Press.

Ministry of Women's Affairs (1991) *Prostitution: A background paper*, Wellington: Ministry of Women's Affairs.

Mulgan, R. (1990) 'The changing electoral mandate', in M. Holland and J. Boston (eds) *The fourth Labour government: Politics and policy in New Zealand*, Auckland: Oxford University Press, pp 11-21.

Nagel, J. (1994) 'What political scientists can learn from the 1993 electoral reform in New Zealand', *PS: Political Science & Politics*, vol 27, p 3.

New Zealand Herald (2003) 'If we encourage prostitution we will get more of it', 18 February, p 7.

Paterson, R. (1996) '"Softly, softly": New Zealand law responds to AIDS', in P. Davis (ed) *Intimate details and vital statistics: AIDS, sexuality and the social order in New Zealand*, Auckland: Auckland University Press.

PLRC (Prostitution Law Review Committee) (2008) *Report of the Prostitution Law Review Committee on the operation of the Prostitution Reform Act 2003*, Wellington: Ministry of Justice, www.justice.govt.nz/prostitution-law-review-committee/publications/plrc-report/index.html

Plumridge, E. and Abel, G. (2000) 'Services and information utilised by female sex workers for sexual and physical safety', *New Zealand Medical Journal*, vol 113, no 1117, pp 370-2.

Plumridge, E. and Chetwynd, J. (1994) 'AIDS policy response in New Zealand: consensus in crisis', *Health Care Analysis*, vol 2, no 4, pp 287-96.

Plumridge, E., Chetwynd, J. and Reed, A. (1997a) 'Control and condoms in commercial sex: client perspectives', *Sociology of Health and Illness*, vol 19, no 2, pp 228-43.

Plumridge, E., Chetwynd, J., Reed, A. and Gifford, S. (1997b) 'Discourses of emotionality in commercial sex: the missing client voice', *Feminism and Psychology*, vol 7, no 2, pp 165-81.

Plumridge, E., Chetwynd, S., Reed, A. and Gifford, S. (1996) 'Patrons of the sex industry: perceptions of risk', *AIDS Care*, vol 8, no 4, pp 405-16.

Plumridge, L. (2001) 'Rhetoric, reality and risk outcomes in sex work', *Health, Risk and Society*, vol 3, no 2, pp 199-217.

Plumridge, L. and Abel, G. (2001) 'A "segmented" sex industry in New Zealand: sexual and personal safety of female sex workers', *Australian and New Zealand Journal of Public Health*, vol 25, no 1, pp 78-83.

Save the Children (1999) *Children's rights: Reality or rhetoric? The UN Convention on the Rights of the Child, the first ten years*, London: Save the Children.

Scanlon, S. (2006) 'Council drops brothel appeal', *The Christchurch Press*, 24 March.

Vowles, J. (1995) 'The politics of electoral reform in New Zealand', in *International Political Science Review*, vol 16, no 1, p 1.

Wall, T. and Garner, T. (2000) 'Sex trade hits suburbs', *New Zealand Herald*, 12 June.

Submissions to Justice and Electoral Select Committee on 2001 Prostitution Reform Bill

Auckland Commercial Massage Operators and Adult Entertainment Owners

Cooper, S.

Miller, R.J.

Submission to the Justice and Law Reform Electoral Select Committee on the 1989 Crimes Bill,

NZPC (New Zealand Prostitutes' Collective) (1989) July.

Submission to the Working Group on Occupational Regulation on the 1978 Massage Parlours Act

NZPC (1990)

FIVE

The Prostitution Reform Act

Gillian Abel, Catherine Healy, Calum Bennachie and Anna Reed

Introduction

As discussed in the previous chapter, the successful lobbying for change in how the sex industry was regulated in New Zealand culminated in a parliamentary vote on 25 June 2003 where the Prostitution Reform Act (PRA) was voted into law by 60 votes to 59 with one abstention. This chapter gives an overview of how sex work was regulated in New Zealand prior to 2003 before discussing the purpose of the PRA and how the specific aims were addressed in a section-by-section discussion of the Act.

Regulation of sex work in New Zealand prior to 2003

Prior to 2003, sex work in New Zealand was not illegal but all related activities were criminalised through the invocation of clauses of a number of existing Acts. Section 26 of the 1981 Summary Offences Act made it an offence for a sex worker to offer sex for money in a public place:

> Soliciting is applicable to any person who offers his or her body or any other person's body for the purpose of prostitution.

However, clients were not criminalised, as it was not an offence to pay or to offer to pay for sex. A double standard existed, therefore, as a sex worker could be convicted of soliciting and incur a criminal record, while, in the eyes of the law, the client had committed no offence.

Section 147 of the 1961 Crimes Act made it an offence to keep or manage a brothel.

(1) Everyone is liable to imprisonment for a term not exceeding five years who –
  (a) Keeps or manages, or acts or assists in the management of any brothel; or
  (b) Being the tenant, lessee, or occupier of any premises, or any part thereof to be used as a brothel; or
  (c) Being the lessor or landlord of any premises, or the agent of the lessor or landlord, lets the premises or any part thereof with the knowledge that premises are to be used as a brothel, or that some part thereof is to be so

used, or is wilfully a party to the continued use of the premises or any part thereof as a brothel.

(2) In this section, the term 'brothel' means any house, room, set of rooms, or place of any kind whatever used for the purposes of prostitution, whether by one woman or more.

If the police raided brothels, the presence of safe-sex literature and condoms could be used as part of a pattern of evidence to achieve conviction against operators of venues and sex workers. With the operation of brothels made illegal, brothel owners ran their businesses under the front of massage parlours, which were a legally permitted enterprise. The 1978 Massage Parlours Act provided for the licensing of massage parlour operators, but did not refer to the provision of commercial sexual services. Sex workers were vulnerable to coercive and exploitative practices by owners or managers of the businesses and had little recourse to the justice system. The Massage Parlours Act also prohibited the employment of individuals under the age of 18 years and people with drug- or sex work–related criminal records in parlours.

Section 148 of the Crimes Act also made it illegal to live off the earnings of the prostitution of another person, which meant that partners or adult children of sex workers could be committing an offence by being supported by their spouse or parent.

Everyone is liable to imprisonment for a term not exceeding five years who knowingly –

(a) Lives wholly or on part on the earnings of the prostitution of another person; or

(b) Solicits, or receives any payment, reward, or valuable consideration for soliciting, for any prostitute.

In addition, section 149 of the Crimes Act made it an offence for any person to procure sexual intercourse for another person:

> Everyone is liable to imprisonment for a term not exceeding 5 years who, for gain or reward, procures or agrees or offers to procure any person for the purposes of prostitution with any other person.

Purpose of the PRA

With the passing of the PRA, all of the clauses in the Acts described above were scrapped. The new legislation represented a shift in policy attitude from a moralistic to a public health and human rights approach. The specific aims of the Act, as stated in section 3, clearly reflected a harm minimisation approach and took into account the human rights of sex workers:

The purpose of this Act is to decriminalise prostitution (while not endorsing or morally sanctioning prostitution or its use) and to create a framework that –

(a) safeguards the human rights of sex workers and protects them from exploitation;
(b) promotes the welfare and occupational health and safety of sex workers;
(c) is conducive to public health;
(d) prohibits the use in prostitution of persons under 18 years of age;
(e) implements certain other related reforms.

Following the enactment of the PRA, the sex industry could operate under the same health and safety rules as any other New Zealand industry. The Department of Labour's Occupational Safety and Health division consequently developed guidelines intended for sex industry owner/operators, the self-employed, employers, managers and workers (Department of Labour, 2004). The development of the guidelines was an inclusive process. The starting point was the guidelines developed in New South Wales, Australia by Scarlett Alliance (a sex workers' rights organisation) and the Australian Federation of AIDS Organisations (Edler, 2000). The New Zealand Prostitutes' Collective (NZPC) collaborated with Scarlett Alliance to enable the Department of Labour to adapt the guidelines for the New Zealand context, in consultation with sex workers and brothel operators. The adapted guidelines include information on the roles and responsibilities of all involved in the sex industry, including operators, managers, receptionists and private and managed workers, under the PRA and the 1992 Health and Safety in Employment Act. They also outline requirements for sex worker health, sexual health education for clients and management and workplace amenities (covering psychosocial factors, such as security and safety from violence, alcohol, drugs, smoking in the workplace, complaints, employee participation and workplace documents).

Health and safety requirements

Operators of businesses under the law are required to adopt and promote safe-sex practices by taking all reasonable steps to ensure that their workers and clients use appropriate protection in all services that carry a risk of acquiring or transmitting sexually transmitted infections (STIs); ensuring that workers and clients are given health information and that this information is clearly displayed in brothels; not implying that a medical examination of a sex worker means that the sex worker is infected with an STI; and taking all reasonable steps to minimise the risk of sex workers or clients acquiring or transmitting STIs (section 8). A business operator who fails to comply with these requirements is liable to a fine of up to $10,000. Advertisements for brothels run prior to the law change had sometimes advertised the women working within their establishments as 'clean'. This implied that sex workers in other establishments may not be 'clean' and that medical certificates guaranteed absence of any STIs. Section 8 acknowledges that medical certificates showing an absence of STIs are only valid at the time of testing and endeavours to counteract discourses of sex workers as 'dirty' by promoting safe-sex cultures within the legislation. This section acknowledges the pressures sex workers are placed under to provide proof of their 'cleanness', which the NZPC argues can in turn lead to demands from clients and operators to provide unsafe sex.

Under section 9, sex workers and clients are also compelled to take all reasonable steps to ensure that they use adequate protection during penetrative and oral sex and minimise the risk of acquiring or transmitting an STI. In addition, sex workers and clients are also required not to state or imply that because they have had a medical examination, they are not infected with an STI. Any person who contravenes section 9 is liable to a fine of up to $2,000. Section 9 stops short of making condoms mandatory. Initially, section 9 was advocated mostly by politicians and was not supported by NZPC, which saw it as creating an environment that would result in the 'policing' of sex workers, such as happens with 100% condom campaigns. Such campaigns are seen to violate the human rights of sex workers without achieving their public health goals (Network of Sex Work Projects, 2003). Nevertheless, NZPC eventually acquiesced as a concession to political reality. NZPC was concerned to keep the legal dynamics of safe-sex confined between the operators and the clients, as they argued that section 9 could be used against sex workers by either clients or operators who had a grudge. The concern was that in such situations, clients and operators are more likely to be believed than sex workers.

Posters and leaflets were developed by the Ministry of Health to promote the objectives of sections 8 and 9[1]. Sex workers were involved in the design of these posters. Separate posters were developed for operators, sex workers and clients. A landmark case was brought before the Christchurch District Court in 2005 when a sex worker laid a complaint with the police about a client who removed his condom during sex without her knowledge. The police prosecuted the client for committing an offence under section 9 of the PRA. The client pleaded guilty to the charge and was fined $400 and a further $130 court costs. To date, no other cases of this sort have come to court.

---

[1] These posters may be viewed at the following web addresses: www.healthed.govt.nz/resources/healthandsafetyinformationforopera.aspx

www.healthed.govt.nz/resources/healthandsafetyinformationforsexwo.aspx

www.healthed.govt.nz/resources/informationforclients1.aspx

The Prostitution Reform Act

Advertising restrictions

Restrictions are placed on advertising for commercial sexual services, with advertisements on radio and television, cinemas and in the print media (with the exception of the classified advertisements section) deemed an offence and liable for summary conviction (section 11). In the case of a body corporate, conviction on the above charges would incur a fine not exceeding $50,000 and in all other cases a fine not exceeding $10,000. Brothels are able to advertise for staff and use the word 'brothel' (although they may not necessarily do so), which makes it clear to potential applicants what is expected of them. Prior to legislative change, obscure advertisements were used that sometimes led people to apply for jobs with no understanding that sex work was involved. Many brothels and individuals are also now advertising on websites, which is not covered under section 11 of the Act.

Territorial authorities delegated powers

Under the PRA, territorial authorities (TAs) were given powers under sections 12-14 to regulate the signage and location of brothels at a local level. Under section 12, a TA can prohibit signage if it is likely to cause nuisance or offence or is incompatible with the character of that area. Any bylaws made under section 12 are made as any other bylaw under the 2002 Local Government Act (LGA). Similarly, bylaws regulating the location of brothels (section 14) may be made under the LGA.

Resource consents, under the 1991 Resource Management Act, are not normally required for land use relating to sex work businesses (section 15), unless specifically noted in the relevant district plan. TAs, in granting or refusing resource consent, must take into account whether the business will cause nuisance or offence to the general public or whether it is incompatible with the character of the area.

In Chapter Nine of this book, Dean Knight examines how TAs have responded to their law-making powers under sections 12-15.

Protections for sex workers

Section 16 provides protection for sex workers by making it an offence, with a penalty of up to 14 years' imprisonment, for anyone to induce or compel another person to provide, or continue to provide, commercial sexual services, or claim any earnings derived from sex work. Individuals, thus, may not use an occupational position or prior relationship with a sex worker to threaten or bribe a sex worker to provide a sexual service. The Act also legislates for the right of refusal to provide commercial sexual services and consent can be withdrawn at any stage in the transaction (section 17). Refusal to work as a sex worker also does not affect any entitlements to a benefit under the 1964 Social Security Act or the 2001 Injury, Prevention, Rehabilitation, and Compensation Act. This also ensures that the state is not forcing someone to work as a sex worker (section

79

18). Sections 16-18 were designed to protect sex workers against exploitative management practices, such as the use of bribes or threats to provide particular sexual services. However, these sections can also provide protection against clients. To date, section 16 has not been tested in court.

Application of the 1987 Immigration Act

Section 19 of the PRA deals with the application of the 1987 Immigration Act. It stipulates that no permit can be granted to a non-resident who provides, or intends to provide, commercial sexual services, or who intends to operate or invest in a commercial sexual business. If the holder of a temporary or limited permit under the Immigration Act does not comply in this regard, the permit may be revoked. NZPC has concerns about this part of the legislation, as it believes that sex workers should be treated like any other migrant worker, and be eligible for work permits. As a result, NZPC has had meetings with Immigration Services. This section was designed to combat trafficking of sex workers. However, Immigration Services has informed the Prostitution Law Review Committee that it has found no cases of trafficking of sex workers to date.

Under-age sex workers

Prohibitions are placed on people who assist anyone under the age of 18 years in providing sexual services, anyone who receives earnings from such services, or anyone who contracts someone under the age of 18 years for commercial sexual services (sections 20-22). The Act allows for a prison term of up to seven years for anyone contravening these sections. No person contravenes sections 20-22 for providing legal advice, counselling, health advice or any medical services to a person under 18 years of age and, in contrast to the situation prior to decriminalisation, no person under the age of 18 years can be charged as a party to the offence. Until the end of March 2008, 92 charges had been brought against people contravening these sections (PLRC, 2008). This does not represent 92 individual cases, however, as in many instances more that one person was charged in relation to the same offence. The highest sentence imposed was for two years' imprisonment, considerably less than the seven-year maximum term for conviction under clauses 20-23. Other sentences have included fines, supervision, community work, home detention and short-term imprisonment (PLRC, 2008).

Powers of entry

Sections 24-33 of the Act deal with powers of entry. Under the PRA, Medical Officers of Health (MOoHs) are designated as inspectors of brothels. A MOoH may appoint a suitably qualified or trained person for his/her district to carry out this task. Under section 26, an inspector may enter premises if they have reasonable grounds to believe that it is being used as a sex work business. However, an inspector may not enter a private home unless he/she has the consent of the occupier or is authorised by a warrant of inspection issued by a District Court Judge, Justice, Community Magistrate or Registrar of a District Court. On entry to any premises under section 26, an inspector must produce identification and evidence of his/her designated power and a warrant (if required). A summary conviction for obstructing an inspector may incur a fine not exceeding $2,000. In Chapter Eleven, Cheryl Brunton provides an account of how MOoHs and public health services have responded in implementing the requirements of the PRA.

Under sections 30–33, police may enter premises with a warrant (issued by a District Court Judge, Justice, Community Magistrate or Registrar of a District Court) if they have reasonable grounds to believe that section 23 has been contravened through the use of persons under the age of 18 years in sex work or if the operator is not in possession of a certificate as stipulated in section 34.

Operator certificates

Sections 34–41 deal specifically with operator certificates: every operator of a sex work business is required to hold a certificate which may be granted by the Registrar of any District Court. Operators not in possession of a certificate are liable on summary conviction to a fine not exceeding $10,000. In many countries that have legalised brothels, a limited number of licenses have been issued, resulting in many brothels operating illegally. In contrast, in New Zealand, under the decriminalised system a Registrar must issue a certificate on application if the applicant pays the prescribed fee, supplies a properly completed application form, attaches a photocopy of a form of official identification, supplies a recent photograph and is 18 years or older. Under section 36, an applicant may be disqualified from holding a certificate if he/she has committed an offence under the 1961 Crimes Act that is punishable by two or more years' imprisonment, an offence under the 1983 Arms Act that is punishable by imprisonment, or an offence in relation to the 1975 Misuse of Drugs Act. An applicant disqualified from holding a certificate may apply for a waiver under section 37 of the PRA. Operator certificates are renewable annually. Registrars may cancel a certificate if the operator is convicted of an offence referred to under section 36 or if a waiver of disqualification is cancelled. Operators are required to produce their operators' certificate if a member of the police produces identification and has reasonable grounds to believe that he/she is operating a brothel (section 40). Under section 41, it is stipulated that court records concerning the identity of applicants for certification, applicants for waivers of disqualification and certificate holders may be searched only by the applicant or holder concerned, the Registrar or the police (but only for the purpose of investigating an offence). Anyone who contravenes this section by obtaining and using information is liable on summary conviction to a fine not exceeding $2,000.

Review of the Act

A review of the operation of the Act within three to five years and the establishment of a Review Committee were legislated for under sections 42-46 of the PRA. The Act requires that the numbers of sex workers in New Zealand be assessed as soon as practicable after the commencement of the Act. Following this, a review of the Act within five years should assess the impact of the Act on the number of persons working as sex workers in New Zealand, assess the nature and adequacy of the means to assist people to avoid or cease sex work, consider whether any amendments to the Act are advisable, consider whether any future review is indicated and report on the findings to the Minister of Justice.

Prior to the enactment of the PRA, in the Second Reading of the Bill in parliament, Tim Barnett highlighted the lack of rigorous research on the efficacy of decriminalisation:

> 'One of the difficulties faced by the Select Committee was that when New South Wales reformed their prostitution law in 1995, they set up no evaluation system and facts have been hard to come by. This has enabled bizarre lies to be told. New Zealand law reform must be and will be better than that.' (Barnett, 2003)

The Prostitution Law Review Committee was appointed by the Minister of Justice and consisted of 11 members. The PRA required that the committee include three people nominated by NZPC, or any subsequent group that represents the interests of sex workers. In Chapter Seven, Paul Fitzharris, the chair of the Review Committee, discusses the formation of the committee and how it carried out the review of the PRA.

Conclusion

Until 2003, New Zealand regulation of the sex industry was consistent with moral perspectives, depicting sex workers as public nuisances and a threat to family values. However, in 2003, after a period of effective advocacy and lobbying from NZPC, other interest groups and some parliamentarians, the government adopted a public health and human rights stance to the regulation of the industry and repealed all laws that effectively criminalised the activities associated with sex work. This was in recognition of the harm caused by these policies. In doing so, New Zealand became one of the few countries in the world to decriminalise sex work and placed itself in the forefront of world interest as to whether this would be an effective strategy in reducing such harm. There is scant research on the impact of decriminalisation on sex workers and the research presented in the following chapters of this book will go some way to redressing that gap in knowledge.

References

Barnett, T. (2003) 'Prostitution Reform Bill – Second Reading speech', www.labour.org.nz/labour_team/mps/mps/tim_barnett/Speeches/speech18/index.html

Department of Labour (2004) *A guide to occupational health and safety in the New Zealand sex industry*, Wellington: Department of Labour.

Edler, D. (2000) *A guide to best practice: Occupational health and safety in the Australian sex industry*, a Scarlett Alliance publication, Sydney.

Network of Sex Work Projects (2003) 'The 100% condom use policy: a sex workers' rights perspective', www.nswp.org/safety/100percent.html

PLRC (Prostitution Law Review Committee) (2008) *Report of the Prostitution Law Review Committee on the operation of the Prostitution Reform Act 2003*, Wellington: Ministry of Justice, www.justice.govt.nz/prostitution-law-review-committee/publications/plrc-report/index.html

SIX

Several sides to this story: feminist views of prostitution reform

Alison Laurie

Introduction

To whore or not to whore? To regard the right to sell sex as an aspect of women's right to choose what she will do with her body, or to see prostitution as degradation and an aspect of male control over women's bodies? To decide to support prostitution law reform as in the best interests of sex workers, or to oppose it as exploitation of women? To recognise sex workers as autonomous women, freely choosing prostitution as employment, or to decry prostitution as an oppressive environment where women are the sexual playthings of men? A patriarchal project to demean women, or a route to economic independence for women? To be for or against? And how to decide?

These were some of the questions New Zealand feminists asked themselves, as politicians and society in general debated prostitution law reform. Some feminists supported reform, others opposed it. Who were they, and what were their arguments? This chapter will explore diverse New Zealand feminist views using examples from the submissions received by the Justice and Electoral Select Committee considering the Prostitution Reform Bill (PRB). The submissions selected are from self-identified feminist individuals or organisations, or from women or men whose arguments could be regarded as drawing on feminist arguments. There were 222 submissions received by the Justice and Electoral Select Committee on the PRB and, of these, 56 are considered by the author to have been written by feminist individuals or organisations or based on feminist arguments. Obviously, this is a personal judgement and is not presented as statistically exact; not does it mean that the writers, organisations or their members all necessarily identify as feminist. This chapter is a guide to understanding the range of arguments based on feminist ideas presented to the committee.

Of the 56 submissions selected, 40 supported decriminalising prostitution and 16 opposed it, and selected examples are included from them to illustrate the feminist ideas in New Zealand prior to decriminalisation. Also included are extracts from a published article by a New Zealand feminist and, because some international feminist literature on prostitution was influential, this is referred to where it is cited in submissions, or where it appears to have informed arguments and recommendations. The focus of this chapter is, however, on the views expressed by New Zealand feminists.

Feminists in New Zealand, as elsewhere, have long engaged with questions about prostitution. Some 19th-century women's rights activists saw prostitutes as 'fallen women' and victims in need of rescue. For example, the Women's Christian Temperance Union (WCTU), founded in 1885, and the National Council of Women of New Zealand (NCWNZ), founded in 1896, campaigned against the Contagious Diseases Acts for 'interfering with the rights and liberties of women only to make it safer for men to sin' and condoning prostitution by ensuring prostitutes were free of venereal disease (Coney, 1993, p 123). Other feminists took a different view. Echoing Cicely Hamilton's *Marriage as a trade* (1981 [1909]), which argued that marriage was a form of private rather than public prostitution, sex educator, Ettie Rout, described marital sex as part of the 'profit system' and regarded marriages of 'convenience' as a form of 'mercenary intercourse' (Rout, 1923, cited in Sutch, 1974). After campaigning for safe sex brothels during the First World War for soldiers on leave in Paris from the front, Rout was reviled and her book *Safe marriage* banned outright (Tolerton, 1992, p 216).

Since the 1970s, second- and, later, third-wave feminists have echoed all these views. One Marxist feminist analysis suggests prostitution is the rental of the body, while marriage is the sale:

> The wife ... differs from the ordinary courtesan only in that she does not hire her body, like a wage worker, on piecework, but sells it into slavery once and for all. (Tong, 1989, p 64)

Other feminists consider sex work degrading and contributing to inequality between men and women. However, US women's studies professor, Wendy Chapkis, concludes from her interviews with sex workers in the US and the Netherlands:

> While feminists have been deeply divided for more than twenty years on whether prostitution should be conceived of as sexual violence or sex work ... all who are concerned with women's rights and well-being might unite around proposals to enhance women's power within the trade and to increase their options beyond it. (Chapkis, 2000, p 200)

Some New Zealand feminists opposing the PRB regarded all payment for sexual services as demeaning and oppressive. They thought that keeping sex work criminal was an effective control for under-age prostitution, some arguing for the 1999 Swedish model of criminalising clients and decriminalising sex workers to decrease demand through fear of legal sanctions. Some New Zealand feminists supporting the PRB thought that sex work must be decriminalised for public health reasons, and to prevent the transmission of sexually transmitted infections. Others argued that decriminalisation would restore human rights for sex workers currently operating in an environment of double standards for women and men. Some believed that decriminalisation would enable and empower sex workers to leave the industry if they wished, as women with criminal convictions for prostitution found it difficult to obtain other employment. Many thought the general culture of criminality surrounding an illegal industry created an environment in which sex workers could be abused.

A number of feminist submissions referred to Article 6 of the Convention for the Elimination of Discrimination Against Women (CEDAW), that 'parties shall take appropriate measures including legislation to suppress all forms of traffic in women and exploitation of prostitution of women'. Some used Article 6 to support the Bill, as they thought that decriminalisation would assist the fight against trafficking, while others used it to oppose the Bill, as they thought the PRB would create increased trafficking.

The following sections explore these and other arguments and recommendations, first, from those opposing the Bill, and then from those supporting the Bill. The author made a submission supporting the PRB. However, for the purposes of this chapter, the intention is to review the range of feminist arguments made both for and against the legislation. It is noteworthy that these submissions have much in common, in that they all proceeded from wanting to promote the best interests of women, but differed in how they thought this could be achieved. New Zealand was the first country to achieve women's suffrage, in 1893, and the first in the then British Empire to admit women to university degrees, in 1877. During the passage of the 2003 Prostitution Reform Act, New Zealand had a woman Prime Minister, Speaker of the House, Governor General and Chief Justice. Conservative women's organisations have a long tradition of influence on New Zealand politics, operating from a mainstream, liberal feminist perspective. Their support of the PRB and the decriminalistion of prostitution was crucial, as was the support of the Ministry of Women's Affairs. The timing was also important, as the centenary of women's suffrage in 1993 and the 1993 Human Rights Act created opportunities during the following decade for a focus on women's lives, especially for broad discussions of women's issues and human rights. For example, the NCWNZ identified financial sustainability, especially employment (including part-time and casual work) and pay equity, as main issues (Page, 1996). From the early 1990s, the New Zealand Prostitutes' Collective (NZPC) (see Chapter Three) worked with women's organisations on issues such as poverty and prostitution. Not all participants agreed that prostitution should be decriminalised, but as a consequence of working closely together, many liberal feminists working in mainstream organisations such as the New Zealand Federation of Business and Professional Women decided to support decriminalisation. Catherine Healy, National Coordinator of NZPC (see Chapter Three) recalls a meeting where she criticised some women's groups who had privately affirmed their support, but who had not done so publicly. Many then rose to the challenge to formally support decriminalisation and subsequently wrote submissions in favour of the PRB (personal communication). It is also significant that the National Collective of Independent Women's Refuges Inc. (see below) acknowledged the role of the NZPC as an advocate for sex workers in its submission. Feminists have argued that people should listen to the voices of women and believe their stories, especially on issues such as rape, sexual abuse, violence and harassment. In this instance, liberal feminists in New Zealand decided to respect the voices and listen to the experiences of the women most affected, and to hear what they wanted. The majority then decided to support the PRB, and even some feminist submissions against the Bill supported decriminalising sex workers.

Arguing against the legislation

One feminist who did not support decriminalisation was Sandra Coney, an Auckland regional councillor, co-founder and editor of the feminist magazine *Broadsheet*, and a long-standing women's health advocate and co-founder of Women's Heath Action, who came to national prominence as co-author of a 1987 article on 'the unfortunate experiment' at National Women's Hospital Auckland, sparking the Cartwright Inquiry (Coney, 1988). In her newspaper column, Coney argued that prostitution was an indicator of gender inequality, stating that 'prostitution reinforces the urge of men to dominate women' and 'there can be no equality between men and women in prostitution and we can never claim we have sex equality while it exists' (Coney, 2001). Her article was appended to the Supplementary Information for the Justice and Electoral Select Committee, described by the committee as providing a 'flavour' of a 'third feminist perspective' on prostitution (Coney, 2001). The committee identified this as a view 'opposing prostitution on the basis that it is immoral and indecent and should therefore be criminalised, differing from two other feminist views supporting decriminalisation' (PRB/JP/1, p 15). Referring to the umbrella organisation NCWNZ, of which the Women's Christian Temperance Union is a member, and which supported decriminalisation, Coney admitted that she was:

> … out of step with many feminists…. Even long-standing women's organisations whose founders fought against prostitution have come around to the fashionable view that prostitution is 'sex work' and should have the protections afforded to other workers. (Coney, 2001)

Despite acknowledging this, Coney did not explain why she thought that continued criminalisation was desirable or why criminalising women sex workers while their male clients were within the law did not represent inequality between men and women. Despite her assertion that gender equality was not achievable while prostitution existed, she made no recommendations in this article as to how it could be eliminated. Coney's article echoes US feminist anti-prostitution theorist Andrea Dworkin (1987), who regards the sale of sexual services as degrading and demeaning. British (now Australian) feminist, Sheila Jeffreys, and Dworkin's former colleagues in the US Women Against Pornography movement, feminists Catherine A. Mackinnon, Kathleen Barry (1995) and Janice Raymond (1995), also take this position on sex work and oppose decriminalisation. Coney cites Jeffreys and Mackinnon that prostitution means female degradation, with compliant patriarchal states making the sale of female sexuality safe for male consumers (Coney, 2001).

Jeffreys herself came to New Zealand, lobbied Members of Parliament and spoke to the media, arguing against the PRB, but it seems that she had little or no influence on the liberal feminist supporters of the Bill, though her concerns were addressed directly or indirectly in some feminist submissions against the Bill. Jeffreys argues that 'prostitution is a form of male sexual violence against women, consistent in its effects on the abused women with other forms of violence, particularly child sexual abuse' (Jeffreys, 1997, p 6). She believes 'the most useful way forward … is to fight prostitution as a violation of women's human rights' (Jeffreys, 1997, p 6). Jeffreys argues that the demand for sexual services must be stopped, as does Christine Stark, who maintains that people promoting 'prostitution as feminist … are acting against the sexual freedom of women and children and they become complicit in the abuse of women and children' (Stark, 2004, p 279).

Coney, rather than making a submission on the PRB, wrote to all Members of Parliament (MPs) on behalf of Women's Health Action, a trust that receives funding from the Ministry of Health to produce a newsletter, lobbies politicians on health concerns and informs women about matters relating to women's health. In the letter, Coney asked MPs to vote against the Bill, based on Article 6 of CEDAW, as decriminalisation would 'make New Zealand a key link in the global trade in women and create the potential for New Zealand to become a prostitution tourism destination'. She did not explain how this might occur, but went on to recommend the Swedish model.

There were some international submissions opposing the PRB. The Coalition Against Trafficking in Women Australia (CATWA), of the international Coalition Against Trafficking in Women (CATW), wrote a submission opposing the PRB, based on Article 6 of CEDAW. Congratulating the New Zealand Government as signatories of CEDAW and ratifying the Optional Protocol to CEDAW, CATWA wanted 'an alternative approach to prostitution which respects women's human rights'. It then recommended the Swedish model, especially retaining legislation prohibiting 'brothel keeping, pimping and procuring'. Citing Barry (1995), the founder of CATW, it stated:

> Pimps can include 'boyfriends' who 'season women' and turn them out into prostitution through a variety of techniques which can include not only violence but also dependency and indebtedness in the victim.

Citing Farley et al. (1998) and Jeffreys (1997), it argued that 'prostitution is not a business like any other', as 'no other business requires women to have sex with strangers on a daily basis'. It maintained that prostitution 'arises from unequal status', and women's 'so-called choice is constructed out of women's subordination', as they 'are not in a position to choose to be prostitutes'.

Echoing points made by Coney, and influenced by Barry (1995), CATWA concluded that 'the sex industry constructs a form of abusive sexuality which is an obstacle to the creation of equality between men and women' (JL/PRB/52, pp 1-3).

Melissa Farley, from Prostitution Research and Education, San Francisco Women's Centers Inc., California, US, submitted against the PRB, arguing that prostitution was:

> ... the hiring of humans to act like sexualized puppets. Prostitution always includes the dehumanization, objectification, and fetishization of women and children.

Stating that she had 'interviewed 854 people in prostitution, from Canada, Columbia, Germany, Mexico, South Africa, Thailand, Turkey, United States and Zambia', Farley denied that sex workers could choose prostitution and claimed that her research showed that 89% 'wished to leave prostitution, but did not have other options'. She recommended New Zealand adopt the Swedish model (JL/ PRB/41, pp 1-2).

Submissions by New Zealanders against the PRB drawing on these international anti-prostitution theorists, included that made by Ruth Margerison, who had worked with WEAVE, a women's educational organisation in Northern Thailand, and who explained that her work had brought her 'into contact with refugee women from Burma faced with ... the lack of any economic opportunity other than the sale of their bodies'. She urged the committee to consider the Swedish model, arguing that CEDAW requires the elimination of violence towards women and children, and that the PRB did not address this debate (JL/PRB/76, p 1). Lesbian Action for Visibility in Aotearoa (LAVA), a small activist group from Christchurch, stated that it 'worked for, not just the well-being of lesbians ... but for the well-being of all women and children in Aotearoa/NZ'. It recommended the Swedish model, citing the Swedish legislation that 'women are not for sale in Sweden' (JL/PRB/152, p 1). In its oral submission, LAVA was the only group recommending the Swedish model to note that it could not 'provide evidence that the Swedish example is working – it has only been in place since the beginning of 1999' (JL/PRB/152a).

LAVA thought that the PRB:

> ... appears to be correcting a law that discriminates against women but ... overlooks the social and economic realities that force women into prostitution and the violence and exploitation that they are then subjected to. (JL/PRB/152)

It supported decriminalising sex workers, and suggested that if the government were concerned about the welfare of women 'forced to sell their bodies on the streets and in brothels, it would be pursuing policies to ensure safe and rewarding employment was available to them' (JL/PRB/152).

Other feminist submissions opposed to the PRB and recommending the Swedish model included that of Marilyn Pryor, an anti-abortion advocate and former National President of the Society for Protection of the Unborn Child. Pryor argued for research to assess

> ... the impact of prostitution on those involved in the sex industry who are most vulnerable to exploitation and violence such a study may reveal that the best we can do for this vulnerable group of people is to enact a law similar to that enacted in Sweden. (JL/PRB/45)

No-one recommending the Swedish model discussed the political, social or historical differences between New Zealand and Sweden, or considered whether these differences could be addressed in New Zealand through social policies and education, or whether they would need to be implemented through increased law enforcement.

A group of three women submitting together (Wakelin, Vautier and Clark) cited the CEDAW resolution as their reason for opposing the PRB, as well as the Convention for the Suppression of the Traffic in Persons and of the Exploitation of the Prostitution of Others 1949, stating:

> Prostitution and the accompanying evil of the traffic in persons for the purpose of prostitution are incompatible with the dignity and worth of the human person and endanger the welfare of the individual, the family and the community.

They claimed the PRB therefore contravened international law and for this reason should not be passed (JL/PRB/219, p 1). Other submissions (McGilvray and Trelive) opposing the legislation on the basis of CEDAW Article 6 used similar arguments (JL/PRB/197; JL/PRB/220).

Streetreach Auckland, a Christian faith-based organisation identifying itself as 'a confidential service for women and girls involved in prostitution', thought that by 'legalising prostitution [this Bill] will bring younger women/girls onto the streets which will increase the risk of disease'. They thought that if the PRB were passed, 'prostitution can be taught in schools as a legal profession', arguing:

> ... normalisation of the 'sex industry' and widening acceptance of the idea that sex is merely a commodity that can be bought and sold ... undermines the value of the sex worker, and does not deal with the reasons of why the sex worker is working on the streets. (JL/PRB/100, pp 1-2)

Pamela Gerrish Nunn, a feminist academic from Christchurch, opposed the Bill, stating:

> I fail to see how any measure which will make prostitution easier to practise or procure can be good for New Zealand … it degrades human relations, exploits women and humours men's worst instincts. (JL/PRB/78, p 1)

Although Nunn argued that prostitution should remain illegal as it was degrading, she made no direct recommendations on the PRB.

Arguing for reform

The support of the mainstream liberal feminist NCWNZ was important for the success of the PRB. In its submission, NCWNZ stated that it was an umbrella organisation representing 43 nationally organised societies, including the Labour Women's Council, New Zealand Federation of Country Women's Institutes, New Zealand Women's Christian Temperance Union, New Zealand Nurses Organisation, Pan Pacific and South East Asia Women's Association, Soroptimist International New Zealand, Zonta International District XVI, Catholic Women's League of New Zealand, Council of Jewish Women of New Zealand and many others such as the Young Women's Christian Association (YWCA), which also wrote separate submissions supporting the PRB. NCWNZ also had 34 branches spread throughout New Zealand, to which women from some 150 societies were affiliated. NCWNZ had supported the decriminalisation of prostitution following its 1996 national conference, although it noted that not all members condoned prostitution, as some questioned 'whether prostitution itself is a human rights violation and suggest it perpetuates the power imbalance between men and women'. It strongly supported the PRB, however, because it:

> … aims to safeguard the rights of women and children, provides for protection from exploitation and seeks to create an environment that promotes public health. It is essential that women working in the sex industry have protection regardless of whether they have chosen the industry as a career or have come into the industry because of a lack of options.

It deemed it grossly unfair that prostitutes, the majority of whom are women, can be charged with offences while their clients, the majority of whom are men, are not prosecuted for using their services. It is high time that this discriminatory practice ceased.

On the question of trafficking, and citing CEDAW Article 6, it thought trafficking:

… typically involved the use of deception to recruit and transport an individual who is held in slave-like conditions or forced or bonded into labour. This may be in the sex industry but also may be in another industry. The deception typically involves the working conditions or the nature of the work.

Only the NCWNZ equated sexual slavery with other kinds of occupational slavery. It supported clauses 7 and 8 on coercion and the right to refuse services and strongly supported the Bill (JL/PRB/113, pp 1- 4).

Many other mainstream, conservative, feminist organisations supported the PRB. Most supported it on grounds similar to those set out by the YWCA of Aotearoa/New Zealand, because it would:

- promote the human rights of women
- assist women to make free choices, including leaving the industry
- assist efforts against trafficking women
- bolster safe-sex education and practice
- be good for public health
- protect young people from exploitation
- reverse a previously inequitable and sexist piece of legislation.

Interestingly, some of these were the same grounds given by opponents of the PRB in their submissions against the Bill. The YWCA explained that it offered a 'Christian feminist perspective' on the Bill, adding that it believed it 'important to make a distinction between morality and law in the case of prostitution'. It stated that 'protection for the marginalised is a core Christian principle', but that it did not condone prostitution and we believe this Bill will actually assist sex workers to leave the industry. There is evidence that significant numbers become trapped in the industry due to criminal convictions, stigma, shame, or coercion. The decriminalisation of the industry will assist women to enter alternative employment.

It addressed input received from the Women's Information Network, representing 22 women's organisations. This included 'a desire for the total eradication of prostitution', which the YWCA thought unrealistic. It rejected the Swedish model, as 'in practice, this option would have an adverse impact on sex workers' and would 'force sex workers to work in more dangerous ways'. It thought the UK 'kerb-crawling laws' increased risks to street workers. Finally, it rejected the suggestion that both clients and workers could be criminalised, because 'workers would still be much more vulnerable than the clients in practice'.

In addition, it rejected the suggestion that decriminalisation would result in increased trafficking, pointing out that the YWCA 'abhors trafficking in women and children as a clear violation of human rights and seeks to ensure New Zealand does not in any way support this appalling trade'. Noting 'Many YWCAs in Asia are actively working against trafficking', they stated that 'in discussion with them, they supported the ideas behind this Bill and recognised the situation in New Zealand is very different from their own countries'. It thought the illegal nature of the industry allows for 'foreign women in bonded labour in the sex industry', and that the Bill would provide 'an opportunity for legal redress for these women', with clause 7 addressing coercion and clause 8 providing for sex workers to decline services (JL/PRB/104, pp 1-8). Its interpretation of what decriminalisation would mean in relation to trafficking was very different from that of CATWA, outlined in the previous section.

The National Collective of Independent Women's Refuges Inc. cited CEDAW, the United Nations Convention on the Rights of the Child and the Beijing Platform for Action (BPFA) as its reasons for supporting the PRB. It supported 'the rights of sex workers and children to be protected against exploitation and violence', acknowledged and supported NZPC as 'the primary organisation providing support services and advocacy for women sex workers', and supported all clauses of the Bill. It especially supported clause 7 because the dynamics of family violence could mean perpetrators used a sex worker's occupation to discredit her and harass her around custody issues, and clause 8 because sex workers should have the power to determine which services they would provide. Commenting on clause 10, it noted that the existing legislation contravened both CEDAW and the BPFA by 'discriminating against women, given the gendered nature of sex work'. It acknowledged:

> Sex work can be viewed as a viable financial option by women – given the cost of education, statistics on unemployment (approx 6%) and significant ethnicity and gender wage disparities to support themselves and their families. For many Maori women in particular, the alternative may be poverty. For women living with family violence (of which financial abuse is a common characteristic) the financial viability may be exacerbated.

It noted how the existing law meant that a conviction for prostitution affected 'a sex worker's ability to obtain alternative employment', noting that the law 'chastises her for being a prostitute but effectively locks her into that identity' (JL/PRB/112, pp 1-3).

The Women's Electoral Lobby (WEL) commented on the double standard operating under existing law, arguing:

> Decriminalisation sees prostitution in terms of consenting behaviour between adults, it allows the same sort of controls and regulations which govern the operation of other businesses. Work places will be free to display safe sex information openly without the risk of police raids. The changes proposed will free police resources to focus on crimes rather than the prosecution of prostitutes for soliciting. A conviction

affects a sex worker's ability to obtain alternative employment, to travel or to obtain mortgage finance and reduces their future options.

WEL supported clause 9, preventing the provision of commercial sexual services by a child, noting Article 34 of the United Nations Convention on the Rights of the Child (JL/PRB/62, p 1).

The New Zealand Federation of Business and Professional Women (BPWNZ), a federation of 40 clubs with 1,400 members, commented that its unanimous policy on decriminalisation from 1994 'may come as a surprise to some people given that many members of BPWNZ could be seen as coming from conservative rural background'. Addressing decriminalisation versus legalisation, it thought the former would ensure that all prostitutes were treated equally before the law, rather than creating a 'class of prostitutes that have been approved ... and another class where their work remains illegal'. They were concerned about 'safety in the workplace' and health issues, and thought that the Bill addressed these. Strongly in support of clause 9, it cited the United Nations Convention on the Rights of the Child and CEDAW. It objected to the definition of 'brothel' in clause 6, as a sole prostitute risked having her family home classified as a brothel. With this exception, it supported the Bill in its entirety (JL/PRB/29, pp 1 -2).

The Wellington Women Lawyers Association, with 300 members, thought that the Bill safeguarded the human rights of women. It acknowledged that the question of whether prostitution was a human rights violation was not addressed, but that 'there may be human rights violations within the practice of prostitution'. Although conceding that 'both men and women are prostitutes', it noted that 'the majority of those exploited by prostitution internationally and ... in New Zealand, are women'. Citing CEDAW and the 1951 Convention for the Suppression of the Traffic in Persons and the Exploitation of the Prostitution of Others, it thought that the Bill would make the conditions of prostitution safer for women. It queried clause 6 in relation to the family home being classified as a brothel, and supported clauses 7, 8 and 9 (JL/PRB/122, pp 1-4).

The Palmerston North Women's Health Collective Inc. noted the double standard of existing legislation, and was concerned that sex workers were exploited by massage parlour operators and escort agencies through lack of access to legal support including employment contracts, or to worker protection as independent contractors. It thought decriminalisation would assist public health (JL/PRB/23, p 1). The Catholic Women's League of New Zealand, representing 3,000 members through 121 rural and urban area branches, made it clear that while not condoning prostitution, it supported the decriminalisation of soliciting. It affirmed that 'while we consider prostitution to be immoral, we do not consider that it should be treated as being illegal as human rights are inequitable under present laws'. It thought that 'the criminal activities and violence which currently flourish under present laws can be better addressed' by decriminalisation. It recommended there be controls over where premises could be located in relation to clause 6 and strongly supported the age protections of clause 9 (JL/PRB/33, pp 1-2).

Importantly for Aotearoa/New Zealand, several submissions from Maori feminists and feminist organisations supported the PRB. The Maori Women's Welfare League Inc., a pan-tribal organisation with 3,000 members and 150 branches throughout New Zealand, thought that decriminalisation allowed sex workers to have the same rights as workers involved in other industries. This will improve their working conditions, and encourage them to attain quality health care. It will also act as a strong deterrent to those who would exploit children through prostitution.

The organisation affirmed its support for clauses 6, 7, 8 and 9 (JL/PRB/65, pp 1-2).

Te Puawai Tapu, a Maori health organisation committed to improving the sexual and reproductive health of Maori, stated that the aims of the PRB provided a 'critical opportunity to make a positive impact on Maori health development, and specifically in regards to the sexual and reproductive health of Maori sex workers', affirmed by the Treaty of Waitangi, which must be 'acknowledged as a key consideration in the passage of the Bill'. In supporting the PRB, Te Puawai Tapu stated that it could 'provide opportunity for rejecting "victim-blaming" and "deficit-thinking" approaches to addressing the sexual and reproductive needs of Maori sex workers', and 'make a positive impact on Maori health development' (JL/PRB/142, pp 1-2).

Professor Ngahuia Te Awekotuku provided a brief historical and cultural context for New Zealand's sex industry, pointing out that after first contact between Maori and Europeans 'sexual favours … were shared, and enjoyed, by both parties', and 'the newcomer would proffer a small gift to his companion … socks (preferably red), foodstuffs … and anything metal or glass, iron nails being the most desirable item'. She affirmed:

> Prostitution has been here in the Maori world since the earliest social encounters with people from the northern hemisphere. During the first encounters … those providing sexual services were in control. The exchange was uncomplicated; the provider set the terms. I would suggest that the proposed Bill puts forward an opportunity for similar arrangements. It has occurred on these islands before; it could happen again. (JL/PRB/116, pp 1-4)

UniQ Victoria, a student group claiming to represent 1,400 gay, lesbian, bisexual and transgendered students, thought that existing laws discriminated against sex workers, who were mostly women, and that the definition of prostitution 'should also be changed to remove connotations which imply prostitution is a taboo and an immoral issue' (JL/PRB/67, pp 1-6).

Criminologist Jan Jordan (see Chapter Two) argued for decriminalisation because it redressed 'a current anomaly in New Zealand law, and to remove a double standard'. She thought:

> The existing legislation is an embarrassment ... based on archaic notions which endorsed a view of men as having uncontrollable sexual needs, and women as being divided into either madonnas or whores.

Jordan argued that because sex workers operated in an 'environment governed by fear and secrecy', they were vulnerable to criminal offences because of their illegality. She supported the Bill as drafted, noting that in the long term it could be desirable 'to promote economic and social measures aimed at reducing the pressures on women to engage in prostitution' (JL/PRB/21, pp 1-3).

Maria Perez-y-Perez, a social work PhD student from Canterbury University, supported decriminalisation based on her in-depth interviews with women in the sex industry and her participant observation as a receptionist at two Christchurch massage parlours. She supported clauses 7 and 8, maintaining that 'the most commonly used means to coerce sex workers into undertaking sexual services against their will is through the withholding of monies.... It is after all a basic human right to say "no."' She opposed a police database of escorts and street workers (JL/PRB/150, pp 1-3).

Other individual submissions included people who had worked on HIV/AIDS programmes. It was argued by Fithian that a decriminalised sex industry would give sex workers equal status with clients and industry operators, and protect public health by encouraging positive behaviour change within the industry through developing and applying occupational safety and health guidelines (JL/PRB/56, pp 1-4). The work of the NZPC was commended. Hicks recommended changes to clause 4 in order to exclude the home of a sex worker from being defined as a brothel, and thought sex workers should be protected from discrimination on grounds of current or previous employment (JL/PRB/30, pp 1-2).

The submissions considered so far in this chapter, whether opposing or supporting the PRB, were from people apparently without personal experience of sex work. Sex workers using feminist arguments also made submissions, including the NZPC, which applauded the PRB because it 'prioritises the human rights of sex workers and promotes their occupational health and safety' and pointed out that sex workers were the people who would be 'most significantly affected by changes to prostitution law'. NZPC noted the four main sectors of New Zealand sex work as massage parlours, escort agencies, private workers and street workers, and described the abuses endemic in parlour and escort work where, it argued, sex workers were often 'treated like overly controlled employees but with none of the rights of recognised employees'. It supported clauses 7 and 8 addressing coercion and the right to refuse to provide commercial sexual service, as these would 'establish a baseline for enhancing the occupational safety and health for sex workers' (JL/PRB/110, pp 1-31).

In its supplementary submission, NZPC noted that after decriminalisation there would be no excuse for an 'out of control' sex industry, and that existing legislation which addressed crimes such as people smuggling or trafficking, rape or sexual violation, sex with minors, slavery, blackmail and so on would not be repealed. However, it warned that repealing all existing laws relating to prostitution, including brothel keeping, procuring and living on the earnings, was essential to establishing health policies and providing safe working conditions for sex workers. It argued strongly against legalisation, as this would result in a two-tiered system, with legal and illegal workers (JL/PRB/110a, pp 1–8). Pride and Unity for Male Prostitutes (PUMP), the NZPC-affiliated project for male sex workers, addressed similar points (JL/PRB/111).

NZPC New Plymouth branch argued that the existing law was discriminatory, condemning the existing police register (JL/PRB/105, pp 1–5), as did NZPC Christchurch, which noted that some sex workers left the industry 'after a short period of time, as the work can be unsuited to them'. The register 'keeps people locked into the industry and for those who leave or want to move on to other employment there is a real fear that their past will be revealed'. It strongly supported clauses 7 and 8 as protections for workers (JL/PRB/99, pp 1–5).

There were several confidential or anonymous submissions, and an anonymous letter to Members of Parliament from a former Maori sex worker, now a university graduate and in full-time employment. She stated:

> I personally was not degraded during my time in the sex industry. The likes of ... Sandra Coney may be horrified to learn that I was actually empowered by working in the sex industry. Being a sex worker gave me financial empowerment. It was the previous lack of money that was more debilitating, but I guess the haves cannot understand how soul destroying it can be to be one of the have-nots. The clients I met for the most part were just lonely people.... My ability to put a little cheer in these people I found rewarding. (Confidential letter, 3 March 2003)

This reflects the views of US writers Annie Sprinkle, Carol Queen, Jill Nagle and others in *Whores and other feminists* (Nagle, 1997), who, as feminists, refute other feminist views expressed from outside the industry that sex work is degrading.

The anonymous letter writer also pointed out that New Zealand's sex industry should not be compared to that of Sweden, Thailand, India or 'many other places too far removed from the experience here to warrant comparison' (Confidential letter, 3 March 2003).

Conclusion

This chapter provides an overview of New Zealand feminist responses to the PRB, as reflected in submissions received by the Select Committee. Some of the 40 submissions based on feminist ideas supporting the Bill were from large organisations with thousands of members, a substantial group reflecting feminist thought within the New Zealand population base of four million. The 16 submissions based on feminist ideas opposing the PRB were from individuals or groups who did not report membership totals. An estimate of the people involved here is far fewer. This is not necessarily statistically accurate, but it does provide a broad picture of New Zealand feminist ideas about sex work. A conclusion from these comparisons is that New Zealand feminists and people basing their arguments on feminist ideas overwhelmingly supported the PRB. From the evidence of their submissions, they did so based on liberal feminist ideas of equal human rights and fair workplace practices for women sex workers. Very few submissions considered men or transgendered sex workers, so from this it may be concluded that the majority were less concerned about these groups. Many feminists who supported the PRB did so because they supported CEDAW and thought that the Bill would reduce the trafficking of women and children into prostitution by removing illegality from the New Zealand sex industry. The majority supporting the PRB thought that sex work should be treated like all other employment. However, almost all submissions supporting the Bill explicitly supported clauses allowing sex workers to refuse services, despite this contradicting the requirements of the 1993 Human Rights Act (HRA) to provide equal access to goods and services for named categories of people protected against discriminatory exclusions. No submissions mentioned the HRA. However, feminist support for these clauses was in most cases explicitly stated to be based on providing protection for sex workers from unscrupulous brothel and parlour owners and operators, and to prevent the use of coercion to force sex workers into unsafe or unwanted working situations.

No submissions from feminists supporting the PRB referred to sex work as degrading or demeaning. However, three organisations stated that while they supported the Bill, they did not condone prostitution – the YWCA and the Catholic Women's League, both operating from Christian feminist principles, and NZNCW, with its diverse organisational membership including Christian feminist groups such as the WCTU.

Those opposing the PRB either explicitly cited overseas feminist ideas, or appeared implicitly influenced by these ideas, particularly those of Sheila Jeffreys, Kathleen Barry and Catherine Mackinnon. Some gave CEDAW as a reason for their opposition, as they believed decriminalisation would increase trafficking. Many denounced sex work as degrading and demeaning, and some thought it increased inequalities between men and women. No-one addressed whether women have the right to control their own bodies and to choose to hire themselves out for sexual services even if they experience this as demeaning and degrading, which workers in other physically demanding occupations such as factory or field work might also argue. Although many opponents of the Bill recommended the Swedish legislation, they did not discuss how this could be implemented in New Zealand. Since 2001, Swedish writer and social commentator, Petra Ostergren (2006), has identified aspects of the current Swedish law that have an adverse impact on sex workers, not considered by the Bill's opponents.

Only a few submissions using feminist arguments were from people stating they had been or were currently employed in the sex industry, with personal experience of sex work in New Zealand. Of these, all supported the PRB. There were apparently no submissions from feminists opposing the PRB who had personal experience of sex work in New Zealand. One submission was from an overseas researcher who had not, at the time of the submission, conducted research in New Zealand; another was from an overseas organisation working on international trafficking, and another from a New Zealander who had worked on trafficking issues in northern Thailand.

   In conclusion, it would appear from the evidence of the submissions received on the PRB that the majority of New Zealanders using feminist arguments did not agree with criminalising sex workers or their clients, and did not agree with feminist analyses of sex work as degrading. Sandra Coney acknowledged this by stating that she was 'out of step' with the majority. Based on their responses to the PRB, it appears most New Zealand feminist organisations proceeded from liberal feminist ideas of equality and fair treatment for women both as individuals and as members of occupational or other groups within New Zealand society.

References

Barry, K. (1995) *The prostitution of sexuality*, New York, NY: New York University Press.

Chapkis, W. (2000) 'Power and control in the commercial sex trade', in R. Weitzer (ed) *Sex for sale*, New York, NY: Routledge, pp 181-202.

Coney, S. (1988) *The unfortunate experiment: The full story behind the inquiry into cervical cancer treatment*, Auckland: Penguin Books.

Coney, S. (ed) (1993) *Standing in the sunshine: A history of New Zealand women since they won the vote*, Auckland: Viking.

Coney, S. (2001) 'No equality between sexes while prostitution exists', *Sunday Star Times*, 12 August.

Dworkin, A. (1987) *Intercourse*, London: Arrow Books.

Farley, M., Barbal, I., Kiremire, M. and Sezgin, U. (1998), 'Prostitution in five countries: violence and post-traumatic stress disorder', *Feminism and Psychology*, 8: 4, 405-426.

Hamilton, C. (1981 [1909]) *Marriage as a trade*, London: Women's Press.

Jeffreys, S. (1997) *The idea of prostitution*, Melbourne: Spinifex Press.

Nagle, J. (ed) (1997) *Whores and other feminists*, New York, NY: Routledge.

Page, D. (1996) *The National Council of Women: A centennial history*, Auckland: Auckland University Press/Bridget Williams Books.

Ostergren, P. (2006) *Porr, horor och feminister (Porn, Whores and Feminists)*, Stockholm: Pocketforlaget.

Raymond, J. (1995) *Report to the Special Rapporteur on Violence Against Women. The United Nations, Geneva, Switzerland*, North Amherst, MA: Coalition Against Trafficking in Women.

Stark, C. (2004) 'Girls to boyz: sex radical women promoting pornography and prostitution', in C. Stark and R. Whisnant (eds) *Not for sale, feminists resisting prostitution and pornography*, Melbourne: Spinifex Press, pp 278-91.

Sutch, W. (1974) *Women with a cause*, Wellington: New Zealand University Press.

Tolerton, J. (1992) *Ettie: A life of Ettie Rout*, Auckland: Penguin Books.

Tong, R. (1989) *Feminist Thought: a comprehensive introduction*. Boulder, Colo.: Westview Press.

Submissions to Justice and Electoral Select Committee on 2001 Prostitution Reform Bill

Catholic Women's League of New Zealand. JL/PRB/33. Supports.

CATWA (Coalition Against Trafficking in Women Australia). JL/PRB/52. Opposes.

Farley, M. JL/PRB/41. Opposes.

Fithian, N. JL/PRB/56. Supports.

Hicks, L. JL/PRB/30. Supports.

Jordan, J. JL/PRB/21. Supports.

Lesbian Action for Visibility in Aotearoa. JL/PRB/152 and JL/PRB/152a. Opposes.

Maori Women's Welfare League Inc. JL/PRB/65. Supports.

Margerison, R. JL/PRB/76. Opposes.

McGilvray, M. JL/PRB/197. Opposes.

National Collective of Independent Women's Refuges Inc. JL/PRB/112. Supports.

NCWNZ (National Council of Women of New Zealand). JL/PRB/113. Supports.

NZPC (New Zealand Prostitutes' Collective). JL/PRB/110 and JL/PRB/110a. Supports.

NZPC Christchurch. JL/PRB/99. Supports.

NZPC New Plymouth. JL/PRB/105. Supports.

Nunn, P.G. JL/PRB/78. Opposes.

New Zealand Federation of Business and Professional Women. JL/PRB/29. Supports.

Palmerston North Women's Health Collective Inc. JL/PRB/23. Supports.

Perez-y-Perez, M. JL/PRB/150. Supports.

Pryor, M. JL/PRB/45. Opposes.

PUMP (Pride and Unity for Male Prostitutes). JL/PRB/111. Supports.

Streetreach Auckland. JL/PRB/100 and JL/PRB/91. Opposes.

Supplementary Information for the Justice and Electoral Select Committee, PRB/JP/1.

Te Awekotuku, N. JL/PRB/116. Supports.

Te Puawai Tapu. JL/PRB/142. Supports.

Trelive, J. JL/PRB/220. Opposes.

UniQ Victoria. JL/PRB/67. Supports.

Wakelin, D., Vautier, A. and Clark, J. JL/PRB/219. Opposes.

Wellington Women Lawyers Association. JL/PRB/122. Supports.

WEL (Women's Electoral Lobby). JL/PRB/62. Supports.

YWCA (Young Women's Christian Association) of Aotearoa/New Zealand. JL/PRB/104. Supports.

Part Two

Implementation and impact of the 2003 Prostitution Reform Act: the first five years

SEVEN

Review of the Prostitution Reform Act

Paul Fitzharris with Aline Taylor

Background

I had a 37-year career in the New Zealand police force, from 1964 to 2001. For two years, during the 1970s, I was appointed Officer in Charge of the Wellington Vice Squad. This role included, among many things, the investigation and prosecution of offences related to prostitution. There were two of us on the squad and we set about our task with enthusiasm and vigour.

The Vice Squad was principally interested in targeting offences relating to prostitution that were visible to the public. Consequently, much of our attention was focused on street-based sex workers, and on sex workers who provided their services to fishing crews on board the growing numbers of Asian fishing vessels that were coming into Wellington at the time – a result of the burgeoning New Zealand fishing industry. Of the sex workers working on the streets, transgendered persons were the most visible to the public. From a police enforcement perspective, they were also the easiest to prosecute because, as the homosexual law reform had not yet been enacted, sexual contact between males was deemed illegal in New Zealand. In prosecutions involving transgendered persons, therefore, all that needed to be proved was that there had been some form of sexual connection between males. The matter of whether or not payment for sexual services had been received was not relevant for prosecution.

A prominent person within the transgender community in Wellington at this time was Carmen. Carmen operated a well-known and respected coffee shop in the heart of the city and, although there was nothing outwardly obvious about Carmen's café to suggest sexual services were being offered within the premises, rumours to this effect circulated widely around Wellington. To people not otherwise involved in the sex industry, such rumours meant that visiting Carmen's café was alluring because it seemed risqué and exciting. We decided to target Carmen to establish whether or not sexual services were being offered on her premises. After establishing that they were, Carmen was arrested along with a transgendered sex worker who had been found working on site.

Following their arrest, a sensational hearing took place in the Wellington courts, during which media attention focused predominantly on the matter of whether the sex worker was male or female. The jury found that she was biologically male, although in every other way a woman, and Carmen and the sex worker were convicted of breaches of the homosexual laws. I felt as though the publicity surrounding this case had merely served to enhance Carmen's reputation and promote her and her coffee shop. Carmen had become an exotic and popular personality around Wellington, and the much-publicised trial did nothing to detract from this.

Carmen never showed any overt antipathy to us following her trial, however, and continued to welcome us into her coffee shop when we carried out further checks. This cordiality continued even after we prosecuted her a second time and, when Carmen celebrated her 70th birthday in Wellington some years later – after the passing of the homosexual and prostitution law reforms – the police were welcomed to the party. In lieu of a gift, Carmen enjoyed a mock celebration of her induction into the Wellington Vice Squad, complete with a pink, sequined police helmet.

Other than 'celebrities' such as Carmen and transgendered street sex workers in general, the other most publicly visible sex workers were those who provided their services to visiting fishing crews. This was because many based their business from a number of prominent coffee shops in Wellington that were known to attract the clientele of easily identifiable Asian fishermen. Prosecuting this group of sex workers was more difficult than prosecuting transgendered sex workers, however, because of the necessity of proving that money was being exchanged for sexual services, and that the sex workers were not simply being – as they claimed – 'very friendly' towards the visiting fishermen. Adding to these complications was the fact that it was almost impossible to use the fishermen as witnesses, as many did not speak English and were only in New Zealand for very short periods of time.

Despite our best efforts, it soon became apparent that our investigations and prosecutions into sex work were not making much of a dent in the Wellington sex industry. In fact, it seemed that all that was really required of us was to obtain some knowledge, for the police, of the milieu that existed around sex work and of city's 'seedy' nightlife. I felt that our task merely entailed 'keeping an eye on the scene', and I did not feel pressure from my superiors to strive to eliminate prostitution completely. We thus did our best as professional police officers in the task we were given.

Other than during this two-year stint in the Vice Squad, the sex industry did not loom large in my career with the New Zealand police. From a personal point of view, my interest in the job on the Vice Squad had emerged predominantly from my ambitions to become a senior police officer – it was just another role and experience in my police career, giving me insight into another side of the community in which I lived. Once I did become a senior officer, complaints regarding prostitution rarely reached my ears and I did not sense any wide community expectation that the police ought to be rigorously enforcing offences against those involved in the sex industry. Strategic plans and public complaints tend to determine where emphasis is placed in allocating resources to enforce the myriad of laws that the police have to deal with and we received more direct pressure to deal with offences related to burglary, violence and mayhem on the roads. In my experience, prostitution was never emphasised in this resource allocation, other than from sporadic instances of disorder that might have occurred around street sex work in large centres such as Christchurch or South Auckland.

Most complaints received by the police concerning sex work revolved around street-based workers. I knew that the New Zealand law made it very difficult to prosecute sex workers soliciting on the street, principally because we needed to prove that the people being solicited were offended. Additionally, a conviction attracted only a minor sanction from the courts – probably reflecting the community's and the courts' lack of opprobrium of this form of behaviour – and, as a result, police prosecuted street-based sex workers only infrequently. Police were nevertheless interested in monitoring the street-based sex work scene, because street sex workers were believed to attract and associate with people involved in other forms of criminal behaviour.

Police interest in the sex industry grew in 1978, when parliament sought to regulate the massage parlour industry through the Massage Parlours Act. Police were responsible for investigating breaches of the Act and for suspending and cancelling massage parlour owners' licences as necessary. In those days, massage parlours were euphemisms for brothels, although this was largely ignored by the police. Criminal investigations were only conducted on particular parlours following community complaints, or following suspected breaches of the Massage Parlours Act, involvement of youth in the industry, drug dealings or other criminal activity. In some cases, undercover officers were sent in to parlours to detect prostitution only if other criminal activity was also suspected. The regular police presence in massage parlours effectively deterred other criminals from becoming involved in the sex industry.

Throughout this time, the police also maintained registers of people working in massage parlours, in an attempt to keep track of individuals involved in the sex industry. I felt, however, that this policy encouraged a number of unanticipated negative responses, such as expanding the escort business and street-based work, as women were driven into these areas thinking they attracted less police attention. In large centres such as Christchurch, however, those involved in the escort business did, in fact, attract police attention, through their need to advertise their services in the local daily newspaper. Rather than attempting to prevent or prosecute escorts for engaging in sex work, the police were interested in monitoring this form of advertising again, solely in an attempt to monitor individuals suspected of being linked to other forms of criminal activity.

I retired in 2001, at the end of a long career with the police, from my role as Acting Deputy Commissioner of Police. In 2003, I was honoured and somewhat surprised to be appointed chair of the Prostitution Law Review Committee (PLRC).

Prostitution Law Review Committee

Section 43 of the 2003 Prostitution Reform Act (PRA) outlines the way in which members are to be appointed to the PLRC. This section stipulates that the committee should comprise 11 members, two of whom are to be nominated by the Minister of Justice, one by the Minister of Women's Affairs in consultation with the Minister of Youth Affairs, and one by the Minister of Health. Two people are to be nominated by the Minister of Commerce – to represent operators of businesses of prostitution – one person by the Minister of Police and one by the Minister of Local Government. The final three people on the Committee are to be nominated by the New Zealand Prostitutes' Collective (NZPC).

In the end, our committee comprised a nun, a number of sex workers, a general practitioner, an academic, a city councillor, a criminologist, a public health official, social workers and myself, a retired policeman. I was appointed chair of the committee. Of the 11 original appointees to the committee, 10 remained from its inception until the completion of its final report in 2008. Sadly, one of the members passed away shortly after resigning in 2004. She was replaced by the then Director of End Child Prostitution, Child Pornography and the Trafficking of Children, who in turn resigned in 2006, following a change in his role. In June 2007, this vacancy on the committee was filled by a Christian, church-based representative who worked in giving confidential support to people in the sex industry.

Few of us knew each other prior to being appointed to committee but, to my mind, the committee members seemed to represent a broad range of views on sex work. As chair, I anticipated that it would be challenging, in the first meeting, to ensure that such a diverse group remained focused on the issues outlined in the legislation. The Committee recognised that the new legislation involved a shift from a moralist approach to sex work to one that focused on the health and human rights of sex workers, and I feared we were likely to deviate from our tasks on to more moralistic or political debates on sex work and the law change. In an effort to remain as objective as possible, I decided that, initially, our discussions should concentrate on specific issues addressed in the PRA: the human rights, welfare and occupational health and safety of sex workers, and the issue of persons under the age of 18 years being involved in sex work.

The specific review process that was to be undertaken by the PLRC is outlined in section 42 of the PRA. The review process broadly consisted of two main tasks, the first of which was to assess the number of persons working as sex workers in New Zealand, and to assess any prescribed matters relating to sex workers or sex work. The committee was required to commence this work as soon as practicable after the commencement of the PRA, and to report these findings to the Minister of Justice. The second task consisted of reviewing the operation of the PRA since its commencement. The committee was required to assess the impact of the Act on the number of persons working as sex workers in New Zealand and on any prescribed matters relating to sex workers or prostitution, as well as assessing the nature and adequacy of the means available to assist persons in avoiding sex work or ceasing to work as sex workers if they so desired.

The committee was also required to consider whether any amendments to the Act or any other laws were necessary or desirable, and whether the system of certification for massage parlours was effective or could be improved. It was to consider whether any other agency or agencies could or should administer this system of certification, and whether a system was needed for identifying the location of businesses of prostitution. Finally, the PLRC was required to consider whether further reviews or assessments of the Act were necessary or desirable. Section 42 of the Act stipulated that the PLRC should undertake this second task at a time no sooner than the expiry of three years, but before the expiry of five years, following the commencement of the PRA. The committee was to report its findings to the Minister of Justice, after which the minister was required to present a copy of this report to the House of Representatives as soon as practicable.

Initially, the committee held monthly meetings at the Ministry of Justice in order to develop coherence and unity between committee members. After completing its first report and setting in place the research needed for its final report, meetings became less frequent and more sporadic. In the later stages of preparing the second report, the committee resumed meetings at least once a month. The first few meetings were spent reaching a consensus on how best to approach the tasks required. I was keen to ensure that each committee member could and would have the opportunity to express their views on any of the topics we discussed and, after several meetings, the group grew more confident that we would be able to work collectively despite our diverse backgrounds. Eventually, we agreed not to engage in discussions based on uninformed speculation or opinion, and agreed that our emphasis should be primarily on substantiating our report with evidence-based research. We were fortunate in receiving advice from the Ministry of Justice and the Crime and Justice Research Centre (CJRC) of Victoria University of Wellington, both of which assisted us greatly by clarifying our role as a committee and advising us on how to approach the tasks required of us. Ministry of Justice staff were particularly good at keeping us grounded on the issues if we appeared to stray too far from the matters with which we were tasked. Their assistance helped bring the disparate committee members together, ensuring that we were able to work together effectively towards a common goal.

During the initial stages of our deliberations, local councils were struggling with how best to respond to the changes in the legislation. A number of regional councils throughout New Zealand enacted bylaws attempting to ban sex work in wide areas of their towns or cities, thereby subjugating the PRA. Some members of the committee thought that this was something we should take a view on and make submissions or public statements about. While these committee members held strong personal views on the councils' approaches – views that were simultaneously being lobbied from within the sex industry – I believed it was too soon for us to take a position publicly, either in favour of or against the councils, as we had yet to complete all of our investigations. We agreed that we felt the councils were acting in an *ultra vires* manner in attempting to ban sex work in their respective cities, and this was ultimately borne out by court decisions.

After the committee had been running for some time, it was brought to our attention – both informally and through submissions made to us by the public – that people suspected us of being biased in favour of the legislation, and of being more likely to lobby for than against it. This view may have been reinforced by the fact that the committee members were able to work so effectively together, without animosity, despite holding such disparate views and coming from a range of diverse backgrounds. The mere fact that the committee included such a cross-section of society should have sufficed to dispel any accusations of a possible bias, but nevertheless these suspicions greatly increased the committee's resolve to support all of its findings and recommendations by rigorous, independent research. Indeed, although I had not come into the committee with any strong moral position in relation to sex work, I had been raised in a conservative, Catholic family, and I considered myself a fairly typical, conservative New Zealander. I was, in fact, initially dubious about the reform, but changed my personal view in support of it after seeing the findings emerge from the research that was being carried out as part of the law review process.

Task one: assessing the numbers of sex workers in 2003

The PRA came into force on 28 June 2003, and the PLRC was appointed at the end of 2003. By the time all the required administrative details were dealt with, the committee held its first meeting in March 2004. Prior to the appointment of the PLRC, the Ministry of Justice had had the considerable foresight to commence research to satisfy the first of the tasks required of the committee – that of assessing the number of sex workers currently working in the New Zealand sex industry. In practical terms, this was taken as the number of sex workers that had been working just prior to the law change. By the time the PLRC was established, this research was well under way and the committee readily endorsed it.

While discussing how best to assess the number of sex workers working in New Zealand, the Ministry of Justice had considered there to be only two agencies with comprehensive knowledge of the New Zealand sex industry: the police and the NZPC. While the NZPC worked intimately with sex workers, the police – with their registers of persons involved in the sex industry and their regular monitoring of street and escort work – were seen as the logical government agency from whom to seek this kind of information. As the sex industry had essentially been operating outside the law, no other agencies appeared to hold any data on this matter.

In April 2005, the PLRC published its first report, entitled *The nature and extent of the sex industry in New Zealand: An estimation* (PLRC, 2005). The use of the word 'estimation' in the title was significant because, as was emphasised throughout the report, not all of the sources used had been able to provide consistently reliable information about numbers of workers in the sex industry. Keeping records was made difficult by the fact that people often move in and out of sex work and the police – particularly in smaller centres – often maintained registers that were cumulative in nature and did not account for people who had left the industry or moved away. This created an inflated number of people involved in sex work and, as a result, police in these centres were only able to make intelligent guesses about the numbers they believed to be involved at the time. These guesses did, nevertheless, prove to be the best approximation of those involved in the sex industry at the time of the change in the legislation, and the final estimates also provided a basis from which to later compare changes within the sex industry following the implementation of the new legislation.

Task two: reviewing the operation of the Act

While the Ministry of Justice was undertaking this research, the committee debated how best to set about its second task – reviewing the operation of the PRA since its commencement. It was soon agreed that the committee required independent expert advice as to how to proceed and, through the Ministry of Justice, it sought expressions of interest from agencies wanting to provide such advice. Eventually, the CJRC was engaged for the task.

In July 2005, the CJRC recommended the committee seek further research into the performance of regulatory authorities in implementing the new legislation, and into sex workers' and business operators' awareness of the impact of the new legal framework, as well as the extent to which they took advantage of their rights and complied with the responsibilities conferred on them by the new legislation. The CJRC also recommended that this research use a mixed-methods approach that incorporated perspectives from multiple informants – including sex workers and others involved in the industry – and that emphasis be placed on the ethical issues associated with the new legislation. It was agreed that the majority of this research would be carried out by the University of Otago, Christchurch School of Medicine (CSoM), CJRC and the Ministry of Justice, using five separate evaluation projects. The research for this second report began in 2006 and was concluded in late 2007.

The CSoM was already involved in a research project on the impact of the PRA on the health and safety of sex workers, which was being funded by the Health Research Council of New Zealand. Initially, this project did not include Auckland, but, following discussions with the committee and the awarding of an additional grant from the Ministry of Justice, the CSoM extended its research to include this major city. At the committee's request, the CSoM also conducted additional research in order to help assess the most current number of persons engaged in the industry at the time.

Throughout the time this work was being carried out, the committee took the opportunity to undertake fieldwork in Auckland, Wellington and Christchurch. This entailed inviting various agencies to meetings in each of the cities, in order to discuss their views on the new laws. In this way, the PLRC obtained the perspectives of local government organisations, police and non-governmental organisations (NGOs). In the evenings, with the help of the NZPC, the PLRC was also able to visit a variety of brothels throughout the cities, and it became clear during this time that NZPC had a deep understanding of the industry and a good relationship with those involved in it at all levels.

During these brothel visits it became apparent to us that the majority of brothel clients were completely unconcerned about the fact that a team of visitors were passing through the premises, questioning and observing the activities that were going on. Indeed, some engaged us in conversations and asked about the role and nature of our work. Likewise, brothel managers were often keen to show us around their premises and discuss management issues they were facing. It seemed that they were keen to be seen to be acting professionally, as any other business in the community.

During this fieldwork period, we also discovered a number of matters that were of significant public interest, but on which the PRA was silent. These included street-based prostitution, trafficking in persons, the links between prostitution, gangs and crime, coercion and drug use within the sex industry, the influence of the media on public perception and the invisibility of clients. Many of these issues had been frequently raised in the media, at the time of the passing of the PRA, and often in ways that emphasised negative aspects of sex work and the likelihood of these being exacerbated by the reform. While the committee's work was, for the most part, guided by the PRA, we did briefly comment on these issues in our report – despite them not having been specifically addressed by the legislation – because of the significant public interest that had surrounded them earlier.

Following this period of fieldwork, the committee discussed how widely it would attempt to obtain views and opinions on the legislation from interested groups and from the general public. We invited interested NGOs and other organisations that had previously made submissions on the Prostitution Reform Bill to provide further submissions for the PLRC to consider. Public notices calling for submissions were also placed in major daily newspapers throughout 2007. While many of the larger NGOs responded to our invitation, few submissions were made by the general public. The committee perceived this lack of response as being due to the fact that the legislation had already been in place for four years and had not generated much public discussion or debate in this time. Throughout the review period, the committee had also made a conscious effort not to comment publicly until all research had been completed, and its low public profile also meant that few people were aware of its existence and purpose.

The committee's second report was finished in 2008 (PLRC, 2008). Although public discussion surrounding the PRA had largely died down by this stage, I was nevertheless surprised by the lack of media interest in both reports, especially since both included commentary on topics that had previously generated sensational media reports. I concluded from this reaction that, other than a few exceptions, the general public had accepted the reform without much difficulty. At the time of writing this chapter, New Zealand was experiencing an election campaign in which sex work had not been raised as a major issue, again probably reflecting the fact that the New Zealand public are resigned to or accepting of these reforms.

Summary of findings of the Review Committee

One of the most common criticisms of the PRA before it was enacted was that numbers of sex workers – particularly street-based sex workers – were likely to increase as a result of decriminalisation. Unsubstantiated claims to this effect continued to be made following the enactment of the PRA, despite the fact that the baseline estimates of the number of sex workers in New Zealand at the time of decriminalisation (PLRC, 2005) and estimates by the CSoM both prior to and post-decriminalisation (Abel et al, 2007, 2009) showed that the PRA had had little impact on the numbers of people working in the sex industry.

In terms of the health, safety and well-being of sex workers, the committee acknowledged the research findings of the CSoM and CJRC, both of which reported high use of condoms and high levels of safe sex within the industry, and awareness by the majority of sex workers of occupational safety and health requirements. Although the committee concluded that there was little the PRA could do in terms of addressing violence in the sex industry, it acknowledged that the improving relationship between sex workers and the police made it easier for sex workers to make complaints following violent encounters.

Another of the tasks required of the PLRC had been to look at how to help people avoid sex work or leave the sex industry if they so desired. The research findings indicated that the predominant reasons for entering the industry were economic and that many sex workers in New Zealand enjoyed and were happy in their jobs and did not want help to leave the industry. The committee nevertheless recommended that a model for best practice to assist people wishing to leave the industry be adopted in New Zealand, as there is currently little support available.

In its 2008 report, the committee also considered the brothel operator certification system. It recommended that the eligibility criteria for holding a certificate remain the same, but that the certificate holder be required to facilitate inspections of their premises as a condition of holding such a certificate. The committee also advised that certificate holders be provided with information on good employment practices. The research indicated some improvement in employment practices of brothel owners/managers, but there were continuing reports of some unfair management practices. The committee recommended that representatives from the sex industry work with the Department of Labour to develop best practice employment contracts that would strengthen the human rights, employment conditions, and health, safety and well-being of sex workers.

With regard to the involvement of under-age people in sex work, the committee considered that the minimum age of 18 years should remain. Despite concerns expressed by some commentators, the committee did not believe that the PRA had increased under-age involvement in sex work. After considering the CSoM findings on under-age sex workers (Abel and Fitzgerald, 2008), the committee recommended that the Ministry of Social Development develop strategies to assist young people considered at risk of entering the sex industry to access alternative sources of financial support.

The PLRC was concerned that some territorial authorities were enacting bylaws within their regions that contravened the intentions of the PRA. In enforcing areas in which brothels were allowed to operate, no distinction was made between small owner-operated brothels (SOOBs) and larger brothels. The committee considered that a SOOB should be regulated in the same manner as any other home-run business.

With regard to street-based prostitution, the PLRC concluded that while such activity was inherently unsafe, it should not be criminalised, as that would be likely to cause the activity to go underground. Instead, street workers should be encouraged to find alternatives such as working from brothels or other premises. Local government, NGOs and the police should also work with those on the street to maximise their safety and adopt practical solutions to minimise public nuisance.

While the PLRC focused on the rights and well-being of sex workers, little emphasis was placed on their clients. There was a feeling that further research was needed to provide a fuller picture of clients' motivations and reasons for buying sex. The committee did, however, comment that there was evidence to suggest that criminalising clients does not appear to deter demand for sex and an unintended consequence of this may be to increase the vulnerability of sex workers.

Other issues that warranted comment were the links between prostitution, gangs and crime, coercion and drug use within the sex industry, and the influence of the media on public perception. These issues were grouped under the heading 'Misconceptions about prostitution', as the research challenged or refuted commonly held perceptions. In summary, the committee found no specific link between crime and prostitution – rather, sex workers were more likely to be victims of crime rather than offenders. In respect of 'coercion', even though there is a perception that all sex workers are made to work by someone else, the CSoM research found that only 4.3% of survey participants had been made to work by someone else. Contrary to popular perception, only 16.7% reported working to support alcohol or drug usage, while 82.3% said they needed the money to support household expenses.

The committee looked at an analysis of media reporting following the implementation of the PRA carried by the CSoM and presented in Chapter Twelve of this book. This analysis showed that the most frequently cited commentators on the PRA in the print media were politicians and that 'crime, drugs and prostitution' were portrayed by the print media as being synonymous with sex work. There was also clear evidence of exaggeration when numbers of sex workers were cited.

In concluding its report, the PLRC felt that the PRA had been effective in achieving its purpose and that the majority of people involved in the sex industry were better off under the PRA than they were under a criminalised system. The PRA has had a marked effect in safeguarding the right of sex workers to refuse particular clients and practices, chiefly by empowering sex workers through removing the illegality of their work. The PLRC acknowledged that progress in some areas was slower than hoped for, but that attitudes and perceptions developed over a number of years could not be changed overnight simply by changing legislation. It may take a long period of relationship building between people involved in the sex industry and those working in organisations that deal with the sex industry before the rights and responsibilities of sex workers and others involved in the sex industry are fully realised. The committee's final recommendation was that the impact of the PRA should thus be assessed again 15 years after its enactment, that is, by the year 2018.

Conclusion

Little over a year after the review was tabled in the New Zealand parliament, there was a change in government. The review sought minor amendments to the law, but generally endorsed the reformed law and recommended some policy changes with continuing monitoring of the sector. The new government has not so far made any changes to the law, but seems to have accepted, to date, the review's recommendation not to criminalise street-based prostitution when asked to do so by some local authorities.

In respect of specific recommendations made by the PLRC, the following has occurred:

- NZPC continues to keep a count of street-based sex workers in the three main centres and monitors the number of brothel and SOOB workers on an annual basis in some areas.
- In the area of human rights, NZPC continues to provide information to sex workers and brothel operators. There has been no formal response from officials on this recommendation.
- The occupational safety and health guidelines have been available online (www.hazsubstancesinquiry.osh.govt.nz/order/catalogue/235.shtml) and the evidence is that sex workers and brothel operators find them helpful. The Ministry of Health, Medical Officers of Health and NZPC continue to build on relationships formed, which allows Medical Officers of Health access to brothels. Similarly, the police continue to build positive relationships with NZPC and sex workers, and have attended functions for the International Day to End Violence Against Sex Workers.
- The government welfare agency does not impose any extra penalties on those who leave the sex industry as opposed to any other industry.
- Best practice guidelines have been developed concerning under-age persons in the sex industry in the South Auckland area, with input from NZPC and other groups. Arrests and prosecutions of clients and brothel operators who hire people under the age of 18 as sex workers continue.

- A large number of city and district councils no longer enact bylaws or make changes to their district plan in order to control the location of brothels. Some that previously had overly restrictive bylaws have realised that these are no longer necessary and have proposed more liberal changes, in some cases revoking them. A very small number of councils have retained bylaws that have reduced options for sex workers to work for themselves from home.
- Employment contracts are becoming more common in brothels.

There still exists in New Zealand a significant body of people who are opposed to the decriminalisation of the sex industry. Some of this group, subsequent to the passing of the legislation, attempted to gather sufficient signatures to force the government to have a referendum on whether decriminalisation should be overturned. To force a referendum, the organisers needed to obtain the signatures of 10% of enrolled electors. They just failed to obtain the numbers of signatures and their campaign lapsed. However, it would not take much to re-energise this campaign, as those people opposed to the sex industry have not lost their fervour. Raised public concern over criminal or antisocial behaviour in the sex industry (such as an increase in the number of young persons being involved in sex work, blatant breaches of liquor licensing or disorderly behaviour in brothels) could easily reignite such a campaign. Similarly, should it be shown that the current high standards of health and safety fail to be maintained within the sex industry in years to come, successive governments are likely to be pressured once again into strongly regulating the industry, thus undermining the significant benefits these reforms have made.

Street-based prostitution remains an issue in Auckland for many citizens, including one local council, which sees it as antisocial and a blight on the city. It associates disorderly and offensive behaviour with street prostitution and considers that this makes the city less attractive. There have been several attempts by the council to have street-based prostitution in their area outlawed.

While the sex industry has been deregulated and generally decriminalised, putting it on the same legal footing as many other industries – even making it even less regulated than some industries in New Zealand – it is my opinion that those involved in the industry need to accept the responsibility they have been given. Those involved in the management, regulating or monitoring of prostitution need to ensure that the industry does not get out of control. Responsibility has been placed on them by the law to ensure that this does not happen. Some government departments did not take an interest in prostitution prior to the change in the law because of illegality (they left it to the police). Those departments with responsibility for labour laws and health and safety, such as Community and Public Health (see Chapter 11) and Occupational Safety and Health indicated to the PLRC that they would be actively carrying out their roles under the PRA. Time will tell.

References

Abel, G. and Fitzgerald, L. (2008) 'On a fast track into adulthood: an exploration of transitions into adulthood for sex workers in New Zealand', *Journal of Youth Studies*, vol 11, no 4, pp 361-76.

Abel, G., Fitzgerald, L. and Brunton, C. (2007) *The impact of the Prostitution Reform Act on the health and safety practices of sex workers: Report to the Prostitution Law Review Committee*, Christchurch: University of Otago www.justice.govt.nz/prostitution-law-review-committee/publications/impact-health-safety/index.html

Abel, G., Fitzgerald, L. and Brunton, C. (2009) 'The impact of decriminalisation on the number of sex workers in New Zealand', *Journal of Social Policy*, vol 38, no 3, pp 515-31.

Pascoe, N., Fitzgerald, L., Abel, G. and Brunton, C. (2007) *A critical media analysis of print media reporting on the implementation of the Prostitution Reform Act, 2003-2006*, Christchurch: University of Otago.

PLRC (Prostitution Law Review Committee) (2005) *The nature and extent of the sex industry in New Zealand: An estimation*, Wellington: Ministry of Justice www.justice.govt.nz/pubs/reports/2005/nature-extent-sex-industry-in-nz-estimation/index.html

PLRC (2008) *Report of the Prostitution Law Review Committee on the operation of the Prostitution Reform Act 2003*, Wellington: Ministry of Justice www.justice.govt.nz/prostitution-law-review-committee/publications/plrc-report/index.html

EIGHT

Brothel operators' and support agencies' experiences of decriminalisation

Elaine Mossman

The material presented in this chapter is based on a research project carried out by the Crime and Justice Research Centre of Victoria University (Mossman, 2007)[1]. The research was commissioned by the Ministry of Justice to assist the Prostitution Law Review Committee (PLRC) in its review of the 2003 Prostitution Reform Act (PRA). The research brief was to interview brothel operators and community support agencies to ascertain their perspectives on the impact of the PRA on sex workers and the sex industry generally.

This particular study was one of a series of research projects outlined in an evaluation framework to review the PRA developed for the Ministry of Justice in 2005 (Mossman, 2005). The framework was created through careful consideration of the content and aims of the PRA as well as the specific review requirements laid out in the Act, with the objective of developing a series of research tasks that would best address the requirements for this review (Mossman, 2005).

What became clear in developing the evaluation framework was the importance of considering a wide range of perspectives. Of key importance were the views and experiences of the impact of the PRA on the sex workers themselves, a topic that was comprehensively studied by the University of Otago, Christchurch School of Medicine (CSoM) in one of the largest pieces of research on sex workers in New Zealand and also internationally (Abel et al, 2007). Details of this study are presented in Chapter Ten and some of the findings are discussed in Chapters Eleven to Fourteen. Another important group were the various government agencies (for example, the police force, Ministry of Health and Department of Labour) and territorial authorities that had specific responsibilities under the PRA. The Ministry of Justice was given the task of assessing the perspectives of these groups, together with special interest groups and the general public. This left the perspectives of two other key groups: the community agencies that are active in providing support, advocacy, education and health services to sex workers, such as the New Zealand Prostitutes' Collective (NZPC), health services, youth organisations, and cultural and religious groups; and the brothel operators, another

---

[1] This project was commissioned by Ministry of Justice; as such, the research and its findings remain the intellectual property of the Ministry of Justice.

group directly affected by the PRA. These two groups had been able to observe first hand the impact of the PRA on sex workers and the sex industry. Their perspectives were the focus of the research presented in this chapter.

Methodology

Interviews with key informants (brothel operators and community agencies) were carried out between January and April 2007 in five regions across New Zealand: Auckland, Hawkes Bay, Wellington, Nelson and Christchurch. These regions covered both the North and the South Islands of New Zealand, and included the three main urban centres with the largest population of sex workers (Auckland, Wellington and Christchurch) together with two smaller, more rural centres (Nelson and Hawkes Bay). These were the same locations as those covered in the CSoM research on sex workers (Abel et al, 2007).

An initial list of potential key informants was proposed by the Ministry of Justice. This was refined with assistance from support agencies in each of the five areas, which provided information on those individuals and organisations that were most actively involved with the sex industry in their region. A total of 86 key informants were interviewed (see Table 8.1).

The aim was to interview similar groups of stakeholders in each of the five sites, although the number of interviews in each region would reflect the relative size of the sex industry and related community agency activity. For example, there were only six interviews in Nelson, which had just two brothels, no evident street work and very few community agencies actively involved with sex workers. In contrast, Auckland City had 26 brothels listed in the Yellow Pages, and 38 in total across the Auckland region as a whole. There are areas where street work occurs in Auckland City and South Auckland, and the number of community agencies actively working with sex workers was higher here than in other areas. The national offices of some of the community agencies are also in Auckland City, such as New Zealand AIDS Foundation, Stop Demand and End Child Prostitution, Child Pornography and the Trafficking of Children New Zealand. As a result, 35 interviews – the largest number of any region – were carried out in Auckland.

Table 8.1: Interviews conducted across research sites

	Auckland	Hawkes Bay	Wellington	Nelson	Christchurch	Total
Brothel operators	14	4	6	2	12	38
Community agencies	21	5	8	4	10	48
Total	35	9	14	6	22	86[1]

Note: [1]Eighty six individuals were interviewed in 73 separate interviews, with some individuals electing to be interviewed together.

Community agencies

The number of community agencies (CAs) identified in each of the areas that were actively working with sex workers was relatively small and it was possible to approach all those identified for an interview. All those contacted agreed to be interviewed[2]. This resulted in a total of 38 interviews conducted with 48 individuals, giving a fairly comprehensive coverage of all relevant community agencies within the five areas.

The interviews covered groups who provided[3]:

- **support, advocacy and counselling for sex workers (n=14)** delivered either through drop-in centres or through outreach;
- **health services (n=21)**, including sexual health checks, provision of condoms and lubricants, and education and health promotion related to the use of drugs and alcohol; and
- **youth-focused support services (n=13)**, including several youth-focused community agencies, two groups concerned with the elimination of sexual exploitation of children in sex work and one group that provided accommodation to youth who had been used in prostitution.

Within these three groups, most CAs worked generically with sex workers from any sector (working from various premises or on the streeet) and any sex or ethnicity. However, 17 agencies were more familiar with experiences of street workers, while 14 worked predominantly with sex workers from the indoor sector. There were also two interviewees who worked specifically with male sex workers, two agencies that worked only with women and four agencies that worked mainly with sex workers who were Maori.

Brothel operators and small owner-operated brothels

Thirty-eight interviews were conducted with operators of brothels[4] and sex workers in small owner-operator brothels (SOOBs)[5]. There were 25 interviews with

---

[2] Two intended CA participants were not available for interview during the period fieldwork was carried out (this included a Maori warden group in Auckland and Streetwise, a local government initiative in Wellington).

[3] For more details of the specific groups interviewed, see Mossman (2007).

[4] The terms 'brothel' and 'parlour' are used interchangeably in this chapter. The term 'parlour' is more common within the industry, but the PRA uses the term brothel rather than parlour. Operators are those who own, operate, control or manage a brothel (for example, the owner, manager and/ or receptionist).

[5] SOOBs are brothels where sex workers are working for themselves (that is, not being managed) and where there are no more than four sex workers working in any premises. Under the PRA, SOOBs are not required to hold an operator certificate, as they are not classified as 'operators'.

larger, commercial brothel operators (BOPs) covering a range of establishments including up-market and more regular brothels, large brothels with over 20 rooms to small brothels with only two rooms, and speciality brothels, providing bondage and discipline, fantasy rooms and Asian sex workers. A further 13 interviews were carried out with workers in SOOBs. These individuals worked from their own private premises as sex workers[6]. Four of the SOOB workers interviewed worked with others, while nine worked alone. They included two sex workers who were dominatrix mistresses and two who were transgender (there were no male sex workers and the ethnicity of SOOB workers was not recorded). Some SOOB workers worked shifts in commercial brothels and were also able to comment on practices there.

Arranging interviews with BOPs/SOOB workers was not quite as straightforward as with the CAs, perhaps unsurprisingly, as people working the sex industry are traditionally suspicious of outsiders. There was considerable reliance on introductions from representatives of NZPC, particularly for the SOOB interviews. A few BOPs/SOOBs could not be contacted. However, many of those who were interviewed commented that they were pleased to have had the chance to provide feedback on the PRA. Only one BOP with whom the researchers made contact refused to be interviewed.

The sample of BOPs/SOOBs included in the research was not fully representative of New Zealand brothels. Assistance from NZPC in recruiting informants was a potential source of bias, although it was evident that BOPs interviewed had varying relationships with NZPC and the research included two brothels where NZPC was not welcome[7]. It is likely that those SOOB workers willing to be interviewed were more experienced, confident and empowered sex workers. Nonetheless, a large number of BOPs were interviewed and coverage in the smaller areas, such as Nelson and Hawkes Bay, was almost complete.

Content of interviews

Interviews were semi-structured with both closed and open-ended questions. With the exception of one phone interview, all were conducted face to face and ranged in length from 30 minutes to, on two occasions, more than three hours. Informed consent was collected from each participant following an explanation of the purpose of the interviews and reassurance of the confidentiality of responses. An interview guide was developed based on the specific aims of the PRA (see

---

[6] As individual sex workers were already the focus of the CSoM study, it was difficult to decide whether sex workers in SOOBs should be included. It was decided that they should, as the impact of the PRA on their ability to operate their own business had not been surveyed and was an important element of this research. However, in terms of numbers of interviews, priority was given to the larger commercial brothel operators.

[7] This was usually because of past disagreements between NZPC and operators over management practices and the treatment of sex workers.

Chapter Five), with questions framed to assess how well these aims were being achieved. Questions were also framed around the two other specific review requirements of assessing how well the system of certification was working, and assessing the means available to assist individuals who wanted to leave the sex industry and those who wanted to avoid entering it.

The intention was not to collect personal opinions with regard to the pros and cons of decriminalisation of prostitution; rather, questions were framed to assess what key informants had *directly observed* or *experienced* following the implementation of the PRA. In other words, they were asked about changes they had seen and areas where they would like to see improvement.

Key informants were encouraged to respond to questions based on their own experience, rather than hearsay. This meant informants were not always in a position to comment on all sections of the interview guide and responses for the different questions varied[8].

Level of support for the PRA

At the start of each interview, individuals were asked to rate, on a scale of one to five (where one indicated they were strongly against the PRA and five that they were very supportive) what their level of support had been for the PRA at two points in time: prior to the Act being implemented, and at the time of the interview (that is, three-and-a-half years after prostitution had been decriminalised). This question aimed to gauge whether their position on decriminalisation influenced their comments on what the impact of the Act had been.

Around 90% of informants (72 out of 84 who responded to this question)[9] said they had been supportive of decriminalising prostitution when it was first proposed. Reasons for supporting the PRA (common across all groups of informants), centred around protecting the basic human rights of sex workers, improving their health and safety and removing the potential negative impacts of having a criminal record for engaging in sex work:

> 'Seeing these women for over eight or nine years … they appeared to have fewer rights than any other group I was aware of. It didn't seem right to me. They couldn't travel because of convictions, couldn't get a mortgage. It was unfair. I don't like the industry, but I see that it will always be there so I supported the Bill for the sake of the women.' (CA – sexual health nurse)

---

[8] For example, informants providing outreach to street workers did not have direct experience of how well the system of certification for brothel operators was working or whether working conditions in brothels had changed, and were not asked these questions.

[9] Three respondents had not been involved with sex workers or the industry before the PRA came into force.

It was also felt that decriminalising prostitution removed a double standard of morality:

> 'The public morality and public discourse had previously been a double standard. On the one hand, it was saying this is illegal and they [sex workers] are criminals. On the other hand, everyone knew and almost accepted it was going on behind closed doors. I think it is better for it to be honestly recognised as happening, whether people like it or not.' (CA – church leader)

Among those who did not support the idea of decriminalisation were two BOPs who were happy with how things were, and two SOOB workers who had concerns over the possible negative impact on business. There were also five CAs that were initially opposed (one health CA and four youth CAs); these were agencies with an ideological stance against sex work that were concerned that decriminalising prostitution would normalise it:

> 'I see prostitution as part of the global system that is encouraging and sustaining violence against girls and women, particularly sexual violence. It is a global problem, and sex trafficking is being fuelled by prostitution. It is all being fuelled by male demand. The Act says it was not morally sanctioning prostitution but by making it legal, it was.' (Youth CA)

When asked what their level of support was at the time of interview, three years after the PRA had been in operation, 77% remained supportive of the Act. Those whose support had waned included eight BOPs and one SOOB, which had experienced a decrease in business following decriminalisation; three of these BOPs were also unhappy about the fact that they had less control over sex workers after decriminalisation. Four CAs (all health-related) gave lower ratings; while still overall supportive of decriminalisation, they expressed concerns over certain aspects of the legislation (for example, the powers given to local authorities for controlling the location of brothels, for example, and the fact that the PRA made sex work illegal for foreign workers). Two SOOB workers reversed their opinion and had now become supportive of decriminalisation, appreciating the associated increased rights and safety for sex workers.

Perhaps, not surprisingly, the basic position of interviewees towards the PRA and the decriminalisation of prostitution typically carried through to their views on how well the Act was achieving its aims. Those who were in support of the Act (the majority) tended to point to positive impacts, whereas those who were unsupportive focused on negative effects. Despite the diversity of key informants and their particular areas of interest (health, youth, human rights or running a profitable business), differences of opinion more often reflected their basic position towards decriminalisation than it did type of informant. However, where differences according to type of informant emerged (regarding, for example, the business concerns of those in the industry), these have been noted.

Welfare, health and safety

A key aim of the PRA was to improve the welfare, health and safety of sex workers. Informants were asked a series of questions around what changes they had seen since the Act had come into operation in relation to safe-sex practices, the general health and well-being of sex workers, access to health information and services, and the safety of sex workers.

The level of observed changes varied according to different aspects of health. However, overall, around two thirds of all respondents (BOPs, SOOB workers and CAs) felt there had been an improvement in some aspect of health for sex workers post-PRA. The most commonly observed impact was an improved sense of well-being in sex workers, attributed to their new rights and to the fact that sex work was no longer deemed 'criminal'. One operator observed:

> 'There's just an increase in confidence now it is legal – been validated. It's hard to explain, but it's something I've seen. When the Act was passed, the girls knew about it. They didn't know the technicalities, but they knew it was legal and the work could be less demeaning.' (BOP)

Safe-sex practices

The PRA made it an offence for sex workers and their clients not to use safe-sex practices. Despite this, three quarters of the informants who felt able to comment were not aware of any substantial change in the frequency of safe-sex practices. However, this was not of great concern to informants, as it was generally felt that most sex workers had adopted such practices prior to the Act, mainly as a result of an effective HIV/AIDS prevention campaign that ran in the early 1980s[10].

While the commitment of sex workers towards using safe-sex practices had remained good, a positive effect of the PRA identified by around a third of informants was the ease with which sex workers were now able to negotiate this with their clients. In this respect, there was wide endorsement of Ministry of Health information stickers that had been printed post-PRA explaining that having unsafe sex with a sex worker was an offence.

> 'There is back-up now. The small sticker that is behind the door or in the bathroom says you must have protected sex. She can point to the bit about the fine. Because it's the law and the law is in print, the client backs down. It's great.' (BOP)

---

[10] The New Zealand Prostitutes' Collective was set up for this purpose in 1987 and is provided with funding from the Ministry of Health for this purpose.

'It's easier to enforce, especially with the persistent clients that try it on. I can say now, "I know the fine won't hurt you, but do you want your name in the paper like the guy down in Christchurch?"' (BOP)

Another positive effect commented on was the easier access for sex workers to condoms and lubricants that could now be displayed in brothels without fear of prosecution (previously, possession of quantities of such items could be used as evidence of brothel keeping).

Under the PRA, brothel operators also have legal requirements to adopt and promote safe-sex practices in their parlours. All operators who were interviewed were aware of this legal requirement and evidence of this was the high visibility of Ministry of Health posters, stickers or similar information in all brothels visited. However, there were concerns from a few CAs, and reports by some SOOB workers, that some managers' support in this area was minimal:

'One time I had a guy in this parlour who took his condom off, and it wasn't the first time either. I told the receptionist who didn't even bat an eyelid [this was after the Act]. They leave it up to the girls. They think they are just renting the rooms to the girls. At home I'd have kicked him out, but you're a bit restricted in parlours.' (SOOB worker)

Access to health information and services

Another aim of decriminalisation was to increase access to health information and services. As with the use of safe-sex practices, no great change was observed by informants, but again this was felt to be because access to such information had been good prior to the PRA. NZPC was seen as taking the lead in providing this information and it was clear that operators both relied on and appreciated what NZPC offered, and felt it should be better funded for the important role it performs.

Two thirds of operators (18 out of 27 who responded to the question) were familiar with the Occupational Health and Safety guidelines published by the Department of Labour shortly after the Act's implementation (www. hazsubstancesinquiry.osh.govt.nz/order/catalogue/235.shtml). These guidelines were generally felt to be useful, although some informants had concerns over the appearance of the guide, which they felt looked like a text book, and wondered whether the information could be made more accessible to those less inclined to read material in this type of format.

Around a third of informants, particularly health-related CAs, felt there was still room for improvement regarding access to health services and information. There were some suggestions on how access could be improved, including more outreach services in brothels, expansion of NZPC offices and/or a dedicated sex worker sexual health clinic in all centres, better internet resources, more user-friendly leaflets in different languages and more opportunities for peer education.

The PRA expressly made it illegal for non-residents to be sex workers. One sexual health nurse was concerned that this was having an unintended negative effect in relation to this group's access to health services. She felt that non-English-speaking sex workers as a group did not seem to have the same degree of appreciation of the importance of practicing safe sex as 'Kiwi' girls:

> 'They say they don't care. It's funny – it's a different culture. I try and explain about infections if they don't use a condom. They say "no problem, it's good money; it doesn't matter if I get an infection".'
> (Sexual health nurse)

This suggests that non-English-speaking sex workers are very much in need of education about safe-sex practices. In this nurse's experience, health professionals had always had difficulty reaching this group, but she (and other informants) were concerned that things had been made worse now that the PRA had expressly made it illegal for non-residents to be sex workers.

Despite improvements, it was generally recognised that there was still a long way to go before the stigma of sex work was eliminated. While stigma remained, it acted as a barrier to further improvements in the health, and particularly the well-being, of sex workers.

Safety issues

Another important aim of the PRA was to improve the safety of sex workers. Opinion on the impact of the Act in this regard differed among informants. Two thirds, mainly BOPs and SOOB workers, felt that the Act was able to do little about the violence that occurred in the sex industry. However, around a quarter felt there had been some improvement, with health-related CAs tending to be the most optimistic in this regard. Differences often reflected the sector of the industry with which informants were familiar. Those primarily involved with commercial brothels, for example, did not feel the situation had changed much, although in their view it had never been a particularly problematic area.

Street workers were seen to be those most at risk of violence, with several CAs reporting acts of violence they had witnessed. There was also considerable concern over two sex workers who had been murdered in Christchurch post-PRA[11]. Ironically, there was a sense among a few informants that things had been made worse, particularly early on, by the increased attention paid to sex workers by the media and the general public following decriminalisation.

> 'It [violence] is still out there. Maybe there is more. This would be a slap in the face to the intention of the Act. People don't like prostitutes. Now

---

[11] There has been a further murder of a sex worker in Christchurch since this research was carried out.

there is more attention on them, and more exposure. It can lead to more problems.' (SOOB worker)

There were mixed views on whether the risks faced by SOOB workers had changed. In general, the SOOB workers interviewed felt safe and in control. However, there were some BOPs who had concerns over the isolated nature of this work and the increased numbers of SOOB workers now potentially at risk:

> 'There have been more girls going private. This is okay if they're switched on, capable of running a business and able to pick the different personalities. If they've got a quick temper, it could be dangerous. You have to know how to talk to people who might be on "P" [Methamphetamine]; they are volatile.' (BOP)

One area relating to safety where an improvement had been noted was in the reporting of violence. There was general acceptance among informants (BOPs, SOOB workers and CAs) that it was now easier for sex workers to report violence to police. Of the informants who felt they able to comment, 70% reported that sex workers were more likely now to do this.

> 'Since the Act … I'd say the incidence of violence has been lessened a little, because the girls can stop a police car now and make a legitimate claim. One night I was in a police car with a senior sergeant and this girl [a sex worker] had just phoned 111 and waved us down.' (CA)

However, while there may have been an improvement, it was acknowledged that barriers still existed to reporting violence, and in particular, following through with a complaint. It was pointed out that when street workers used illegal drugs, it made them reluctant to ask for assistance from the police. For others, fear of being publicly exposed as a sex worker was still a significant barrier. One SOOB worker spoke of deciding against making a complaint when a policeman asked how she would feel if her name were in the newspaper. There was also a perception that police might not take sex workers seriously:

> 'Reporting has increased. Or at least they will give more consideration to reporting. But although they can, they often don't as they are concerned with how the police will treat them. They still expect to be treated disrespectfully, due to the stigma that still exists.' (CA)

Relationships with the police were seen to have improved post-PRA in some regions, with perceptions of the police changing from 'prosecutors' to 'protectors'. In other regions, informants felt relationships still needed to improve.

Positive relationships between those in the industry and the police in Christchurch had made possible the implementation of a 'Phone Text' safety initiative: sex workers could voluntarily supply a mobile phone number to NZPC, and if NZPC received information of a potentially violent client (and the information was verified by the police), it sent out alerts to those registered on the Phone Text system.

Conditions of employment

Decriminalising prostitution means that sex workers are now entitled to the same employment rights and subject to the same responsibilities – such as paying tax – as those working in other industries. Prior to the PRA, brothel keeping was illegal, so there was no legal redress for sex workers if they had been unfairly treated, coerced or exploited by those running the brothel. To ensure that sex workers are protected against such treatment, there are specific provisions included in the Act that make it an offence to coerce a sex worker to provide commercial sexual services. The Act also specifies that sex workers have the legal right to refuse clients (sections 16 and 17).

The general impression gained from interviewing those familiar with working conditions in brothels before and after the implementation of the Act was that brothel operators who had treated their workers fairly prior to the PRA continued to do so, but those with prior unfair management practices had also continued.

> 'Nothing has changed here because we've always been good. Elsewhere, who knows? But you hear lots of stories still of poor management, workers having to have sex with the boss as part of the interview, money taken off girls, personal details used to blackmail them if they try to complain or cause trouble....They [operators] threaten to "out" them to their families.' (BOP)

A common management practice prior to the Act included charging a sex worker a bond that they were supposed to get back when they finished working for the brothel. In practice, the bond was more commonly used to try to control behaviour – for example, by deducting a fine from the bond if workers turned up late for a shift. The Act explicitly makes illegal any form of coercion to provide commercial sexual services. In asking how management practices had changed post-PRA, several of the brothel operators reported they had now ceased using this practice, with some operators commenting on how this had made running their business more difficult.

> 'Girls choose which shifts they work and what hours. I get cross though, if they don't turn up for a shift they're supposed to do, unless they phone in that they're sick or something. We used to fine them … a $200 bond was good in a way … it was useful in managing the business. We knew when she was finishing: "I'll take my bond on

Friday". Now, you never know when they are finishing. They just don't turn up.' (BOP)

'You can't control the girls now – sometimes they are not here when clients arrive. You can't run a business like that.' (BOP)

Other operators appeared to have adopted slightly modified versions of financial control:

'Workers have to say if they can't meet the terms of their contract. For example, there's a $70 infringement fee if they can't come in. It's set out in the rules.' (BOP)

'We no longer charge any fines or shift fees. We still operate "bonds", but call it a banking deposit. If they do a runner, we get paid.' (BOP)

Operators' frustrations over difficulties in 'controlling' workers and the impact this had on their ability to run a viable business were clearly evident. However, the use of more conventional management practices, such as a system of warnings prior to a worker being dismissed, did not appear to be commonplace.

Brothel operators were aware that sex workers now had the right, at any time, to refuse to provide commercial sexual services. Most operators interviewed appeared to accept this, but six of the 25 BOPS interviewed prefaced this with "but they have to have a good reason":

'If they do refuse, we need an explanation. We won't allow nationality to be the reason – they don't have a right to discriminate. If the client is intoxicated or abusive, they don't have to if they don't want [to].' (BOP)

However, in some cases, it appeared difficult to refuse regardless of the reason:

'One 18-year-old worker had just finished a job. A big Samoan guy was waiting who she had not even had a chance to check out. He was really rough with her, held her down by her throat. She went out to complain to the manager who told her to "go back in".' (SOOB worker)

One BOP observed that while practices in some brothels were slow to improve, the Act had provided sex workers with more options to control their working environment:

'Girls have started to stand up for themselves. They've got some leverage now. They can either refuse to pay fines, choose to move on, work private or they can take the boss to court. Some managers still try it on, but they haven't got a leg to stand on if they are challenged. Some girls, though, unfortunately still buckle in.' (BOP)

A key to assessing whether the PRA is achieving its aims is to ascertain whether sex workers are aware of their new rights. Research with sex workers post-PRA found that 90% were aware they had more employment, occupational health and safety, and legal rights, although some were still confused over what their rights actually were (Abel et al, 2007).

System of certification

The PRA requires that every operator of a prostitution business must hold a 'brothel operator's certificate' that is approved and issued by the Registrar of the District Court at Auckland. Owners, managers and receptionists are all considered to be operators; sex workers in SOOBs are not, as by definition they are working for themselves. There was much debate prior to the Act as to whether a system of certification would result in a two-tier system of illegal and legal operators, as had happened in Victoria, Australia (Sullivan, 1999; CMC, 2004). This two-tiered industry of legal (licensed) and illegal (unlicensed) brothels was attributed to the system of certification being overly onerous and expensive, resulting in high levels of non-compliance (Sullivan, 1999; Jordan, 2005). None of those interviewed for this research was aware of this happening in New Zealand.

Of those who responded to questions on the system of certification (predominantly BOPs and SOOB workers), nearly all (87%, n=26) were supportive of some sort of system of certification. They felt it was important to have some control over people running businesses that placed them in a position of power over sex workers. Certificates were not seen to be difficult to obtain, and neither were they considered expensive (at $200). In addition, compliance appeared to informants to be good.

There were some areas of dissatisfaction, particularly from BOPs. Almost all operators interviewed wanted a more convenient reapplication process. Currently, they have to reapply each year, requiring a recent and authenticated piece of photo identification (such as a passport photo) signed by a Justice of the Peace. Despite making the effort to obtain a certificate, most operators had not had their certificate checked, and felt a more rigorous checking process would be appropriate. Around half thought that for the certificate to have any real value, the criteria and process of obtaining it should be more demanding, by including appropriate skills and knowledge tests, for example.

NZPC offered a counterview with respect to standards for certification. They cautioned that making the system too onerous may result in fewer operators applying for certification, increasing the risk of the two-tier system of illegal and legal operators.

Leaving the sex industry

The Prostitution Law Review Committee (PLRC) was required to assess the means available to assist sex workers to leave the industry. While the PRA took a neutral moral stance by neither endorsing nor sanctioning the sex industry in the process of decriminalising prostitution, it did implicitly promote measures to help sex workers leave the industry (PLRC, 2008). A criminal record is a significant barrier to finding employment and repealing prostitution-related offences from the criminal code was, therefore, intended to assist sex workers in this respect.

Assessing the impact of the PRA in this area proved to be a difficult task. Many within the industry felt that leaving sex work was not an issue - in their view, sex workers left "when they wanted to". In fact, an issue of greater concern for operators was how to retain workers. This was supported by SOOB workers, who did not feel that any assistance with leaving the industry was necessary. It was also pointed out that being a SOOB or sex worker was a career choice many were content with:

> 'I don't have a problem, I can come and go as I please, I've got qualifications, BSc, MA.... But I'd rather do two clients a day, earn $200 and be able to watch TV for the rest of the day.' (SOOB)

It was also suggested by NZPC workers that it could be demeaning to discuss how sex workers might best be helped to exit the industry:

> 'It is offensive to talk about exiting – it's a right to be able to be a sex worker. We don't need rescuing. For some it is just three to five years for an average career – a means to a goal. Get the money for the degree and then move on.' (CA, NZPC)

Those who responded (BOPs, SOOB workers and CAs) were all able to identify services that could be accessed by a sex worker who wanted assistance to exit the industry. Informants were given the opportunity to say what type of services they felt were most effective. Responses included:

- access to mainstream support services. This was seen as more effective than providing dedicated services that singled out sex workers and risked further stigmatising them;
- availability of emergency accommodation and half-way houses;
- access to alcohol and drug (A&D) services, budgeting advice, careers counselling; and
- opportunities to develop relationships and trust, such as through outreach and drop-in centres, so that when sex workers were ready to exit, they were comfortable about asking for assistance.

One area of difficulty, noted by several CAs, was how exiting sex workers accounted for their time in the industry when preparing CVs or going for a job interview. It was felt that it would be some time before sex work would be acceptable for inclusion in a CV.

Many of the themes emerging from the interviews mirrored those in international literature on models of best practice in relation to exiting that was recently reviewed for the Ministry of Justice (Mayhew and Mossman, 2007). These included the question of how many sex workers actually want to exit and the considerable financial barriers to doing so. The types of provision identified above (housing options, and access to A&D treatment in particular) have also been strongly endorsed in other countries.

Persons under 18 years

The issue of the number of young people who might enter sex work as a result of decriminalisation was a key concern when the PRA was passed. The Act makes it an offence for anyone to purchase sexual services from someone under 18 years of age, or for anyone to assist someone under 18 years of age to provide commercial sexual services. It is not, however, an offence for a person under the age of 18 years to provide commercial sexual services, but by doing so they are legally considered to be the victim of an offence.

Informants interviewed had mixed views on whether decriminalisation had affected the number of young people entering sex work. The PLRC acknowledged the difficulties in determining the number of under-age people working in the sex industry, but in reviewing the available evidence, concluded that the Act had not increased the involvement of under-age persons in sex work (PLRC, 2008).

There was consensus among key informants, those within the industry and CAs supporting sex workers that persons under 18 years of age should not be working as sex workers. However, there were mixed views on the impact of decriminalising prostitution on those under 18 years of age. Opinions on whether it had had a positive or negative impact were fairly equally divided.

A few CAs were concerned that young people were interpreting the Act as meaning 'I'm not doing anything wrong', which, it was feared, could encourage their involvement in prostitution:

> 'I was talking with one young person who was telling me she wasn't doing anything wrong. It was like when the government passed the law. It was saying prostitution is okay. It's like drinking – it's illegal until you're 18 years, but it's okay as an adult. So you're being grown up if you do it before 18.' (CA)

However, other CAs took a more positive position, including many of those who worked closely with young people who were engaging in sex work, either providing them with outreach services or accommodation. Their view was that if young people felt they were not doing anything wrong, it made them easier to contact so as to provide support and assistance:

> 'They are much easer to make contact with now – they stand in the light. We can provide them with information, resources, and get them to come to clinic so we can work with them on personal hygiene. The Act provided us with a tool. We are now able to openly discuss what is going on.' (Youth CA)

> 'There are ups and downs to things like this. It is negative if young people are taking on an identity that says it's okay to be a sex worker. But deep down they don't want that – so by being legal and in the open, it allows for an open dialogue. Our girls here want to get out of it. As a result they don't want to talk about it. Most of them were doing it as "survival sex". But in general, if there is open dialogue, you can challenge their identities. If it's illegal, you don't have the same opportunity to talk about it.' (Youth CA)

There was also acknowledgement among some informants that an unintended effect of the Act was that, for those under 18 years of age and determined to work in the industry, it was now more difficult for them to work in brothels so they would be limited to working on the street, where the risk to safety was the highest.

The message sent by the Act to those inclined to use young people to provide commercial sexual services, particularly brothel operators, was much clearer. Operators were aware of the penalties and were very particular when it came to asking for age identification, although it was pointed out that sometimes age was difficult to assess when young people looked older than they were and had fake ID.

> '… it is difficult sometimes with fake ID … managers are now aware of how careful they have to be, they can't afford to make mistakes, they could go to prison. The owners are often doing the hiring themselves these days, because they don't trust the managers to get it right.' (BOP)

One youth CA questioned whether men were aware that they were breaking the law if they picked up a girl who was 16 or 17 years old:

> 'We've got concern over a lack of awareness in New Zealand on what is legal by the public and clients. I don't think many of the clients really understand that they are breaking the law if they pick up a girl who is maybe 16. Most men understand that sex with someone under 16 would be illegal, but they don't see the difference between that and paying someone 16–17 for sex. I don't think guys out there make the connection. They don't see is as criminal act. How do we legally educate people in NZ?' (Youth CA)

Prosecutions

Prosecutions of brothel operators facilitating the prostitution of those under 18 years old was viewed positively, with informants pleased in particular with a successful prosecution of a brothel operator in Christchurch who had girls under 18 years old working in his premises. However, some youth CAs were frustrated over the lack of prosecutions against men who were picking up girls under 18 years old from the street:

> 'Enforcement has been very poor. There has been no attempt by police to reduce the demand for child prostitution. Police know there are young people out there. They've been given licence plate numbers, and there is CCTV that picks them up. Maori Wardens also collect information and make it available. Some of these men even turn up in work cars. How hard can it be? There is one girl who is now 14 years old who has been prostituting since she was 12 – every night for two years. She is still going to school, but has been introduced through the gang scene. Nothing is being done. (Youth CA)

Focusing on stopping demand through more arrests by the police was not seen as the solution by NZPC, which cautioned that this could result in offenders and young girls moving to places that were less visible and less safe. NZPC would rather see resources put into support services for young people to help them avoid entering the industry or to leave it.

One agency was in favour of making it an offence for those under 18 years to work as sex workers. This stemmed from its frustration over the perceived lack of action from government agencies, and a feeling that making it an offence for the young person may pressure welfare agencies and the police to take action. However, criminalisation of young people in this way was not an option supported by others interviewed.

Preventing entry

All groups of informants acknowledged that preventing young people from entering the industry was a challenge. The complex and difficult family backgrounds of many was frequently mentioned:

> 'You have to ask why they feel safer on the streets than at home. No youths should have to support themselves.' (CA)

> 'It's the abuse in homes. The young people think if I'm going to be abused I might as well at least get paid for it. In South Auckland there is a huge amount of violence and abuse in homes.' (Youth CA)

'Transgender youth are a special concern. Because of conditions at home they move out, but they can't get an Independent Youth Benefit. The family says they are willing to support them, but "only if he acts like the man he should be". There's a real "trans-phobia" that needs to be addressed.' (CA)

This last quote points to a particular concern shared by several CAs. Transgender young people were seen to be at particular risk of ending up on the streets engaging in sex work. One transgender ex-worker explained the difficulties in finding acceptance among peers at school or from family members; as a result, transgendered individuals are drawn to the streets where they find support from other transgendered peers.

Specific suggestions offered to prevent young people turning to sex work included:

- ensuring that adequate financial support was available to young people in need and in particular making the government youth benefit easier to obtain;
- providing young people with both emergency and long-term accommodation options; and
- providing drug and alcohol treatments specifically for young people.

Territorial Authority (local government) responses

The Act included provisions that enabled territorial authorities (city and district councils) to enact bylaws to regulate the location and signage of brothels (see Chapter Nine). Territorial authorities (TA) across the country varied widely in their response to the PRA. Some did nothing, while others enacted bylaws in response to concerns raised by their local communities.

Informants were asked to discuss their experience of actions taken by their TA in response to the Act. Their comments reflected the unique characteristics of the region they were in, and, in the case of BOPs and SOOB workers, whether they personally had been affected by a bylaw. Informants in Wellington, Hawkes Bay and Nelson were either happy with the response of their TA or had no comments. The reaction was different in Christchurch and Auckland, locations where the TAs had enacted restrictive bylaws, albeit subsequently quashed by the High Court. Here, informants spoke of the stress experienced (in the case of BOPs and SOOB workers) or observed (in the case of CAs) as a result of TA actions. These had resulted in brothels either closing or reverting back to illegal operations, thus eliminating any intended positive impacts of decriminalisation.

Monitoring and enforcement

A key theme that emerged throughout the interviews was that while the majority of those interviewed applauded the PRA, there was also a high degree of frustration that the provisions of the Act were not being adequately monitored and enforced. The main areas of concerns relating to:

- young people under 18 years of age being used in prostitution;
- unfair management practices used by some brothels, such as the use of bonds, fines, intimidation and sexual harassment;
- clients trying to have unprotected sex; and
- the health and safety practices of some in the industry.

The effectiveness of any legislation depends not only on its provisions, but also on the effectiveness of the regulatory body responsible for implementation (CMC, 2004; Mossman, 2005). The Act decriminalised sex work, recognising that providing commercial sexual services was a legitimate business. Regulation of the industry is through existing statutes and regulations that apply to all businesses and individuals in New Zealand. The only exception is the brothel operator licensing system (certification of brothel operators), which is specific to the sex industry.

Interviews revealed considerable confusion over who was responsible for overseeing the various aspects of the Act. For example, only one in five informants were aware of who was responsible for ensuring appropriate standards of occupational health and safety. This confusion is perhaps understandable when one considers that there are at least six different government agencies with relevant roles (including the police, the Ministry of Health, Inland Revenue, and the Department of Labour and Immigration). In addition, TAs have powers to regulate the location of brothels and signage through local bylaws. Operators reported that they had been subject to virtually no checks in relation to operator certificates, occupational health and safety, employment conditions or anything else. Only one of the 25 BOPs interviewed had had their operator's certificate checked, with most having had no checks of any type.

'I've no idea who checks, as I've never been checked.' (BOP)

'I read about OSH [Occupational Safety and Health division of the Department of Labour] supposed to be coming around to show us how to do the job without hurting your back – I'm still waiting, though! Parlour owners need to know what to do if a girl has a condom break; there are lots of myths out there like to use a bottle of coke.' (BOP)

'Never had anyone ask about our license for prostitutes. Had liquor checks but not a check for operators of brothels.' (BOP)

The exception to this was operators in Auckland's North Shore, who were subject to a local licensing system in addition to a having to obtain a brothel operator's certificate. This involved a series of inspections prior to being granted a licence.

It appeared that one of the reasons for this lack of compliance checks was that, in the main, the regulatory system is essentially 'complaint driven'. For example, a Medical Officer of Health will investigate a health issue only if a complaint has been made (see Chapter 11). Similarly, concerns over employment issues, such as unfair dismissal, rely on a complaint being made to the appropriate agency. Police also rely heavily on complaints being made in order for them to be able to follow up on such things as illegal coercive practices or the hiring of persons under 18 years of age. Some informants were concerned over the appropriateness of such a system for the sex industry when 'complaining' could lead to difficulties for the complainant, such as retaliation or public exposure.

Conclusion

It is difficult to directly attribute any observed changes, whether positive or negative, to the PRA itself from this research. Changes in broad social policy, community health initiatives or rates of unemployment could equally affect many of the areas researched. Another consideration is whether there has been sufficient time for the Act to achieve its stated purpose – some intended outcomes, such as those dependent on sex workers becoming aware of their rights and for their confidence to develop sufficiently to then assert these rights, may take longer than the three years that had elapsed prior to the research.

The overall picture gained by these interviews was that those with the most direct experience of working with sex workers or of working directly in the sex industry were, in the main, happy with what had been provided for by the Act. The few who were dissatisfied tended to be BOPs who were finding running and managing a profitable business more difficult post-PRA and informants from organisations who had remained ideologically opposed to prostitution and its decriminalisation.

Positive impacts that informants attributed to the Act were seen as significant. These included the fact that sex workers were no longer considered to be criminals, that they had the same rights as those working in other industries, and that it was easier for them to negotiate safe-sex practices. There were also areas where improvements were seen as needed, such as eliminating poor management practices, protecting those under 18 years from being used in prostitution, and better administration of the brothel operator system of certification. Other issues that arose included whether it had been appropriate to criminalise foreign sex workers (those without New Zealand residency) and how to protect and improve the situation for transgender youth. However, the majority of informants were pleased with the Act and felt that, with more time and an increase in monitoring and enforcement of its provisions, the positive intentions behind the PRA could be more fully realised.

References

Abel, G., Fitzgerald, L. and Brunton, C. (2007) *The impact of the Prostitution Reform Act on the health and safety practices of sex workers'*, Christchurch: University of Otago, Christchurch School of Medicine.

CMC (Crime and Misconduct Commission) (2004) *Regulating prostitution: An evaluation of the Prostitution Act 1999 (QLD)*, Queensland: Crime and Misconduct Commission.

Jordan, J. (2005) *The sex industry in New Zealand: A literature review*, Wellington: Ministry of Justice.

Mayhew, P. and Mossman, S.E. (2007) *Exiting prostitution: Models of best practice*, Crime and Justice Research Centre report prepared for the Ministry of Justice, Wellington: Ministry of Justice.

Mossman, S.E. (2005) 'Evaluation framework for the review of the Prostitution Reform Act 2003', Unpublished Crime and Justice Research Centre report prepared for the Ministry of Justice, Wellington.

Mossman, S.E. (2007) *International approaches to legalising and decriminalising prostitution: Review of the literature*, Crime and Justice Research Centre report prepared for the Ministry of Justice, Wellington: Ministry of Justice.

PLRC (Prostitution Law Review Committee) (2008) *Report of the Prostitution Law Review Committee on the operation of the Prostitution Reform Act 2003*, Wellington: Ministry of Justice.

Sullivan, B. (1999) 'Prostitution law reform in Australia: a preliminary evaluation', *Social Alternatives*, vol 18, no 3, pp 9-14.

NINE

The (continuing) regulation of prostitution by local authorities

Dean Knight

Introduction

This chapter examines the local government response to the 2003 Prostitution Reform Act (PRA). First, it identifies the local regulatory options – bylaws, district plan rules, decisions on resource consents – that continue to be available following the decriminalisation of prostitution by the PRA. Second, it discusses the degree to which local authorities have adopted these regulatory initiatives, along with the legal challenges to them. To date, there have been three notable challenges (two successful and one unsuccessful) to bylaws enacted by local authorities. The chapter concludes by assessing the state of affairs around local regulation and briefly touching on the tension arising from the local ambivalence towards the national countenance of prostitution.

The continuing role for local regulation of brothels and the business of prostitution

The PRA fundamentally shifts the nature and locus of the regulation of the business of prostitution. The central feature of the PRA was the repeal of the various offences prohibiting solicitation and prostitution. But room remains for the regulation of sex work. Consistent with the purpose of the PRA (section 3), the welfare and occupational health and safety of sex workers are managed nationally through a centrally driven regulatory framework of licensing and inspection of brothels.

Regulation of the perceived neighbourhood or environmental effects of prostitution was left to local communities through their territorial authorities (city and district councils). Territorial authorities are one of the forms of local or municipal government in New Zealand. The responsibility for sub-national governance and regulation generally is shared between 73 territorial authorities (city and district councils) and 12 regional councils (see Mitchell and Knight, 2008, paras 7-11). The allocation of the duty to manage the effects of prostitution to territorial authorities is consistent with the standing brief of territorial authorities. In particular, territorial authorities have a general mandate to promote the well-being of their communities under the 2002 Local Government Act, including legislative power to pass bylaws to achieve this purpose. They also possess an important role to sustainably manage the use, development or protection of land and natural and physical resources within their district under the 1991 Resource Management Act. This is principally implemented through the legislative power to promulgate objectives, policies and rules in district plans (their central regulatory instrument for planning or land-use management) and the responsibility, as consent authorities, to grant resource consents (effectively permits or dispensations) for activities that do not meet those rules (see generally, Nolan, 2005, chs 3 and 4). Consistent with the usual raison d'être of local government, territorial authorities are charged with enabling democratic local decision making on behalf of their communities when undertaking their functions; among other things, they are required to consult and take account of the views of their communities when making significant decisions.

Following the passing of the PRA, the particular regulatory methods by which local authorities can continue to address aspects of the business of prostitution or activities associated with prostitution are as follows:

• regulation of the location of brothels under section 14 of the PRA;
• regulation of the signage of commercial sexual services under section 12 of the PRA;
• regulation of the business of prostitution under the 1991 Resource Management Act, augmented by section 15 of the PRA; and
• regulation of activities, to the extent possible, under generic law-making and approval processes available to local authorities.

Regulation of the location of brothels

The most controversial regulatory method is the regulation of the location of brothels. Section 14 of the PRA specifically allows territorial authorities to pass such bylaws:

> **s14 Bylaws regulating location of brothels**
> Without limiting section 145 of the Local Government Act 2002, a territorial authority may make bylaws for its district under section 146 of that Act for the purpose of regulating the location of brothels.

While the reforms of local authorities and their law-making powers in 2002 sought to simplify and generalise the scope for bylaws (2002 Local Government Act, section 145; Knight, 2005a), local authorities continue to have specific bylaw-making powers in a narrow range of specific areas (2002 Local Government Act, section 146). The conferral of such a power by the PRA therefore is not unique, and needs to be seen in this broader context (see, for example, Mitchell and Knight, 2008, paras 132-9).

The conferral of a bylaw-making power such as this delineates, in jurisdictional terms, the scope for local regulation of the activity. Local authorities are entitled to develop their own local responses – whether permissive or restrictive – as long as they do not exceed the jurisdictional limits of the empowering provision. In this case, the limits are constructed by first, the governance injunction 'regulat[e]', and, second, the defined subject-matter 'location of brothels'. The governance injunction adopted was relatively soft. There is long-standing authority for the proposition that the power to 'regulate' does not include the power to prohibit or effectively prohibit (*Municipal Corporation of the City of Toronto v Virgo* [1896]). Therefore, while the local community is entitled to pass laws controlling location, an outright ban on brothels throughout the entire district is beyond its power. This basic proposition was central to the litigation about bylaws promulgated by some local authorities and a point to which we return later. Second, the subject-matter was defined in terms of 'brothels', defined in terms of premises (PRA, section 4(1)):

> brothel means any premises kept or habitually used for the purposes of prostitution; but does not include premises at which accommodation is normally provided on a commercial basis if the prostitution occurs under an arrangement initiated elsewhere.

Notably, the definition of brothel, and therefore section 14, does not draw any distinction between small owner-operator brothels and other larger brothels, unlike some other licensing provisions in the PRA. The specific bylaw-making power does not confer, or speak directly to, any power in relation to the regulation of sex workers individually. Whether there remains the ability to regulate these matters under the general empowering provision and whether the specific power to regulate the location of brothels affects that question is considered below. Further, the reference to 'location' only contemplates spatially based regulation.

Although bylaws represent the local community's articulation of the rules applying to their district, local authorities usually retain the ability to formally condone non-compliance in individual cases. Typically expressed as a dispensing power, bylaws usually provide the generic power to grant permits or otherwise dispense with the application of any rule in a bylaw. For example, the *Model General Bylaws* contains the following template provisions (Standards New Zealand, 2007, clause 7):

Dispensing power

Where in the opinion of the Council full compliance with any of the provisions of this Bylaw would needlessly or injuriously affect any person, or the course or operation of the business of, or bring loss or inconvenience to any person without any corresponding benefit to the community, the Council may, on special application of that person, dispense with the full compliance with the provisions of this Bylaw;

provided that any other terms or conditions (if any) that the Council may deem fit to impose shall be complied with by that person.

Potentially, this allows any brothel operator finding themselves operating in a location in contravention of a bylaw, or wishing to establish in a prohibited location, to apply for formal permission to operate regardless. Vociferous local opposition to brothels may mean the prospects of successfully obtaining a dispensation are not high. Any refusal is capable of being challenged in the courts, however, on the basis that it is unlawful (for example, if the dispensation test was not faithfully applied or a blanket rule against dispensations was adopted) or is otherwise manifestly unreasonable.

Unlike resource management rules, there is no explicit requirement that bylaws recognise or preserve 'existing use rights' (Caldwell, 2004; Knight, 2005b). That is, existing businesses operating lawfully before a bylaw is enacted are not automatically exempted from the requirements of any new bylaw. That said, the impact on existing businesses is a factor the courts will take into account when considering whether a bylaw is reasonable or not. A failure to accommodate existing businesses within the new bylaw (either through specific exemptions or a transitional regime) may force a court to conclude that the severity of the bylaw outweighs any positive outcomes such that the bylaw is unreasonable and invalid.

The scope of mandate for local authorities to regulate the location of brothels was initially uncertain. There was some speculation that restrictive bylaws promulgated by some local authorities, provoked by vocal anti-prostitution groups, might have exceeded the express and implied limits set by the bylaw empowering provisions. To some extent, a series of challenges to different brothel bylaws – two successful, one unsuccessful – clarified how far local authorities could go in regulating the location of brothels. However, this is complicated by the fact that the outcomes in the three cases are difficult to reconcile.

Bylaws can be challenged in various ways: a direct challenge to the bylaw under special provisions in the 1908 Bylaws Act, an application to judicially review the local authority's process and decision to adopt a bylaw, or by raising the invalidity of the bylaw collaterally as a defence to enforcement action based on the bylaw (Knight, 2005a). In general terms, the courts' role is two-fold. First, the courts review whether the bylaw is 'lawful', including whether it falls within the scope of the empowering provision, whether it is not repugnant (that is, 'fundamentally inconsistent') to other laws and whether it is consistent with the 1990 New Zealand Bill of Rights Act (under section 155(3) of the 2002 Local Government Act, bylaws must not breach the Bill of Rights Act). Second, the courts assess whether the bylaw is 'reasonable'. The lawfulness of the bylaw is typically scrutinised closely by the courts to determine whether the parameters set by parliament have been correctly observed. In contrast, the assessment of whether, viewed in the round, the bylaw is reasonable is calibrated more deferentially and is designed to provide some latitude for the choices and judgements made by the primarily mandated decision maker, that is, the local authority. Historically, this has been framed in terms of a particularly convoluted legal test or calculus found in a case from the beginning of last century, *McCarthy v Madden* [1915]. In basic terms, it allows the courts to judge whether the productive benefits of the bylaw outweigh the negative effects. But it also reminds the court that locally elected members are mandated, and better placed, to make the judgement about whether a bylaw is suitable; the courts are directed to take a deferential approach, except in a narrow range of circumstances where greater scrutiny may be justified (Knight, 2005a).

The first case, *Willowford v Christchurch City Council* [2005], involved a challenge to a Christchurch City bylaw that: (a) permitted brothels in a small designated area of the district only (in general terms, part of the central business district amounting to about 1% of the city); (b) treated small–owner operator brothels in the same way as larger brothels; and (c) made no provision for existing use rights for existing brothels or for new brothels to apply for dispensations (except for three particular long-standing massage parlours/brothels that were specifically exempted from the location requirements). The bylaw was challenged by a prospective brothel operator who owned land both within and outside the designated area.

Ultimately, the High Court ruled that the degree of restriction, in particular the effective prohibition on small owner-operated brothels, was too severe and amounted to impermissible prohibition such that it was unreasonable and/or unlawful. On the one hand, Pankhurst J was reluctant – 'by quite a margin' – to conclude that the local authority's definition of the designated area within which brothels could operate was unreasonable or impermissibly small (*Willowford*, 2005, para 71). He placed some weight on the scope of the designated area reflecting the 'considered view' of the Council subcommittee reached after full public consultation. The view of the community weighed strongly in favour of confining brothels to the central business district and their concern was 'understandable' (*Willowford*, 2005, para 71). On the other hand, he took issue with the effect of the small designated area on small owner-operated brothels. He took the view that the bylaw prohibited sex workers from, in the words of the famous *Virgo* statement on non-prohibition, 'plying their trade at all in a substantial and important part of the city no question of any apprehended nuisance being raised' (*Willowford*, 2005, para 94). Particular weight was placed on the uncontested evidence from the New Zealand Prostitutes' Collective that a private home, discreetly situated in suburban areas, was the natural habitat of small owner-operated brothels and that as many as 50 or 60 sex workers would find themselves unable to work lawfully under the bylaw.

The judge was agnostic about whether the finding of invalidity was properly characterised as being based on 'unreasonableness, [impermissible *Virgo*-style] prohibition, or unreasonable restraint of trade' (*Willowford*, 2005, para 94), although there are a number of hints in the judgement that suggest his driving concern was that the local authority had exceeded the critical legislative mandate. In particular, the judge pointed to the findings of the local authority's own subcommittee (ultimately rejected by the council itself) that small owner-operated brothels had previously existed essentially in residential areas and done so without causing 'significant problems'; he described the subcommittee's original proposal to allow small owner-operator brothels in residential areas as representing 'a realistic squaring up to the clear intent of the Act' (*Willowford*, 2005, para 93) – especially because the PRA recognised that brothels would exist in residential dwellings and exempted them from the need to obtain an operator's certificate.

In the course of his decision, Pankhurst J rejected arguments that the bylaw breached a constitutional or common law right of sex workers to work. His Honour recognised the right of sex workers to engage in the business of prostitution, but accepted that the right was qualified, both generally (regulational restrictions on the right to work being 'commonplace') and specifically (the legislation provided for the regulation of the location of brothels) (*Willowford*, 2005, para 83). Pankhurst J concluded that the bylaw did not intrude 'to any significant degree' on sex workers' right to work (*Willowford*, 2005, para 83), except to the extent he had earlier found that the bylaw improperly restricted the ability of small owner-operated brothels to operate.

The second case, *JB International* v *Auckland City Council* [2006] involved a challenge to a bylaw that restricted the operation of brothels, including small-owner operated brothels, to a few prescribed zones within Auckland City. The bylaw further restricted the operation of brothels in close proximity to designated schools, churches, transport or community facilities, or existing brothels; within the central business district, it also prohibited operation of brothels at street level. As well as challenging the bylaw, the operator of a brothel outside the designated areas challenged the local authority's refusal to grant a dispensation from the requirements of the bylaws.

Heath J ruled that the bylaw was invalid, essentially because the spatial restrictions were too severe. His Honour also ruled that the refusal of the dispensation was unlawful because there was insufficient evidence to suggest that good reasons existed to prevent the operation of the brothel. The close proximity rules meant that an operator faced 'considerable obstacles' in establishing discrete premises in the central business district and, outside that, there were 'only three (relatively) small pockets of land on which brothels could be established' (*JB International*, 2006, paras 85 and 87). 'The Act envisaged', the judge said, 'that both smaller owner-operated brothels and larger enterprises will operate within the jurisdiction of territorial authorities' (*JB International*, 2006, para 92). The power to regulate the location of brothels must 'be exercised on legal (not moral) grounds', with the purpose of meeting the general objectives of territorial authorities set out in the 2002 Local Government Act (namely, addressing nuisance, public health and safety, and offensive behaviour) and traditional resource management objectives (*JB International*, 2006, para 92). Adopting the analysis of Pankhurst J in *Willowford*, Heath J expressed particular concern that the bylaw effectively forbade small owner-operator brothels from operating in their natural habitat – suburban homes – contrary to the outcome contemplated by the PRA. Concerns were also expressed that the restrictions might force brothels to operate in less discreet and safe areas, thereby undermining the safety purposes of the PRA. The judge noted that the grounds on which the bylaw was found invalid overlapped; the *Virgo* non-prohibition principle was breached, the purpose of the PRA was undermined and the nature of regulation could be characterised as unreasonable (*JB International*, 2006, paras 76 and 99).

The third case, *Conley* v *Hamilton City Council* [2006, 2008], involved an unsuccessful challenge to a bylaw that (a) restricted the location of brothels to three zones within Hamilton City (the city centre, a commercial zone and an industrial zone); and (b) prohibited the operation of brothels within 100 metres of 'sensitive sites' (churches, schools, marae (sacred Maori meeting places) and so on). The challenge was brought by the operator of a large brothel employing 12 sex workers that had operated for 19 years; the brothel was located just outside the permitted zones of operation and the operator had failed to secure other premises within which she could lawfully operate the brothel.

The challenge was rejected in the High Court (*Conley*, 2006) and subsequently rejected on appeal to the Court of Appeal (*Conley*, 2008), largely on the basis that the degree of restriction was not so grave as to be unlawful. Significantly, both the High Court and Court of Appeal accepted the evidence that there were over 2,500 'potential occupation units', both commercial and residential, within the zones from which brothels could lawfully operate (*Conley*, 2008, para 68). The Court of Appeal noted that it would still be a 'challenge' to find suitable premises for small owner-operated brothels. But it said it was not prepared to rule that in the circumstances the degree of restriction amounted to an objectionable prohibition (*Conley*, 2008, para 68). Further, the court recorded the contextual differences between the *Conley* case and the situation in other cities. First, the Hamilton bylaw fell short of the 'virtual prohibition' found in the *JB International* case. Second, the evidence presented about the natural habitat of small owner-operated brothels differed: in *Willowford*, uncontested evidence was presented that around 50-60 workers in such brothels would be forced to operate illegally under the bylaw; in the *Conley* case, however, the evidence on the impact on such sex workers was more equivocal, with some acceptance that the natural habitat in Hamilton for small owner-operated brothels included discreet apartments in the central city or mixed-use areas where brothels were permitted.

Finally, the Court of Appeal emphasised the need for deference towards the judgements of elected local members when grappling with the appropriate limits of such bylaws. Hammond J said (*Conley*, 2008, para 75):

> [E]ven if this were a close run case, in our view where as here the choices being made are distinctly ones of social policy..., a court should be very slow to intervene, or adopt a high intensity of review. A large margin of appreciation should apply. Parliament entrusted the location of brothels to local authorities, which are elected bodies, and Parliament has itself decided to maintain a measure of ongoing review of prostitution.

A number of points can be drawn from these cases, but first they need to be put in their wider context. These cases represent one of the first contemporary opportunities for the courts to deliberate on their appropriate methodology when reviewing local government legislative action, particularly in the light of the 2002 local government reforms. Fundamental to this question is the degree of intensity or scrutiny the courts will apply to local government questions. Historically, courts were relatively vigilant when reviewing bylaws and were not timid about intervening to overturn decisions of elected bodies if they were concerned about the deleterious effects of the bylaw. This was in part because the bodies and their decision-making deliberations being reviewed were not necessarily viewed with the greatest esteem and it was necessary for the courts to play an active role to protect the rights and interests of citizens. However, modern jurisprudence – spurred by the reforms of local democratic processes – reflects the belief that greater deference should be accorded to decisions made through participatory processes by elected members who are ultimately accountable to the electorate. The line of brothel cases arises in a time of uncertainty and form part of the vanguard of the establishment of the modern approach for reviewing bylaws (see Knight, 2005b). The most authoritative statement comes from the Court of Appeal, where Hammond J stressed the need for judicial restraint so that local communities, through their elected officials, are properly empowered to set the limits on this matter of social policy.

Second, the limits of local authority regulation in this area remain opaque. At first blush, it appears difficult to reconcile the different results in the cases. A number of factors feed into this uncertainty. Local democracy contemplates different outcomes in different districts. As Hammond J noted in *Conley*: 'The whole point of the parliamentary delegation is that the appropriate requirements for the particular locales may very well vary ...' (*Conley*, 2008, para 76). Overlaying that fundamental point is the fact that the nature of judicial supervision of these local decisions is quite open textured and ultimately a matter of judgement. The question of whether the extent of a bylaw is so restrictive that it amounts to impermissible prohibition is a finely balanced judgement call. Whether a bylaw fundamentally undermines the purpose of, or is 'repugnant' to, the PRA is not a simple or definitive question. Assessing the 'reasonableness' of a regulatory measure requires a judgement based on variable and contested cost-benefit factors and weightings. Each of these questions involves the evaluation, in the round, of a bylaw and its effects; whether the bylaw passes muster is a matter of fact and degree.

To some extent, the reluctance of the courts to clearly articulate the ground for striking down bylaws has exacerbated this uncertainty, a point noted by the Court of Appeal (*Conley*, 2008, para 44, adopting Knight, 2005b). Clarity about the basis for intervention is critical for developing a body of jurisprudence about the limits in this area. For example, if a bylaw is quashed due to the local authority exceeding the legislative mandate in section 14 because it effectively prohibits small owner-operated brothels, that judicial ruling should be of universal application; no local authority can, as a matter of law, effectively prohibit small owner-operator brothels, regardless of local conditions. However, if a bylaw is quashed because the negative effects of the bylaw are not generally proportionate to the positive outcomes (or vice versa), the central issue is the reasonableness of the regulatory initiative; this will be an assessment dominated by local conditions, along with desired community outcomes and views.

Third, as it stands, it is difficult to predict whether a bylaw will be treated as being valid or not. The general theme that can be discerned from the various cases is that local authorities can legitimately respond to community concerns about the location of brothels but cannot set their regulation too aggressively such that it makes it practically impossible for brothels, particularly small owner-operated (typically suburban) brothels, to operate. It is difficult to state the scope and limits of the local authority bylaw-making power with any greater certainty that this. Finally, it is worth noting that, following this line of case, the general uncertainty about the limits of permissible regulation was considered by the Prostitution Law Reform Committee (PLRC, 2008, pp 145-6). The committee took the view that the decisions in *Willowford* and *JB International* better reflected the philosophy of the PRA, although it accepted that the *Conley* case turned on its own facts. It noted that the jurisprudence is 'still developing' and suggested it would be 'premature' to amend the Act to attempt to provide any greater certainty (PLRC, 2008, p 146). In particular, it said it would be 'fictional' to amend the terminology to exclude small owner-operated brothels from the definition of a brothel in order to exclude them from location controls and it was concerned that such a change might produce 'unintended consequences' (PLRC, 2008, p 146). Further, variable geographical situations and population spreads made it difficult to provide hard-and-fast rules for controlling the location of brothels.

Regulation of signage

Section 12 of the PRA specifically empowers territorial authorities to regulate signage advertising commercial sexual services:

12 Bylaws controlling signage advertising commercial sexual services

(1) A territorial authority may make bylaws for its district that prohibit or regulate signage that is in, or is visible from, a public place, and that advertises commercial sexual services.

(2) Bylaws may be made under this section only if the territorial authority is satisfied that the bylaw is necessary to prevent the public display of signage that—

    (a) is likely to cause a nuisance or serious offence to ordinary members of the public using the area; or

    (b) is incompatible with the existing character or use of that area.

(3)   Bylaws made under this section may prohibit or regulate signage in any terms, including (without limitation) by imposing restrictions on the content, form, or amount of signage on display.

(4)   Parts 8 and 9 of the Local Government Act 2002 (which are about, among other things, the enforcement of bylaws and penalties for their breach) apply to a bylaw made under this section as if the bylaw had been made under section 145 of that Act.

In this provision, 'commercial sexual services' carries the statutory definition as set out in section 4(1), that is, sexual services that:

(a)   involve physical participation by a person in sexual acts with, and for the gratification of, another person; and

(b)   are provided for payment or other reward (irrespective of whether the reward is given to the person providing the services or another person).

Prior to the PRA, local authorities already had some scope to regulate signage under the general power to make bylaws for the purpose of 'protecting the public from nuisance' or 'minimising the potential for offensive behaviour in public places' (2002 Local Government Act, section 145) or, arguably, the power to regulate 'trading in public places' (2002 Local Government Act, section 146(a)(v)). However, the specific provision in the PRA is slightly different. First, the scope of the provision is potentially broader. It covers signage that is not only in public places but also 'visible from' public places. This enlarges the signage capable of being regulated to include signs on private property; therefore, the threshold before regulation is permitted is lowered. Although the provision replicates the general power by permitting regulation where signs are likely to cause a 'nuisance' (cf 2002 Local Government Act, section 145(a)) or likely to cause 'serious offence' (cf 2002 Local Government Act, section 145(c)), the additional jurisdictional ground of 'incompatibility' with the existing use or character of the area is added. A signage bylaw could potentially be challenged if it regulated signs in circumstances that fell short of those mentioned in section 12(2). However, the jurisdictional terms ('serious offensive', 'nuisance', 'incompatibility' and 'character') have a degree of vagueness or ambiguity that mean it would be difficult to overturn a local authority's judgement that a particular case has been made out for a signage bylaw to be adopted.

Second, the specific bylaw-making power clarifies that this type of regulation can include an absolute prohibition or restrictions of various kinds. This avoids any bylaws being attacked on the basis that they overreach under the *Virgo* principle (although the broader 'purpose' injunction in section 145 might have ameliorated that possibility anyway).

Third, bylaws made under section 12 (in contrast to bylaws made under section 14) need not be consistent with the 1990 New Zealand Bill of Rights Act. Ordinarily subordinate legislation such as bylaws must not breach the Bill of Rights (2002 Local Government Act, section 155(3); *Drew* v *Attorney-General* [2002]), that is, any bylaws restricting rights like the freedom of expression are only permissible if they are enacted in the pursuit of an important government objective and any restrictions on the rights are proportionate with that objective (Rishworth et al, 2003, ch 5; Butler and Butler, 2005, ch 6; *R* v *Hansen* [2007]). However, section 13(2) of the PRA contained an express provision exempting compliance with the Bill of Rights for signage bylaws.

[A] bylaw may be made under section 12 even if, contrary to section 155(3) of the Local Government Act 2002, it is inconsistent with the New Zealand Bill of Rights Act 1990.

In many respects, the provision was adopted out of an abundance of caution. Although any signage bylaws would prima facie restrict people's expressive rights under section 14 of the Bill of Rights, bylaws would have been potentially justifiable and therefore lawful. But perhaps there was not the mood for such challenges – even potentially futile challenges. The exemption provision avoided any doubt.

A number of local authorities have enacted bylaws incorporating restrictions on signage advertising commercial sexual services, either specifically addressing brothels (for example, North Shore City) or more generally as part of a broader package regulating the advertising of sexual services or offensive advertising (for example, Wellington City). While the form of the regulation varies between local authorities, the regulation has been relatively restrictive, although not entirely prohibitive. For example, North Shore City prohibits signs displaying anything other than the name of the brothel proprietor and imposes strict controls on the size and illumination of the sign (2008 North Shore City Bylaw, clause 25.4.1). In contrast, Wellington City requires approval for all signs, based on criteria largely focused on depiction of sexual activity, nudity and offensiveness (2008 Wellington Consolidated Bylaw, Part 5, clause 10).

Land use regulation under the 1991 Resource Management Act

Local authorities have the power to regulate brothels under the 1991 Resource Management Act, either by promulgating rules specifically to regulate brothels or through judgements made on individual applications for resource consents.

Section 15(3) of the PRA expressly left open the power of territorial authorities to develop land use controls regulating the business of prostitution or brothels:

> Subsection (1) does not limit or affect the operation of the Resource Management Act 1991 in any way, and it may be overridden, with respect to particular areas within a district, by the provisions of a district plan or proposed district plan.

Local authorities have the legislative power to promulgate objectives, policies and rules in district plans to manage 'the effects of the use, development, or protection of land and associated natural and physical resources of the district' (1991 Resource Management Act, sections 31 and 72). As with other businesses or home enterprises, the operation of a brothel, regardless of size or nature, constitutes the 'use' of land, thereby allowing local authorities to regulate any adverse effects of the activities on the environment. This potentially allows the regulation of the location of brothels, along with the management (or prohibition) of adverse effects of prostitution businesses, including signage, parking and so on.

With the key terms – 'effects' and 'environment' – being framed broadly (notably to include amenity values and community well-being, not just ecological factors) (1991 Resource Management Act, sections 2 and 3) a wide degree of regulation is, in theory, permissible. However, any proposed rule regulating activities must, on a case-by-case basis, pass muster under section 32 of the Resource Management Act. This evaluation subjects any rule (and associated provisions) to relatively intense scrutiny to ensure that it is consistent with the purpose of the Resource Management Act (viz 'sustainable management') and, having regard to their efficiency and effectiveness, it is the most appropriate method to achieve that purpose – broadly inviting a cost-benefit assessment of any rule (1991 Resource Management Act, section 32; see Nolan, 2005, para 3.91). Critically, the section 32 assessment of a local authority is subject to appeal to the Environment Court on a *de novo* basis, effectively allowing the court to reach a fresh and independent evaluation of the appropriateness of the rule (1991 Resource Management Act, section 290 and schedule 1, clause 14).

Further, regulation through district plan rules comes with an additional complication for local authorities. Any controls on brothels or the business of prostitution only operate prospectively; any brothels or businesses already established before any rule was promulgated are entitled to 'existing use rights', thereby exempting them from the application of any new controls. Existing use rights arise where a land use was 'lawfully established' before any rule was formally notified to public and where the effects of the land use are the 'same or similar in character, intensity, and scale' to those which existed before the rule was notified (1991 Resource Management Act, section 10). There was a question-mark about whether brothels or businesses of prostitution would be able to establish that they were 'lawfully established' when, even though they were not typically addressed in previous resource management controls, prostitution and brothels were effectively unlawful under the criminal law. However, this became moot with the passing of the PRA, as brothels and such businesses became lawful and therefore capable of relying on existing use rights when the Act came into force on 28 June 2003. With the minimal lead-time before the Act came into force, few, if any, local authorities were able to notify district plans provisions in time to prevent existing use rights applying to existing brothels.

Although regulation through district plan rules remains available to local authorities, the narrower mandate, more intense supervision of any proposed controls and impact of existing use rights mean this type of regulation is less attractive to local authorities. Few local authorities have adopted this regulatory approach.

The second resource management tool available to local authorities to regulate brothels and prostitution businesses is the express power to take into account additional effects when considering an application for resource consent relating to a 'business of prostitution' (PRA, section 15(1) and (2)):

Resource consents in relation to businesses of prostitution

(1) When considering an application for a resource consent under the Resource Management Act 1991 for a land use relating to a business of prostitution, a territorial authority must have regard to whether the business of prostitution–

(a) is likely to cause a nuisance or serious offence to ordinary members of the public using the area in which the land is situated; or

(b) is incompatible with the existing character or use of the area in which the land is situated.

(2) Having considered the matters in subsection (1)(a) and (b) as well as the matters it is required to consider under the Resource Management Act 1991, the territorial authority may, in accordance with sections 104A to 104D of that Act, grant or refuse to grant a resource consent, or, in accordance with section 108 of that Act, impose conditions on any resource consent granted.

Obviating the need for local authorities to change their district plans to specifically direct the consideration of these matters, this provision gives local authorities the power to address any potential 'nuisance', 'serious offence' and 'character incompatibility' when assessing applications for resource consent for brothels and prostitution businesses. In some cases, depending on the nature of the relevant district plan rules, local authorities could have ordinarily taken these matters into account; however, this provision avoids any doubt about the power to do so and extends the circumstances in which these matters can be taken into account.

These additional factors can be considered in any case where an application is made for a resource consent application 'relating to the business of prostitution' (prostitution having been defined as 'the provision of commercial sexual services' (section 4)). The reach of the section 15 has yet to be definitively settled by the courts, but the language suggests it has broad application. The qualifier 'relating to' suggests a wide interpretation and transcends the customary demarcation between 'development' (the construction or alterations of buildings or facilities) and 'use' (the activity that takes place in those buildings), and applies in both cases. Further, the need to obtain a resource consent need not arise from a failure to comply with a district plan rule specifically regulating brothels or prostitution (such as a spatial prohibition of the operation of brothels in certain zones); it may arise from a failure to comply with rules regulating general matters not specific to brothels or prostitution (such as bulk and location of buildings, parking requirements, size of business and so on).

Finally, the provision allows for an application to be declined, or conditions imposed, in circumstances where ordinarily that would not be possible. Absent this provision, the 1991 Resource Management Act circumscribes, based on a prescribed hierarchy, when certain matters can be taken into account in the decision about whether to grant a resource consent and what type of action can be taken as a result. At one end, for activities listed as 'controlled activities' or 'restricted discretionary activities' in a district plan, a local authority may only consider certain effects specifically listed in the district plan. In the case of the former, they can only impose conditions to address the effect, not decline the application and, in the case of the latter, they can impose conditions or decline the application. For example, an activity may be treated as being controlled if it only proposes to provide 80% of the required number of car-parks, or restricted discretionary if it only proposes 60% of the required number. In such cases, the conditions or matters required to be taken into account would typically be restricted to car-parking, the size of the business and other expressly recorded related effects. At the other end, for activities listed as 'discretionary' or 'non-complying' activities, any effects can be taken into account and the application could be declined or any conditions imposed. For example, for such activities, an application could be declined for any reason, such as noise, even if the need to obtain a resource consent arose solely because of a failure to provide the (unrelated) required number of car-parks. Section 15, therefore, allows local authorities to take into account 'nuisance', 'serious offence' and 'character incompatibility' relating to brothels even if, in the case of controlled or restricted discretionary activities, they were not specifically listed in district plans. Further, in the case of controlled activities, section 15 allows an application to be declined, even though ordinarily this would not be permissible. The reach of section 15 is, however, not comprehensive. The additional matters to be considered can only be considered when an application for a resource consent is required. If a brothel or prostitution business is a 'permitted activity' under a district plan such that it can be undertaken lawfully without applying for a resource consent, there is no ability for a local authority to control the brothel or business under section 15.

The effect of this provision has, to date, only been considered in one judicial decision: *Mount Victoria Residents Association Incorporated* v *The Wellington City Council* [2009]. Members of a local residents' group challenged Wellington City Council's decision to grant a resource consent for the expansion of an existing brothel located in a residential zone – The Lovely Lilly – from three sex workers to five. In its decision to grant consent, the council had focused solely on traditional resource management effects, such as provision for car-parking, and did not refer to the compatibility, nuisance or serious offence matters mandated by section 15 of the PRA. This failure was fatal. The council had ambivalently argued that even though it had not directly referred to these matters, they were still indirectly assessed or partially considered in the standard assessment of the effects. But that was insufficient. The court reiterated the 'tolerably clear' intention of parliament, expressed in section 15, that compatibility matters were to be taken into account over and above the usual resource management considerations (*Mount Victoria Residents*, 2009, para 10). As there was no contest to the fact that the application was one relating to the business of prostitution, the council's failure to directly turn its mind to these matters, both when deciding whether to publicly notify the application and when deciding whether to grant the application, led to the resource consent for the brothel being quashed. Dobson J was, however, careful to note that it should not be assumed that section 15 matters would automatically mean that every application relating to the business of prostitution would need to be publicly notified or that the application must be declined; there was still the need for 'case by case consideration' (*Mount Victoria Residents*, 2009, para 26).

Generic law-making powers and approval processes

Local authorities also possess a number of generic law-making powers or responsibility for approval processes. Some local authorities have sought to utilise these general powers to regulate brothels and prostitution activities.

A number of local authorities have enacted bylaws seeking to prohibit the 'touting' or 'solicitation' of commercial sex services, either solicitation of services per se (Rodney District Council and Rotorua District Council) (Caldwell, 2004, p 136; PLRC, 2008, p 140) or touting of brothel-related services (Grey District Council) (PLRC, 2008, p 140). Others have sought to specifically prohibit street prostitution (Carterton District Council and Queenstown Lakes District Council) (Caldwell, 2004, p 136; PLRC, 2008, p 140).

The lawfulness of these regulatory responses is, in some cases, unclear, and, in other cases, dubious. Local authorities possess the power, at least in a jurisdictional sense, to enact such bylaws under their general bylaw-making powers (that is, 'protecting the public from nuisance', 'protecting, promoting, and maintaining public health and safety' and 'minimising the potential for offensive behaviour in public places'; 2002 Local Government Act, section 145), their specific bylaw-making powers governing the regulation of street trading or hawking in the 2002 Local Government Act (that is, to 'regulate ... trading in public places'; 2002 Local Government Act, section 146(a)(vi)), or their general bylaw-making power under public health legislation (that is, 'improving, promoting, or protecting public health, and preventing or abating nuisances'; 1956 Health Act, section 64(1)(a)). As a matter of jurisdiction, these provisions are broad enough to provide an initial foundation for these measures. However, there remains a question of whether doing so is fundamentally inconsistent or repugnant to the PRA (Caldwell, 2004). This point has yet to be tested in the courts.

Local authority-led law reform

It seems clear that there is not universal satisfaction among local authorities with the extent to which prostitution can be regulated, even with the relatively potent power of local authorities to continue to regulate aspects of the prostitution business. Some local authorities favour greater powers to regulate the perceived concerns about prostitution.

Most dramatically, this was demonstrated by the attempt by Manukau City Council to lobby parliament to enact a local Bill prohibiting street prostitution within its district. The Manukau City Council (Control of Street Prostitution) Bill was introduced by local Member of Parliament, George Hawkins, in November 2005. It proposed to make it illegal for both sex workers and clients to 'solicit for prostitution in a public place' within Manukau City. The proposed Bill was designed to respond to local concerns about the high number of sex workers operating on the street (estimated at over 150) and the associated negative effects of street sex work (Hawkins, 2005). Ultimately, the Bill was voted down by 73 votes to 46 (New Zealand Parliament, 2006, p 5653), after an adverse report from the Local Government and Environment Select Committee (Local Government and Environment Select Committee, 2006). While the Select Committee acknowledged some of the concerns that led to the Bill being promoted, the majority of the Committee suggested there were better ways to address concerns about street safety without undermining the purpose of the PRA or enacting a location-specific law.

Conclusion

Local authorities continue to have the power to regulate the business of prostitution, either through specific measures brought in the package of reforms in the PRA or through their generic law-making or administrative powers. The bundle of powers available to local authorities varies in their potency. Militant regulation of brothel advertising is permitted, while the power to regulate the location of brothels is more circumscribed (and uncertain). Some local authorities have sought to aggressively utilise their available powers, although not all attempts have been sanctioned by the courts, with some bylaws governing the location of brothels being overturned. The propriety of some other bylaws, particularly those effectively prohibiting solicitation, have not yet been definitively tested before the courts.

Local authority regulation has arguably now become the main locus for debate about the merits of regulating (or, rather, restricting) prostitution. That locus is framed by awkward tensions: a national, philosophical direction to ensure a safe and healthy environment for sex workers to legitimately operate within; strongly held views by some elements of local communities against prostitution and its effect on local amenity; and uncertainty and variation from the courts about how to mediate between national commands and local concerns, particularly where central government has mandated some degree of role for local responses.

References

Butler, A. and Butler, P. (2005) *The New Zealand Bill of Rights Act: A commentary*, Wellington: LexisNexis.

Caldwell, J. (2004) 'Bylaws regulating the sex industry', *Resource Management Bulletin*, issue 5.

Hawkins, Hon G. (2005) *New Zealand Parliamentary Debates*, vol 628, p 651.

Knight, D. (2005a) 'Power to make bylaws', *New Zealand Law Journal*, May, p 165.

Knight, D. (2005b) 'Brothels, bylaws, prostitutes and proportionality', *New Zealand Law Journal*, December, p 423.

Local Government and Environment Select Committee (2006) *Report on Manukau City Council (Control of Street Prostitution) Bill*, www.parliament.nz/en-NZ/PB/Legislation/Bills/2/c/a/00DBHOH_BILL7085_1-Manukau-City-Council-Control-of-Street-Prostitution.htm.

Mitchell, C. and Knight, D. (2008) 'Local government (reissue 1)', in Hon J. McGrath (ed) (1991) *The laws of New Zealand*, Wellington: LexisNexis.

New Zealand Parliament (2006) *New Zealand Parliamentary Debates*, vol 634.

Nolan, D. (2005) *Environmental and resource management law in New Zealand* (3rd edn), Wellington: LexisNexis.

PLRC (Prostitution Law Reform Committee) (2008) *Report on the operation of the Prostitution Reform Act 2003*, Wellington: Ministry of Justice.

Rishworth, P. et al (2003) *The New Zealand Bill of Rights Act*, Oxford: Oxford University Press.

Standards New Zealand (2007) *Model general bylaws: Introduction*, NZS 9201.1:2007, Wellington: Standards New Zealand.

Cases

Conley v *Hamilton City Council* [2006] Unreported, High Court, Hamilton, CIV-2005-419-1689.

Conley v *Hamilton City Council* [2008] *New Zealand Law Reports*, vol 1, p 789.

Drew v *Attorney-General* [2002] *New Zealand Law Reports*, vol 1, p 58.

JB International v *Auckland City Council* [2006] *New Zealand Resource Management Appeals*, p 401.

McCarthy v *Madden* [1915] *New Zealand Law Reports*, vol 33, p 1251,

Mount Victoria Residents Association Incorporated v *The Wellington City Council* [2009] Unreported, High Court, Wellington, WN CIV-2008-485-1820.

Municipal Corporation of the City of Toronto v *Virgo* [1896] *Appeal Cases*, p 88

R v *Hansen* [2007] *New Zealand Law Reports*, vol 3, p 1.

Willowford v *Christchurch City Council* [2005] Unreported, High Court, Christchurch CIV-2004-409-2299.

TEN

Christchurch School of Medicine study: methodology and methods

Gillian Abel, Lisa Fitzgerald and Cheryl Brunton

Introduction

This chapter provides a detailed account of the methodological approach and the methods used in carrying out a study at the University of Otago, Christchurch School of Medicine (CSoM) into the impact of the 2003 Prostitution Reform Act (PRA) on the health and safety practices of sex workers. Chapters Eleven to Fourteen draw on the findings from this study. This chapter begins by discussing community-based participatory research (CBPR), which is an approach regarded as best practice when doing research with marginalised groups of people such as sex workers. This approach underpinned all the methods utilised in the research.

Mixed-methods research, utilising both quantitative and qualitative methods, was undertaken and the merits of doing this are described. The description of the methods used in the research begins by discussing the quantitative arm of the research, with the development of the questionnaire, the methods used to sample the survey population, the process of quantitative data collection and analysis of the questionnaire data. A description of the qualitative arm of the research gives attention to the selection of the samples, the semi-structured in-depth interviews undertaken to collect data and the theoretical thematic analysis of the data. The methods to analyse print media are also described.

This study was able to draw some comparisons before and after decriminalisation in health and safety practices of sex workers. In 1999, CSoM had carried out a survey of Christchurch female sex workers. An estimation of the number of workers in the Christchurch sex industry done prior to the survey in 1999 yielded a total of 375 workers (Plumridge and Abel, 2000). The survey sampled to saturation and was able to collect information from 303 sex workers, which represented 81% of the estimated population. Similar techniques were used to sample sex workers in Christchurch in the post-decriminalisation study and some questions in the questionnaire remained unchanged so that comparisons could be made between Christchurch female sex workers' reporting of health and safety practices before and after the PRA.

The study done in the 1990s cemented a relationship between the lead author and the New Zealand Prostitutes' Collective (NZPC). This relationship was essential in carrying out the research after decriminalisation. NZPC were partners in the research, contributing in several ways, from the development of the research aims to the writing up and dissemination of the data.

Community-based participatory research

CBPR is a partnership approach to research, in which all partners contribute their own unique strengths in order to enhance the 'understanding of a given phenomenon and the social and cultural dynamics of a community, and integrate the knowledge gained with action to improve the health and well-being of community members' (Israel et al, 2003, p 54). The goals and methods used in participatory research take into account the structures controlling people's lives, not only focusing on the negative aspects, but also revealing the positives and working for social justice (Wallerstein and Duran, 2003).

Internationally, there is increasing interest in developing innovative, multi-methodological approaches to explore marginalised populations[1] and the approaches that are finding increasing popularity are those that are collaborative and truly 'community *based*' (original emphasis) (Minkler and Wallerstein, 2003; Benoit et al, 2005). These approaches require a shift in the purpose of doing research, from merely amassing knowledge for the use of academic and policy audiences to actually benefiting the populations or communities involved, where participants are active players in the social construction of knowledge, empowerment and social change (O'Neill, 1996; Lewis and Maticka-Tyndale, 2000).

Traditional research methods can serve to strengthen inequality, taking an 'outside expert' approach that often leads to community interventions that are disappointing (Minkler and Wallerstein, 2003). Their concepts and findings very often represent the perspective of elite groups, are accessible primarily to experts and devalue personal experiences and everyday knowledge held by non-elite people (Cancian, 1992). Such research methodologies involve researchers identifying particular 'problems' within communities or populations, posing research questions, making decisions on research methods to be utilised in the collection and analysing of data and developing interventions or recommendations for the alleviation of the 'problem'. Members of the research population participate as subjects in the research and have little influence on the research process and the

---

[1] Marginalised populations are those populations that are disadvantaged and that tend to be excluded from the social rights enjoyed by other residents (Romero et al, 2003; Beiser and Stewart, 2005). These populations share common characteristics. They are often stigmatised and marginalised from the rest of society, are distrustful of outsiders and often unwilling to participate in research (Benoit et al, 2005; Liamputtong, 2007). These characteristics can pose problems for traditional research methods, which are often ineffective with marginalised populations and raise a number of ethical problems, risks and challenges (Romero et al, 2003).

reports and publications produced by the research (Lewis and Maticka-Tyndale, 2000). In many instances, the 'problem', as seen from the perspective of the researcher, differs from the community perspective and resultant interventions are often not successful.

In contrast to traditional research methods that place the participant as subject, CBPR involves an active and ongoing partnership between the researchers and the community at all stages of the research process, with the aim of improving public health. Through the direct involvement of the participants in the research process, there is a sharing of power, which means that participants are less likely to be exploited in the research relationship (Liamputtong, 2007). It is argued that health improvements will only be achieved where research is embedded in the local knowledge and with the active support of community members (Baum, 1995).

Traditional researchers are often uneasy with methodologies that give control of research to untrained participants, arguing that this does not constitute 'good' research and compromises scientific rigor. Others argue, however, that participatory methods do not necessarily undermine scientific rigor (which is often predicated on objectivity), but offer alternative and strengthened scientific standards (Cancian, 1992; Bradbury and Reason, 2003; Fadem et al, 2003). Cancian (1992, p 633) suggests that '… drawing on the active participation and collective knowledge of community members will produce more valid descriptions and explanations'. Both Cancian (1992) and Bradbury and Reason (2003) provide alternative possibilities for assessing the scientific standard or quality of participatory research, claiming that maximising participation in the decision-making process, ensuring that methodological and methods choices are appropriate and relational, incorporating social action into the research, legitimating knowledge by showing that it works in a practical situation and improving opportunities for debate among diverse groups of researchers by challenging previous assumptions and presenting new interpretations all have profound implications for the validity of the research. Less control over the research does not necessarily equate to less scientific rigor. It is important to recognise the differences between the researcher and the community in understanding an issue and the impact that this may have in practice. What is required by such methodological approaches is more time, patience and ability to negotiate with community partners (Allison and Rootman, 1996). The research process may be slower in the initial phases because of the emphasis on participation, but with vigilance and the guiding hand of the researcher, the research can achieve a high degree of rigor (Denner et al, 1999). Some compromises may have to be made along the way, but by building relationships with community groups and working in partnership, research is more likely to reflect the perspectives of marginalised populations.

This is not to say that CBPR is without its difficulties. Studies on the sex worker population in Canada that have utilised this approach have documented several challenges faced during the course of the research (Lewis and Maticka-Tyndale, 2000; Benoit et al, 2005; Shaver, 2005). It takes time to develop a relationship based on trust between academics and community members and researchers have to work hard to allay the community's initial suspicions (Lewis and Maticka-Tyndale, 2000; Benoit et al, 2005). The priorities and timelines required by research funding agencies may not fit with the timeline of the community (Lewis and Maticka-Tyndale, 2000). The intricacies of the research process are foreign to community groups and there can be impatience with the need to follow a rigorous procedure. Yet despite these challenges, there is an agreement that the advantages to taking a participatory approach outweigh the challenges and that this approach addresses many of the ethical challenges in doing research with a marginalised population (Lewis and Maticka-Tyndale, 2000; Benoit et al, 2005; Shaver, 2005).

The study was funded by the Health Research Council of New Zealand and received additional funding from the Ministry of Justice. Ethical approval was granted for the study by the Multi-region Ethics Committee.

Study design

The study utilised a quantitative and qualitative approach in a complementary way to provide a broader understanding of the impact of decriminalisation on the lives of sex workers. In so doing, the complexity of sex workers' lives was better revealed in a multi-dimensional way. In addition, qualitative interviews with Medical Officers of Health who had acquired the role of inspectors of brothels under the terms of the PRA were carried out, as well as an analysis of their submissions to city councils regarding bylaws.

Quantitative approach

Questionnaire development

It is important to involve research partners in the design of research tools, such as questionnaires or interview guides. Local knowledge ensures that the questions posed are relevant and appropriate, and that the language used is pertinent to the target audience (Lewis and Maticka-Tyndale, 2000). NZPC and the CSoM research team developed their questionnaire in a collaborative manner. The starting point for the development of the questionnaire was the questionnaire used for the study of Christchurch sex workers in 1999. Some questions from this survey remained unchanged to allow for some direct comparisons to be made between pre- and post-decriminalisation data, while others were changed to allow for better wording and additional questions were added. The final questionnaire consisted of 68 questions with a number of sub-questions[2].

---

[2] For a copy of the questionnaire, please refer to Abel et al, 2007, pp 189-221.

Quantitative sample

It is very difficult to gain a statistically representative sample of marginalised populations such as sex workers (Lewis and Maticka-Tyndale, 2000). In countries where activities associated with sex work are criminalised, sex workers constitute a hidden population and thus there is no adequate sampling frame (Heckathorn et al, 2001; Romero et al, 2003; Benoit et al, 2005; Liamputtong, 2007). This makes random sampling impossible and purposive sampling is more likely to be used when researching populations such as sex workers (Benoit et al, 2005). In New Zealand, the sex worker population is newly licit and as such, it is arguable that sex workers are no longer 'hidden'. However, societal acceptance of sex work as an occupation is often underpinned by moral judgements and for this reason many sex workers continue to keep their occupation secret (Weir et al, 2006). Although this study had estimated the number of workers in the geographical locations of the study (Abel et al, 2007, 2009) and it may have been possible to attempt to randomly select private workers and individuals on the street and in brothels, the disadvantages of doing so outweighed the advantages. NZPC maintained that random sampling would elicit a level of distrust among those selected to participate and the response rate would likely be very low, thus compromising the external validity of the study. In taking a CBPR approach, it is understood that sometimes compromises have to be made that may affect the rigour of a study, but the knowledge organisations such as the NZPC have about their community is of utmost importance and cannot be overlooked. This study, therefore, did not utilise random sampling, but there was still a need to represent the overall cultural make-up of the population within the sample (Berg, 1999).

There are strategies that can be employed to increase the likelihood of reflecting the diversity of the sex industry. A robust estimate of the size of the sex industry[3] within the locations of the research, as well as the gender and sector make-up of the workers within each location (Abel et al, 2007, 2009), allowed informed sampling within each micro-grouping. Having community partners with an in-depth knowledge of the industry in each location also improved the likelihood of gaining access to the diversity of sex workers. However, the representativeness of the sample cannot be assessed, which does pose a problem for external validity.

The target population for this research was sex workers in Auckland, Christchurch, Wellington, Napier and Nelson. Auckland, Christchurch and Wellington are the three largest cities in New Zealand and are the centres where the majority of sex workers are located. Street-based sex work rarely occurs outside of these cities. The smaller cities of Napier and Nelson were selected to provide comparisons between the experiences of workers in small and larger cities post-decriminalisation. There was only one exclusion criterion: sex workers whose English was not sufficient to understand the questions without the aid

---

[3] For details on the researchers' estimation of the size of the industry, including the methods used to do this, please refer to Abel et al, 2007, 2009.

of an interpreter, were excluded from the study. There were three reasons for this decision. First, because of the sensitive nature of the topic and the personal questions asked within the questionnaire, having an interpreter present would have compromised the confidentiality of the participants. Second, there were no funds available to employ translators. Third, foreign sex workers are a particularly vulnerable and marginalised population, because of their occupation and minority ethnicity status, and some may not be working legally. It was felt that they would be distrustful of the research and would be less likely to participate.

Different sampling strategies were undertaken in the different research locations. In Christchurch, as many participants as could be recruited into the study were sampled. The study done in Christchurch in 1999, prior to decriminalisation, employed this sampling strategy, and in order to make comparisons in the city pre- and post-decriminalisation, a similar strategy had to be used. As there are fewer male and transgender workers than female workers, and fewer street-based workers than workers operating from indoor venues, all male, transgender and street-based workers who could be identified in all the locations of the study were invited to take part in the survey. This was done in order to make meaningful comparisons between sectors and gender. As Napier and Nelson have smaller numbers of workers, this method of sampling was employed in these locations to enable the investigation of any significant differences between small-city and big-city workers. Although it would have been beneficial to the study to sample female private and managed workers in Auckland and Wellington in a similar way, financial constraints and the logistics of recruiting sufficient NZPC staff to conduct the interviews within a relatively short timeframe meant that it was only possible to sample a proportion of these populations. In Auckland, the study aimed to sample 315 of the female private and managed sectors, which represented 25% of this population. In Wellington, where the sex worker population is smaller than in Auckland, the study aimed to recruit 120 participants, which represented 42% of the population of female private and managed workers. These sampling strategies resulted in unequal selection probabilities that may introduce bias into the study. This was controlled for by weighting the sample to a known population distribution. Disproportionate sampling and inequalities in the selection frame and procedures create unequal selection probabilities and are corrected by weights inverse to those probabilities (Kish, 1965). Weighting of a sample to a known population distribution will adjust for differences in sampling rates and will also adjust for the difference in response rate of different sectors of the industry (Kalton, 1983). Unequal weights were applied to control for bias. However, although bias is controlled, the unequal weights also increase imprecision through increasing the standard error of the estimates. Therefore, SAS Survey Procedures were used, as these use weights for point estimates and also take into account weights for standard errors.

Quantitative data collection

Recruitment of participants into the study and the collection of reliable information are more readily accomplished when working in partnership with relevant community organisations, making use of peer interviewers. Community partners can vouch for the trustworthiness of the researchers and the relevance of the study, which works to benefit the research (Lewis and Maticka-Tyndale, 2000). Once trust has been established with initial participants, obtaining additional participants is more easily achieved (Lewis and Maticka-Tyndale, 2000).

Information sheets were provided to all participants giving details of the study. Participants were reimbursed with a cash payment of $15. The questionnaire took between 35 and 45 minutes to complete. Questionnaires were delivered face to face by a trained peer interviewer. The locations in which the interviews took place varied. Sex workers who accessed NZPC were asked to participate in an interview when they accessed one of the branches. If the time was not appropriate, they were asked to return at a more convenient time. Interviewers approached brothel workers through their routine outreach visits and several interviews took place in the lounges of brothels. Brothels that were not open to NZPC visits were telephoned and brothel managers asked to relay information about the study to their workers. Several brothels placed flyers with details about the study and contact details on their notice boards. Private workers were telephoned and asked to come into NZPC branches to participate in the interview or were offered the possibility of an interviewer coming to their home. Street outreach workers approached street-based workers on the street. Many completed the questionnaire at nearby cafés or in the interviewers' parked cars and others went back to NZPC community bases with the interviewers. In the smaller cities of Nelson and Napier, interviewers from Christchurch and Wellington travelled to the respective locations to undertake the interviews. These interviews either took place in participants' place of work, their homes or in the interviewers' motel rooms.

A total of 772 questionnaires were completed across the five locations of the study. In Auckland, 22% of the estimated population of sex workers completed the questionnaire. In Christchurch, the proportion of the estimated sex worker population that participated was 63%, in Wellington 40%, in Hawkes Bay 31% and in Nelson 48%. Different venues for sex work were then collapsed into a street sector, a managed indoor sector (comprising brothel and escort workers) and a private indoor sector (comprising workers who worked privately on their own or from shared premises or other venues such as bars) (see Table 10.1). This distinction was made to provide for comparisons between workers who work under a system of management and those who do not, as the literature proposes that the dynamics of work in the different sectors has differential impacts on the health and safety experiences of sex workers.

Table 10.1: Location and numbers of street, managed and private workers

Location	Total number in survey	Street	Managed indoor	Private indoor
Auckland	333	78	180	75
Christchurch	246	92	100	54
Wellington	151	33	70	48
Napier	23	0	15	8
Nelson	19	0	13	6
Total	**772**	**203**	**378**	**191**

Qualitative approach

Qualitative sex worker sample

The qualitative phase of this study included one-on-one, in-depth interviews. Fifty-eight sex workers were sampled across the five locations of the study. In terms of a qualitative study, this is a large sample size (Britten, 1995; Hansen, 2006). Unlike quantitative studies where a large, representative sample is often desired, qualitative samples are large enough if the data collected is rich enough to support a highly detailed, in-depth analysis (Rice and Ezzy, 1999; Hansen, 2006). Sex workers were sampled purposively, using maximum variability sampling, within all the locations of the study. This method of sampling provides for information-rich cases to be included in the study and captures the diversity of the industry within the final sample (Hansen, 2006). This strategy is useful for identifying common patterns that cut across the diversity of the sample and also allows for exploration of the differences (Patton, 1990). Potential participants were approached either through telephone calls or when outreach workers made contact with them in NZPC offices, brothels, escort agencies, streets or private homes. Attention was given to gaining participation of female, male, transgender, street, managed and private sex workers as well as small-city and big-city sex workers. Efforts were also made to contact potential participants who had no affiliation to NZPC, so as to truly reflect the diversity of the industry within the sample.

Regulatory officer sample

Nine regulatory officers were sampled purposively from different areas of New Zealand. They were identified by Cheryl Brunton, a principal investigator on this research project. Dr Brunton is Medical Officer of Health for the West Coast of the South Island and was a member of the Ministry of Health's Prostitution Reform Working Group. She made an initial approach to Medical Officers of Health at their national meeting in May 2006 to identify which of them undertook the role of inspector of brothels in their respective districts. She then invited the Medical Officers of Health from each of the study locations to participate. In Christchurch, two sexual health promoters who carried out the inspector of brothels role on behalf of the Medical Officer of Health and an occupational health officer from the Department of Labour were also invited to participate.

Sample of public health submissions on territorial authority bylaws

Existing territorial authority bylaws under the PRA, or district plan rules regulating location and/or signage of brothels, were identified through territorial authority websites (a complete list of which was obtained from Local Government New Zealand's website www.lgnz.co.nz). The websites were searched for an index of bylaws and these in turn were scanned for bylaw titles including the words/ phrases 'prostitution', brothels' or 'commercial sex premises'. In addition, the websites were searched electronically using their embedded search engines and the same three words/phrases as search terms. Dr Brunton then contacted the Medical Officer of Health in each of the districts with bylaws or relevant district plan rules by email, asking if they had made a submission on the bylaw or plan change and requesting a copy of their submission if they had done so. Copies of 19 bylaws and four relevant district plan rules identified by search of territorial authority websites were either downloaded from these websites or obtained in hard copy. Copies of 11 public health submissions were obtained from Medical Officers of Health, including those from each of the main study locations.

Qualitative data collection with sex workers

A semi-structured interview guide was developed, following analysis of preliminary focus group discussions with NZPC staff, volunteers, sex workers and associates. Semi-structured interviews are flexible, loosely structured and have areas of interest defined for exploration in the course of the interview (Britten, 1995). Questions are phrased in an open-ended, non-directive manner with probes used to encourage elaboration (Hansen, 2006). Their flexibility allows the adjustment of the interview guide after some interviews have been completed to incorporate the exploration of new ideas that may have emerged from the earlier interviews (Hansen, 2006).

Semi-structured interviews take the form of a conversational narrative, which is created jointly by the interviewer and the interviewee (Romero et al, 2003). They enable the exploration of the meanings and interpretations participants give to their experiences in sex work in a confidential manner (Rice and Ezzy, 1999). Sex workers are often suspicious of researchers and how the information they provide will be utilised. For this reason, peer interviewers were utilised to carry out the interviews, as rapport with the participant is vital in the collection of rich, in-depth information.

Participants were provided with information sheets and written or oral consent was taken to participate in the study. Each participant was reimbursed with $30 cash in appreciation of their time. The interviews lasted between 30 and 120 minutes, with the average interview taking an hour to complete.

Regulatory officer data collection

A semi-structured interview guide was developed following discussion at the national Medical Officers of Health meeting in May 2006. Interviewees were asked about a range of topics, including their experience of proposed territorial authority bylaws, their roles as inspectors of brothels under the PRA, their relationships with regulatory officers from other agencies in relation to implementing the PRA, how they dealt with complaints and their views on the effectiveness of the PRA. Two in-depth interviews were conducted by Dr Brunton in face-to-face meetings in Christchurch: one with the two sexual health promoters who carried out the inspector role on behalf of the local Medical Officer of Health and the other with an occupational health officer from the Department of Labour. Six other interviews were conducted over the telephone with Medical Officers of Health in various parts of the country.

Qualitative analysis

The interviews with sex workers and regulatory officers were digitally recorded and transcribed to word accuracy. A theoretical thematic analysis was undertaken. Thematic analysis is a method used extensively in qualitative research to identify, analyse and report patterns in data (Aronson, 1994; Braun and Clarke, 2006). Meaning is sought in the accounts and/or actions of participants, taking into account how the broader social and political context impinge on these meanings (Holloway and Todres, 2003; Braun and Clarke, 2006). In many instances, researchers undertaking thematic analysis have taken a passive stance, where they are guided by the data rather than pre-established hypotheses or assumptions (Daly et al, 1997; Rice and Ezzy, 1999; Hansen, 2006). However, as Braun and Clarke (2006) assert, analysis does not take place in an epistemological vacuum and the underlying assumptions, ideas and conceptualisations of the researcher are theorised as shaping or informing the data. A theoretical thematic analysis takes a constructionist approach where events, realities, meanings and experiences of the participants are examined as effects of a range of discourses operating within society (Braun and Clarke, 2006). It is understood that meanings and experiences are socially produced and the analysis '… seeks to theorise the sociocultural contexts, and structural conditions, that enable the individual accounts that are provided' (Braun and Clarke, 2006, p 85). Although this is an inductive analytical method where themes or patterns identified as being important to the participants were coded for, theoretical and analytical interests played an important role in the identification of themes.

   Names of all participants have been changed in the presentation of the qualitative analysis to protect their identity.

Media analysis

In addition to the study described above, a content analysis of print media in the national newspapers of New Zealand was conducted between June 2003 and December 2006. This was done to provide a snap-shot of the media messages surrounding the implementation of the PRA. NZPC representatives regularly collected print media articles around sex work in New Zealand and had noticed an increase in the number of print media articles being written about the sex industry at the time. This perceived increase had also been noted by both research participants and the principal investigators of the study.

A content analysis of coverage of the PRA in the main newspapers of New Zealand, including the *Dominion Post*, *National Business Review*, *New Zealand Herald*, *Otago Daily Times*, *Sunday Star-Times*, *Independent Financial Review*, and *The Christchurch Press*, was conducted to establish general trends across news items (Hodgetts et al, 2005). Published material was located by searching Factiva, an online database. The initial search was undertaken by a research student for articles that contained the world 'prostitution' in the headline or lead paragraph and excluded republished news, obituaries, sports, calendars and recurring pricing and market data. This strategy recovered 520 published items, which were narrowed down to 440 by means of an initial brief reading that eliminated articles that were not concerned with the PRA or issues arising from it and pertained to sex work in general in New Zealand. The 440 articles were ordered chronologically and read to inform the creation of coding categories. This process was also informed by the reading of existing literature on sex work and critical media analysis in social science literature. All articles were read and their content systematically coded on the basis of criteria identified from the literature and repeated readings of the media articles. The coding framework was established in a series of analysis meetings with the principal investigators and research student and in these meetings refinement to the coding of articles was made and a diary was kept of any coding/categorisation decisions to facilitate the uniform application of the coding schema. Where necessary, items were re-read and recoded to ensure consistency throughout the process to provide intercoder reliability. The total number of items read and coded in the sample was 361. A list of major themes found in published items, assumptions/assertions made, sources cited and the identifying characteristics of each item was entered into a Microsoft Access database, which was used to store, organise and retrieve data. Themes were itemised into what was defined as textual and contextual (Lupton, 1992). Textual themes refer to the explicit content or story of the article such as 'charges /prosecution under the PRA', or 'court action due to local law changes following PRA'. Contextual themes were underlying broader discourses associated with sex work embedded in the article, such as 'sex work as a threat to dominant morality' and 'sex work as a public health issue'. Such an approach is similar to Hodgetts et al (2005) 'text and context' approach, where the aim is to move beyond the description of a news article to broader observations about socio-cultural processes underlying such representations in the form of broader discourses. With the PRA being new policy, the researchers were interested in assumptions/assertions made about what would occur post-PRA, which parties were cited (as examples of symbolic power) and each article's disposition towards the PRA.

The following three chapters draw on the findings from the analysis of the survey of 772 sex workers, the in-depth interviews with 58 sex workers, the in-depth interviews with nine regulatory officers, the document analysis of 11 submissions made by regulatory officers and the content analysis of 361 news media articles published between June 2003 and December 2006. Chapter Eleven explores the experiences of the regulatory officers post-PRA and provides an analysis of regulatory officer' submissions. Chapter Twelve draws on the content analysis of the media, as well as perceptions of sex workers on media reporting post-PRA drawn from the qualitative interviews. Chapter Thirteen provides a public health perspective of the impact of the PRA, drawing on both the quantitative and qualitative data collected from sex workers. Chapter Fourteen completes the chapters from this research by examining stigma as experienced by the sex workers in the study post-decriminalisation.

References

Abel, G., Fitzgerald, L. and Brunton, C. (2007) *The impact of the Prostitution Reform Act on the health and safety practices of sex workers: Report to the Prostitution Law Review Committee*, Christchurch: University of Otago, www.justice.govt.nz/prostitution-law-review-committee/publications/impact-health-safety/index.html

Abel, G., Fitzgerald, L. and Brunton, C. (2009) 'The impact of decriminalisation on the number of sex workers in New Zealand', *Journal of Social Policy*, vol 38, no 3, pp 515-31.

Allison, K. and Rootman, I. (1996) 'Scientific rigor and community participation in health promotion research: are they compatible?', *Health Promotion International*, vol 11, no 4, pp 333-40.

Aronson, J. (1994) 'A pragmatic view of thematic analysis', *The Qualitative Report*, vol 2, no 1, online journal.

Baum, F. (1995) 'Researching public health: behind the qualitative-quantitative methodological debate', *Social Science and Medicine*, vol 40, no 4, pp 459-68.

Beiser, M. and Stewart, M. (2005) 'Reducing health disparities: a priority for Canada', *Canadian Journal of Public Health*, vol 96, Supplement 2, S4-S7.

Benoit, C., Jansson, M., Millar, A. and Phillips, R. (2005) 'Community-academic research on hard-to-reach populations: benefits and challenges', *Qualitative Health Research*, vol 15, no 2, pp 263-82.

Berg, J. (1999) 'Gaining access to underresearched populations in women's health research', *Health Care for Women International*, vol 20, pp 237-43.

Bradbury, H. and Reason, P. (2003) 'Issues and choice points for improving the quality of action research', in M. Minkler and N. Wallerstein (eds) *Community-based participatory research for health*, San Francisco, CA: Jossey-Bass.

Braun, V. and Clarke, V. (2006) 'Using thematic analysis in psychology', *Qualitative Research in Psychology*, vol 3, no 2, pp 77-101.

Britten, N. (1995) 'Qualitative interviews in medical research', *British Medical Journal*, vol 311, pp 251-3.

Cancian, F. (1992) 'Feminist science: methodologies that challenge inequality', *Gender and Society*, vol 6, no 4, pp 623-42.

Daly, J., Kellehear, A. and Gliksman, M. (1997) *The public health researcher*, Melbourne/Oxford/Auckland/New York, NY: Oxford University Press.

Denner, J., Cooper, C., Lopez, E. and Dunbar, N. (1999) 'Beyond "giving science away": how university-community partnerships inform youth programs, research and policy', *Social Policy Report: Society for Research in Child Development*, vol 13, no 1, pp 1-20.

Fadem, P., Minkler, M., Perry, M., Blum, K., Moore, L. and Rogers, J. (2003) 'Ethical challenges in community-based participatory research: a case study from the San Francisco Bay area disability community', in M. Minkler, M. and N. Wallerstein (eds) *Community-based participatory research for health*, San Francisco, CA: Jossey-Bass.

Hansen, E. (2006) *Successful qualitative health research: A practical introduction*, Crows Nest, NSW: Allen & Unwin.

Heckathorn, D., Broadhead, R. and Sergeyev, B. (2001) 'A methodology for reducing respondent duplication and impersonation in samples of hidden populations', *Journal of Drug Issues*, vol 31, no 2, pp 543-64.

Hodgetts, D., Cullen, A. and Radley, A. (2005) 'Television characterizations of homeless people in the United Kingdom', *Analyses of Social Issues and Public Policy*, vol 5, no 1, pp 29-48.

Holloway, I. and Todres, L. (2003) 'The status of method: flexibility, consistency and coherence', *Qualitative Research*, vol 3, pp 345-57.

Israel, B., Schulz, A., Parker, E., Becker, A., Allen, A. and Guzman, J. (2003) 'Critical issues in developing and following community-based participatory research principles', in M. Minkler and N. Wallerstein (eds) *Community-based participatory research for health*, San Francisco, CA: Jossey-Bass.

Kalton, G. (1983) *Introduction to survey sampling*, Newbury Park: Sage Publications.

Kish, L. (1965) *Survey sampling*, New York, NY: John Wiley & Sons.

Lewis, J. and Maticka-Tyndale, E. (2000) *Escort services in a border town: Transmission dynamics of STDs within and between communities. Methodological challenges conducting research related to sex work*, Windsor: University of Windsor.

Liamputtong, P. (2007) *Researching the vulnerable: A guide to sensitive research methods*, London: Sage Publications.

Lupton, D. (1992), 'Discourse analysis: a new methodology for understanding the ideologies of health and illness', *Australian Journal of Public Health*, 16: 2, 145-150.

Minkler, M. and Wallerstein, N. (2003) 'Introduction to community-based participatory research', in M. Minkler and N. Wallerstein (eds) *Community-based participatory research for health*, San Francisco, CA: Jossey-Bass.

O'Neill, M. (1996) 'Researching prostitution and violence: towards a feminist praxis', in M. Hester, L. Kelly and J. Radford (eds) *Women, violence and male power: Feminist activism, research and practice*, Buckingham/Philadelphia, PA: Open University Press.

Patton, M. (1990) *Qualitative evaluation and research methods*, Newbury Park/ London/ New Delhi: Sage Publications.

Plumridge, L. and Abel, G. (2000) *Safer sex in the Christchurch sex industry. Study 2: Survey of Christchurch sex workers*, Christchurch: University of Otago, Christchurch School of Medicine.

Rice, P. and Ezzy, D. (1999) *Qualitative research methods*, New York, NY: Oxford University Press.

Romero, M., Rodriguez, E., Durand-Smith, A. and Aguilera, R. (2003) 'Twenty five years of qualitative research on mental health and addictions with hidden populations. First part', *Salud Mental*, vol 26, no 6, pp 76-83.

Shaver, F. (2005) 'Sex work research: methodological and ethical challenges', *Journal of Interpersonal Violence*, vol 20, no 3, pp 296-319.

Wallerstein, N. and Duran, B. (2003) 'The conceptual, historical, and practice roots of community-based participatory research and related participatory traditions', in M. Minkler and N. Wallerstein (eds) *Community-based participatory research for health*, San Francisco, CA: Jossey-Bass.

Weir, T., Abel, G., Fitzgerald, L. and Brunton, C. (2006) *The impact of the Prostitution Reform Act on the health and safety practices of sex workers. Report 1: Key informant interviews*, Christchurch: University of Otago, Christchurch School of Medicine.

ELEVEN

Becoming inspectors of brothels: public health authorities' experience of implementing the Prostitution Reform Act

Cheryl Brunton

'I mean it was all very well for me to go into this place but how could I judge it if I'd never been into a parlour before.... So I realised there was just no way I could have any ability to use the legislation constructively (a) if I wasn't known and our role wasn't known and (b) if I had no idea of how the sex industry worked and of what, where it actually was and who was in it and what a brothel, actually what you would expect to find in a brothel. I nearly dissolved the first time I saw a client, but by the time I got to the last brothel, I was cheerily saying "good morning" to them.' (Medical Officer of Health, Waikato)

Introduction

The passage of the 2003 Prostitution Reform Act (PRA) brought with it new and somewhat unexpected responsibilities for public health authorities, particularly Medical Officers of Health. The architects of the legislation clearly saw public health as an important consideration in regulatory reform of the sex industry (see Chapter Five) and indeed, Part 1, section 3 of the Act states that the purpose of the Act is to create a (legislative) framework that, among other things, 'is conducive to public health' (section 3(c)). The PRA makes Medical Officers of Health, who are designated officers under the 1956 Health Act, inspectors of brothels and gives them powers in relation to that function, including the appointment of other inspectors. Medical Officers of Health, and the public health services in which they work, have also made submissions to local authorities on proposed bylaws under the PRA, as they do on other bylaws and council plans relating to public health.

This chapter begins by outlining the statutory roles of Medical Officers of Health under the PRA and examines the early responses of public health authorities to implementing the legislation. The focus of the chapter is on the views of Medical Officers of Health and other public health and occupational health workers regarding their roles under the Act and their experience of its implementation.

The various approaches taken by public health services to implementing the legislation are also discussed, including the approach to complaints and interactions with other agencies. The latter part of the chapter analyses the content of public health submissions on proposed bylaws under the PRA and discusses the effect these submissions had (or in some cases, failed to have) on subsequent bylaws.

Public health authorities and their role in the PRA

In New Zealand, regional public health services are delivered by 12 District Health Board-owned public health units. Public health units focus on 'core public health services', as specified in the Public Health Services Handbook (Ministry of Health, 2003a), including: environmental health, communicable disease control, tobacco control and health promotion programmes.

Many of these services include a regulatory component performed by designated officers appointed under statutes (mainly the 1956 Health Act). These statutory officers are employed by District Health Boards but are personally accountable to the Director-General of Health.

Medical Officers of Health

Medical Officers of Health are designated officers of the New Zealand Ministry of Health who work in regional public health units. They are registered medical practitioners who have specialist training and qualifications in public health medicine. Regional public health units usually have more than one Medical Officer of Health; they may share duties across their districts or, in larger metropolitan units, specialise in particular aspects of work such as communicable disease control. Section 25 of the PRA made all Medical Officers of Health inspectors of brothels and gave them powers in relation to that function, including the appointment of other inspectors:

> 25 Inspectors
>
> (1) Every person designated as a Medical Officer of Health by the Director-General of Health under the Health Act 1956 is an inspector for the purposes of this Act.
> (2) A Medical Officer of Health may also appoint persons as inspectors for his or her health district, on a permanent or temporary basis, for the purposes of this Act.
> (3) A Medical Officer of Health may appoint a person as an inspector only if satisfied that he or she is suitably qualified or trained to carry out that role.
> (4) That appointment must be in writing and must contain-
>   (a) a reference to this section; and
>   (b) the full name of the appointed person; and

(c) a statement of the powers conferred on the appointed person by section 26 and the purpose under section 24 for which these powers may be used.

This role under the PRA has some parallels with other inspectorial functions under the 1956 Health Act, although these cannot necessarily be delegated. Health Protection Officers (formerly known as Health Inspectors) are also designated officers under the Health Act and they carry out many inspectorial functions. However, they were not specifically created inspectors of brothels under the PRA, although some have been appointed as such under section 25(3) (see above). Both Medical Officers of Health and Health Protection Officers have enforcement training in respect of their regulatory responsibilities. Their duties are generally undertaken using a risk management approach, responding to complaints and targeting enforcement activities in areas where adverse impacts on public health are greatest or more readily preventable.

Many of the powers granted to inspectors under section 26 of the Act are similar to those in other legislation such as the 1956 Health Act and the 1992 Health and Safety in Employment Act:

26 Powers to enter and inspect compliance with health and safety requirements

(1) An inspector may, at any reasonable time, enter premises for the purpose of carrying out an inspection if he or she has reasonable grounds to believe that a business of prostitution is being carried on in the premises.

(2) For the purposes of the inspection, the inspector may –
    (a) conduct reasonable inspections;
    (b) take photographs and measurements and make sketches and recordings;
    (c) require any of the following persons to provide information or assistance reasonably required by the inspector:
        (i) A person who operates the business of prostitution, or an employee or agent of that person,
        (ii) a sex worker or client of the business of prostitution.

(3) An inspector may seize and retain any thing in premises entered under this section that the inspector has reasonable grounds to believe will be evidence of the commission of an offence against section 8 or section 9.

(4) Nothing in this section limits or affects the privilege against self-incrimination.

(5) An inspector may take any person acting under the inspector's direct supervision into the premises to assist him or her with the inspection.

The options provided for under subsection 2(b) caused some amusement among Medical Officers of Health:

> 'I'm not sure I have the artistic skills really … makes us sound a bit like Toulouse Lautrec hanging around brothels making sketches.' (Medical Officer of Health, Wellington)

> 'What exactly, pray, do they think we will measure?' (Medical Officer of Health, Otago)

The Department of Labour

The Department of Labour is the government agency responsible for oversight of workplace health and safety in New Zealand. The principal legislation under which it operates is the 1992 Health and Safety in Employment Act. The department uses its enforcement powers when it is unable to get voluntary compliance with the law or the matter is such that a duty-holder needs to be held accountable for failure to meet minimum standards. Enforcement is used as a complement to other strategies such as education.

Department of Labour occupational health and safety inspectors investigate complaints about health and safety, notifications of serious harm, notifications of occupational disease and incidents that might have harmed someone. Inspectors come from a variety of backgrounds: some are former factory inspectors and a few are occupational health nurses. The department does not investigate every event reported to it. Most of the resources available for investigation are devoted to the more serious events.

Once sex work became decriminalised by the PRA, the sex industry and sex workers became subject to the requirements of the 1992 Health and Safety in Employment Act.

> 'No, it's not an issue for me at all really. It's an industry that's been around forever. It's not going to go away. There are circumstances where staff will be taken advantage of. Um … there are significant health issues and I think it's just another workplace.' (Occupational health nurse, Christchurch)

There are potential areas of overlap between occupational health and safety and public health in the sex industry, notably in regard to the safety and well-being of sex workers and their ability to practice safe sex.

> 'I mean, the legislation has opened the door … I mean, I think OSH [Department of Labour Occupational Safety and Health division] should be a partner in this. I think it's a total cop-out for OSH to say, "no, we don't do that 'cause it's sex". I mean, we don't do health and

safety in employment 'cause it's work ... here is a classic case where I think it should be a dual approach. Probably the best thing would be, you know, Health and OSH inspecting together.' Medical Officer of Health, Waikato

Despite this, according to the study's interviewees, dual inspections have seldom happened, although there have been attempts to coordinate the approaches of various agencies to regulating the sex industry both nationally and locally (see below).

Initial public health responses to the PRA

In early July 2003, shortly after the PRA was passed, a few Medical Officers of Health wrote to the Ministry of Health to attempt to clarify its expectation of their new role as inspectors under sections 25 and 26 of the PRA.

'I must say it kind of did come sort of, um, kind of came from the side really when we realised that we were going to be there, you know, sort of named, you know, named within the Act. It would have been good to be involved earlier.' (Medical Officer of Health, Wellington)

Initial guidance was issued to public health services and Medical Officers of Health on 19 August 2003, which provided background to the legislation and an outline of the new powers for Medical Officers of Health under the PRA.

Around the same time, staff in the Ministry of Health's Public Health Directorate moved to set up a Prostitution Reform Working Group to:

- identify existing health information (information on safe-sex practices and on services for the prevention of sexually transmissible infections) that is available for operators of the businesses of prostitution for sex workers/clients;
- identify and prioritise the necessity to revise and develop specific health information requirements for operators of businesses of prostitution, sex workers, and clients;
- identify processes for comment and feedback on drafts of new information and advice developed.

In addition to staff from the Ministry of Health, the working group included representatives from the New Zealand Prostitutes' Collective (NZPC), two Medical Officers of Health, representatives of operators of businesses of prostitution, a representative from the NZ Venereological Society and from Te Puawai Tapu, and representatives from the Department of Labour's Occupational Safety and Health (OSH) division. It met on 3 September 2003 and, in addition to considering the matters listed above, it also discussed how public health complaints under the PRA could be handled. Subsequent to the meeting, further work was done by the Department of Labour on developing occupational safety and health guidelines (see Chapter Five) and the Ministry of Health secured funding for the development of health information resources about the requirements of the PRA for operators of businesses of prostitution and clients (Ministry of Health, 2003b).

A circular letter was sent from the Ministry of Health on 12 December 2003 to Public Health Service Managers and Medical Officers of Health further clarifying their roles under the PRA and draft enforcement guidelines were sent to Medical Officers of Health on 16 December 2003.

> The Ministry of Health's role in enforcement of the PRA is based on the protection of public health, which includes the health of both sex workers and clients.

> The approach the Ministry of Health wishes to take with regards to the enforcement of the PRA is essentially one of education and encouragement to achieve compliance with the requirements of sections 8 & 9 of the Act. (Excerpt from draft enforcement guidelines, 16 December 2003)

Training

It was not until the following year that formal training in their new role was provided for designated officers. A training workshop for Medical Officers of Health and other public health service staff involved in work under the PRA was held on 29 June 2004 in Wellington by the Ministry of Health and its contracted training provider, Southern Monitoring Services Ltd. The presenters included Ministry of Health staff and representatives of NZPC. There was a total of 27 attendees from public health services: a mix of Medical Officers of Health, Health Protection Officers, sexual health promoters and public health nurses. The training had a strong focus on prosecutions under the PRA and the printed course material contained hypothetical case studies and generic enforcement advice. The Medical Officers of Health interviewed in this part of the study spoke of this training workshop:

> 'Oh the training, I mean it was fairly generic, I thought, especially for the few public health nurses who haven't been, um, haven't done any enforcement work and they found it quite useful. (Medical Officer of Health, Auckland)

> … I saw the folder that was produced, it was, um, a curious document in that it was mostly about prosecution. And I guess the Act sort of leads into dealing with complaints and prosecution, but, um, I mean from a public health point of view … I want to be having some guidance about how to work with sex workers and indeed their clients, and

particularly their management about, um, you know, good old Ottawa Charter stuff about, you know, creating a supportive and healthy environment for the sex industry to operate in. (Medical Officer of Health, Waikato)

Interviews with regulatory officers

The author attended a national meeting of Medical Officers of Health in Wellington on 18 October 2005. She gave a presentation on the research and its various components and requested information from those present about the extent of their involvement with implementation of the PRA. She also requested information about their involvement with regulatory officers from other agencies in their regions in relation to the PRA.

The extent of involvement reported by Medical Officers of Health at the meeting was highly variable, from those who had had no involvement at all to those who had been involved in local intersectoral groups to discuss protocols and one who had visited all their local brothels and met regularly with NZPC workers. Eleven Medical Officers of Health from seven districts (including the five main study locations) agreed to be interviewed further about their involvement with the PRA.

A semi-structured interview guide was developed following further discussion at the national Medical Officers of Health meeting in May 2006. Interviewees were asked about a range of topics, including their experience of proposed territorial authority bylaws, their roles as inspectors of brothels under the PRA, their relationships with regulatory officers from other agencies in relation to implementing the PRA, how they dealt with complaints and their views on the effectiveness of the Act. Two in-depth interviews were conducted by the author in face-to-face meetings in Christchurch: one with the two sexual health promoters who carried out the inspector role on behalf of the local Medical Officer of Health and the other with an occupational health nurse from the Department of Labour who worked as an occupational safety and health inspector. Six other interviews were conducted over the telephone with Medical Officers of Health in various parts of the country. All interviews were audio-recorded and transcribed to word accuracy.

Early experience with implementation

Much of public health services' reported early experiences of implementing the PRA involved making submissions on proposed local bylaws (see the second part of this chapter). Some Medical Officers of Health initiated local meetings with other agencies, including NZPC, and undertook to provide training on the PRA locally.

'…I know in discussions we had around the time the Act was getting, um, you know, coming into play, we met with local police guys and stuff like that ... and we were, um, you know, pushing the advantage of the health and safety for workers and that kind of thing.' (Medical Officer of Health, Nelson)

'I think the law passed in June, and in November of that year we had a, um, meeting here and, um, invited all the local operators to come and go through the Act … we invited someone from city council and OSH to come along too. The council declined. They decided not to do it, because they were in the middle of their bylaw struggle thing, so they thought it might not be very good for the operators, who were angry with them, and if certain operators had turned up there could be a fight basically … and they (the operators) were sort of a bit hesitant at first, but we just said, "Well we just thought it would be good to meet you and go through the law and tell you what our side of it is", and we had a cup of tea and biccies and just tried to make it very normal, you know, not a big deal at all.' (Sexual health promoter, Christchurch)

'The Prostitutes' Collective, who initially we worked with, our local branch, we did training sessions for everybody, the police, the local authorities, OSH, ourselves, and we had a good network.' (Medical Officer of Health, Otago)

Around this time, some public health service managers and Medical Officers of Health sought clarification from the Ministry of Health about whether or not there would be additional funding to assist them with their new functions under the PRA. The response was that the new requirements were a statutory function and that they would need to be carried out within existing resources.

''Cause remember the Medical Officer of Health way back wrote to the Ministry saying, "Is there any extra money or staff coming with this?", because, you know, at that stage it was like, "Well okay, the Act's passed, great. Who's going to do the work?" And there was no extra money, no extra staff, and so … it was just considered that we, we'd react to complaints basically rather than going in, you know, every so often.' (Sexual health promoter, Christchurch)

'Um, sort of, a couple of managers have said, "There's no resources. Will you tell me what people are going to stop doing to enable you to do this?".… What we were proposing was quite a small time investment, which I think could have helped establish relationships and rapport so that if, you know, if there are big issues we would have been in a better position to do something about it.' (Medical Officer of Health, Wellington

'I mean if we suddenly got in a, you know, heaps of complaints or a whole lot of brothels setting up and people wanted us to inspect them, then it might be an issue.' (Medical Officer of Health, Bay of Plenty)

Public health service approaches to implementing the PRA

Almost all public health services took a largely reactive approach to implementation of the public health role under the PRA, apart from the initial local meetings and training mentioned above. This approach was determined, at least in part, by limited resources, rather than an unwillingness to take a more active role.

'We were told by the Ministry not to be proactive … [our manager] was hoping that we could take a more proactive role so we did actually discuss this issue of doing something more active. But in the end with the HPOs [Health Protection Officers] involved we decided that none of it was feasible really.… We did not have the resources.' (Medical Officer of Health, Auckland)

One notable exception was in Hamilton, where the Medical Officer of Health and a Health Protection Officer visited all the brothels in the district. This happened after they responded to a complaint about one local premises.

'And the Prostitutes' Collective representative rang me about this particular premises and gave me quite a lot of background about it and about concerns the sex workers have had working there for a long time. And, um, so, um, with tremendous trepidation – I mean I don't think I've ever been so nervous – but I mean I visited, armed with large male Health Protection Officer, who's even slightly more mature in years than me. And the pair of us tip-toed into this place, which we'd been told was one of the less satisfactory premises around. And I meant it was all very well for me to go into this place, but how could I judge it if I'd never been into a parlour before? So that was what led to me into the process of visiting all our other parlours.' (Medical Officer of Health, Waikato)

Some Medical Officers of Health also identified a potential problem if they were to attempt to take a more proactive approach to their work. This was how they could go about identifying the brothels in their district. The PRA makes no provision for the identity of licensed operators or premises to be disclosed to Medical Officers of Health; indeed, section 41(1) appears to preclude this. One

Medical Officer of Health sought clarification of this from the Registrar of the Auckland District Court. Its response was as follows:

> As you note, section 41(1) of the Prostitution Reform Act restricts access to information about operators held by the Court. While it may be possible to provide some statistical information this may not in fact be helpful for your purpose. This is because when an application of an Operator's Certificate is made under the Act all that we can seek from the applicant is a postal address. We do not hold any details about the premises that the operator may be managing and fact the postal address could well be outside the area of where the applicant may be operating. (We know of one applicant, of the six received to date, whose address is in one area but owns premises in 3 other areas. We are only aware of this because the applicant discussed the situation with one of our staff). (Excerpt from a letter to Dr Cheryl Brunton from I.D. Wilson, Administration Officer, Auckland District Court, January 2004)

Although in one district with a bylaw requiring licensing of brothels, the territorial authority supplied the local Medical Officer of Health with a list of licensed premises, most other public health services have identified brothels in their districts through a combination of searches of the Yellow Pages, the local knowledge of sexual health educators/promoters and NZPC. This is in contrast to other issues where Medical Officers of Health have regulatory responsibilities, such as the Sale of Liquor Act (1989), where the location of licensed premises and the contact details of owners and operators are a matter of public record and routinely available from the licensing authority.

At least one Medical Officer of Health also questioned the priority that should be given to PRA-related work in relation to other areas of work.

> 'I mean certainly in terms of outcomes, if you had to put up a case for doing it in terms of what health, what actual shown risk has there been, and it's so low, so it would be low on the scale of things.' (Medical Officer of Health, Otago)

Dealing with complaints

Only one of the Medical Officers of Health interviewed had not yet dealt with a complaint under the PRA.

> 'I resolved fairly early on that I'd respond to any complaints that come through and well, I've never had any.' (Medical Officer of Health, Bay of Plenty)

All the rest commented that complaints had been infrequent and none had dealt with more than 10 distinct complaints in total (on occasion, more than one complaint had been received about a particular premises, or one complainant had complained multiple times). None had actively sought complaints or promoted their role in responding to them.

> 'To be honest it's not something we push, as in "we are the first ones to contact for complaints about brothels", because a lot of complaints would fall outside our powers of inspection.' (Medical Officer of Health, Otago)

One Medical Officer of Health for a large metropolitan area (which may well have the largest number of brothels in the country) thought he had dealt with no more than one complaint per year. Most complaints were either about unsafe sex practices or matters of hygiene, such as the unavailability of washing facilities or dirty sheets or towels, and some complaints involved both.

> 'But it was around an unsafe work environment, the, um, and the unsafeness related to both kind of, you know, hygiene things. They weren't clean sheets, there wasn't a process of, you know, laundering sheets and towels and things like that. Um and also the physical location of the work area was down a long dark corridor across the road from the main area, very poor lighting, no kind of alarm bells, no one else working over there. So there was a real risk of violence towards sex workers. So we referred that on to, um, the Department of Labour for OSH to follow up.' (Medical Officer of Health, Wellington)

Almost all complainants were anonymous and Medical Officers of Health commented that this made it very difficult to take action unless adequate detail was supplied to them.

> 'There was, for instance, one guy kept ringing. He'll ring me, he'd ring an HPO [Health Protection Officer], he'll ring everybody, um, saying that he's got concerns about, um, unprotected sex, and that he would send us a video of their promotional material and all sorts of things, but nothing came out. Just wouldn't give us the details of the premises.' (Medical Officer of Health, Auckland)

> 'There's none of our complaints, we've never had anyone that we can identify, you know, who's willing to give a name and a contact. They're anonymous. They're just about all, all by phone....You can't go further with them really. And it's good to keep them, because you can get a pattern if one place is consistently getting them. 'Cause you know, it could be a competitor wanting to shut down someone else's business.

And it could be a disgruntled client or disgruntled worker. And one of them was from a worker who was actually still working in the place, and um, you have to be very careful then how you approach it, 'cause they, even though they don't like some of the things, they want, they need the job. So you can't ring and say, "One of your workers". You've just got to say, "An anonymous someone that we can't, you know", and you can honestly say, "We don't know".' (Sexual health promoter, Christchurch)

'One was from a member of, a member of the public, who had visited a brothel and was um didn't, wasn't able to see the posters. He'd obviously read things, and, um, he told us he'd been offered sex without a condom. Now, we were obviously very concerned about that and wanted from him some details of, um, both the location of the venue, the times, the date, the name of the sex worker, the description, any details about him. And he wasn't prepared to provide any details, um, and the conversation, he very rapidly hung up.' (Medical Officer of Health, Wellington)

Unsurprisingly, perhaps, none of the complaints that had been investigated by Medical Officers of Health had resulted in a prosecution. The experience of the occupational safety and health inspector was similar, in that he had also had few complaints to investigate:

'… since the launch of the guideline, for instance, I've probably only had two or three inquiries or investigations that I've had to carry out actually in some of the places around town.

One of them related to a place in town where one of the women that worked there had said there were … no adequate facilities for hand washing.' (Occupational health nurse, Christchurch)

Relationships with other agencies involved in implementing the PRA

All the interviewees made generally positive comments on their relationships with other agencies also involved in implementing the provisions of the PRA: the police, territorial authority officers, and the Department of Labour's OSH division. However, the issue of potential overlap of functions with the Department of Labour was raised by some interviewees.

'I mean it's a grey area. Um, but because OSH is separate from regulatory public health services … the working conditions of the workers … as a public health risk to clients. But I mean they could take the OSH, um, role. OSH applies to the workers and the people that are working, people visiting the premises. Therefore OSH should be responsible for it all, but then should OSH be responsible for ensuring – well I suppose it is health behaviour?' (Medical Officer of Health, Otago)

'We have good relationships with OSH locally … and, um, I hoped that we might be able to team up with them a bit over the, you know, sort of physical aspects of brothels. Um, but regrettably the colleague with whom we work mostly on this, was as scared of it as we are and, um, said they'd be really happy to deal with things like dangerous facilities and showers, and, you know, lethal surfaces that were slippery. But, um, he ran a mile from the sex side of it.' (Medical Officer of Health, Waikato)

Most interviewees also highlighted the importance of the role of NZPC. Several alluded to the professional support for sex workers provided by NZPC and the assistance and information they provided to regulatory officers.

'Um, we've kept in contact with the NZPC and I've tended to feel that's probably the best way to go because I'm not, I'm not an expert in the industry.... I think the NZPC are the people who have got an actual good grasp of what the realities are.' (Occupational health nurse, Christchurch)

'I think their [NZPC's] role is very fundamental in that they are, that they provide advocacy for the workers and are intent on raising the standards, um, within the profession.' (Medical Officer of Health, Otago)

The role of Medical Officers of Health under the PRA

When asked to comment about the Medical Officer of Health's role under the PRA, all the interviewees expressed now having a level of comfort with it and feeling that it was an appropriate role for them.

'… I'm very comfortable with that role. You know, I don't have any, um, ethical or moral qualms about it, and in fact, you know, I fully support anything that could be done, you know, around, you know, improving work conditions.... There's certainly potential there and, you know, we would like, certainly like to do more in this area, both from, you know, exactly, you know what we've got under the Act here, but also from, you know, there's going to be other potential health gains from it for a whole lot of reasons.' (Medical Officer of Health, Wellington)

'Yeah, I mean it is, it is actually. I think it sits comfortably with the role of Medical Officers of Health, yeah.' (Medical Officer of Health, Otago)

Several interviewees made reference to the need to be non-judgemental in carrying out this work. The comments of two sexual health promoters were typical:

C   'There's just no way you could begin a dialogue in this industry if you weren't really comfortable with the issues and the reality of it all and how it is really.'

D   'Mmm, oh absolutely, and because if you were going in there with some sort of judgemental, moralistic attitude, you know, it just wouldn't work. You wouldn't, you wouldn't build up that kind of relationship with people where, you know … people could ring up and have pretty easy conversations about things. And that's what we want – people to be able to ring us too and you know, if they've got any issue or questions they feel safe to ring us. So absolutely, I mean, we've done years of work in sexual health, so …'

C   'We're unshockable.' (Sexual health promoters, Christchurch)

Only three of the Medical Officers of Health interviewed had formally appointed other staff as inspectors of brothels (as they are able to do under section 25(2) of the Act) and the type of people they had appointed were Health Protection Officers, public health nurses and sexual health promoters/educators. One Medical Officer of Health had temporarily appointed a public health medicine trainee in his absence.

'… well the only time we've used it, we've actually used these powers, was about a year ago when there was a issue raised through, um, the sexual health educator … they were concerned about a new operator in the field who had very little knowledge of how to keep his brothel clean and how to function … and OSH was involved but they wanted a Medical Officer of Health to go along just to have a look at the facilities…. Now neither [the other Medical Officer of Health] or I could go because we had other things….And so we actually delegated the registrar to go and do it.' (Medical Officer of Health, Otago)

Perceptions of the impact of the PRA on health and safety in the sex industry

All interviewees were asked about their perceptions of the impact of the PRA on health and safety in the sex industry. Most felt the impact had been positive, although there were some reservations.

'Oh, I think these kind of predictions of once it becomes legalised that all sorts of things are going to be dreadful and into drugs and all sort of things. You know, it was kind of "and the sky will fall in too" ... and it doesn't appear to have happened.' (Medical Officer of Health, Wellington)

'Well honestly, I do not know how much of an impact it has had. I mean, it started off with a bang of guidelines and produced information material with them. How compliant they are I don't really know.' (Medical Officer of Health, Auckland)

'I think it has, it has actually improved their conditions ... which is sort of the safety side of it. I'm not sure about the health side of it ... because, I mean, in principle by encouraging safer sex, that's great. But then if either clients have too much power, if you like, if the clients can say, "Well, I'll give you a lot more money under the counter if you don't use protection", then short of doing random inspections to see what's going on ...' (Medical Officer of Health, Otago)

All the interviewees were aware of the OSH guidelines document, although the Department of Labour staff member interviewed for this research commented on the limits to its usefulness.

'... there was a comment made that it was rather big. It was like a telephone book. Some of the people felt it was like a telephone book and that it just needed to be a small brochure, pamphlet for people. But I mean this is really there to be able to answer any, pretty much any enquiry an employer might have or somebody who's dealing in an industry. It's not the sort of book that you'd give one of the girls on Manchester Street.' (Occupational health nurse, Christchurch)

He also commented on a suggestion that had been made to him by a local NZPC representative that OSH does an assessment of all the brothels and made similar observations to those of the Medical Officers of Health about the priority given to this work and limits on resources.

'Um, X had actually wanted that. We go and do an assessment of all of them and give them all, you know, make sure that they've got information and have an assessment of all of them. But, which is probably a good idea, but it's not one of the priorities for us for this year. We sort of are involved in a range of other health priorities at the moment.' (Occupational health nurse, Christchurch)

Local bylaws under the PRA and public health

As discussed in Chapter Nine, sections 12, 13 and 14 of the PRA give territorial authorities (city and district councils) the ability to make bylaws regulating advertising and signage of commercial sexual services and the location of brothels. Medical Officers of Health and the public health services in which they work made submissions to local authorities on proposed bylaws under the PRA.

Identifying territorial authority bylaws

Existing territorial authority bylaws under the PRA, or district plan rules regulating location and/or signage of brothels, were identified through territorial authority websites (a complete list of which was obtained from Local Government New Zealand's website, www.lgnz.co.nz). The websites were searched for an index of bylaws and these in turn were scanned for bylaw titles including the words/phrases 'prostitution', brothels' or 'commercial sex premises'. In addition, the websites were searched electronically using their embedded search engines and the same three words/phrases as search terms.

Copies of 19 bylaws and four relevant district plan rules identified by search of territorial authority websites were either downloaded from these websites or obtained in hard copy.

Bylaws in the main study locations

Territorial authority bylaws under the PRA exist (or existed) in all five main study locations. In the greater Auckland region, North Shore City (2000 North Shore City Bylaw: Part 20 – Brothels), Auckland City (2008 Auckland City Bylaw: Part 30 – Brothels and Commercial Sex Premises), Manukau City (1992 Manukau City Consolidated Bylaw: Chapter 28 – Brothels) and Rodney District (1998 Rodney District Council General Bylaw: Chapter 22 – Brothels and Commercial Sex Premises) all had bylaws, although Waitakere City and Papakura did not. Auckland City's bylaw was the most comprehensive and prescriptive of the four and initially contained provisions regulating both location and signage of brothels, although the location provisions are no longer in force. Both the Manukau City and North Shore City bylaws also regulated location and signage of brothels. However, Auckland City and Rodney District's bylaws both included sex workers working from home as a home occupation, or a private residence where any sex worker is working, in their definition of a brothel for the purposes of the bylaw, although all four included small owner-operated brothels (as defined in the PRA) within their bylaw's definition of a brothel. All four bylaws also made provision for licensing of brothels, although only three (Auckland, Manukau and Rodney) included health and safety considerations, such as hygiene of the premises and washing facilities, in their requirements for licensing. The draft versions of both the Auckland and Manukau City bylaws included contagious and notifiable infectious disease provisions that were inconsistent with the provisions of the 1956 Health Act and human rights legislation and this was highlighted in the submissions of the Auckland Regional Public Health Service.

> The Service notes that it is unlikely that clause 7.13 of the Draft Bylaw (the communicable disease provision) is justifiable. The purpose of the Prostitution Reform Act is, among other things, to safeguard the human rights of sex workers and protect them from exploitation. It does not provide a legislative frame work for restricting the movement (based on possible or confirmed presence of communicable disease) of sex workers or their clients. The Service considers it is extremely unlikely that this subsection of the Bylaw also meets the other two criteria of justifiable discrimination.

> Of particular note is Section 21(1)(h)(vii) of the Human Rights Act that prohibits discrimination on the grounds of disability, including the presence in the body of organisms capable of causing illness. (Excerpt from Auckland Regional Public Health Service submission on Manukau City Council's 2004 Draft Brothel Control Bylaw)

These provisions were deleted before the bylaws were passed.

In Hawkes Bay, neither Napier City nor Hastings District Council had bylaws under the PRA, although Napier City changed the rules in its district plan in 2005 to restrict brothels from operating in the central business district (CBD). Napier City's original proposed plan change would also have prohibited small owner-operated brothels from operating but the council was encouraged to exempt these by the local Medical Officer of Health (see below).

In the Wellington region, the Hutt City and Kapiti District Councils did not have bylaws under the PRA. Wellington City Council had a bylaw, which had been in force since before the PRA was enacted, regulating commercial sex premises but not brothels per se, and Upper Hutt City was the only territorial authority to have a bylaw under the PRA in the Wellington region (2003 Upper Hutt City Council Brothels Bylaw). This bylaw prohibited brothels being located in a residential zone or the CBD or within 200 metres of sites such as churches, schools, play areas or retirement homes. It also regulated brothel signage but did not impose any requirement for brothels to be licensed.

Nelson City had a bylaw (Nelson City Council: Advertising Commercial Sexual Services Bylaw No 208) made under the PRA regulating the advertisement of commercial sexual services (including brothels), but this had no provisions relating to location or licensing of brothels. Neither of the neighbouring Tasman or Marlborough districts had bylaws under the PRA.

In Christchurch, the city council initially passed a bylaw (2004 Christchurch City Brothels (Location and Signage) Bylaw) that regulated signage of brothels and restricted the location of brothels (including small owner-operated brothels) to a defined zone of the CBD (clause 6), and exempted existing brothels in the designated area (clause 7) only if their activities did not change in character, scale or intensity. These clauses were later quashed by the High Court of New Zealand on 29 July 2005, as they related to location of brothels.

Public health submissions on local bylaws

Medical Officers of Health in each of the districts with bylaws or relevant district plan rules were contacted by email, asking if they had made a submission on the bylaw or plan change and requesting a copy of their submission if they had done so.

Copies of 11 public health submissions were obtained from Medical Officers of Health, including those from each of the main study locations.

The submissions made by Medical Officers of Health on local bylaws or district plan changes under the PRA throughout New Zealand had several common features. Almost all referred to the purposes of the PRA as outlined in section 3(a), (b) and (c) and most stressed that it was important that councils did not create local bylaws or plan changes inconsistent with the aims and purposes of the Act.

> I would like to see local governments concentrate their deliberations on the health and well being protection and improvement goals of the Prostitution Reform Act, and consider what statutory tools you have available to meet these goals…Councils might better invest their resources by finding out what concerns are currently impacting on the health, well being and protection of sex workers, and working with them to find discreet and acceptable ways of managing these risks. (Excerpt from a letter to all territorial authority Chief Executives in the region from the Waikato Medical Officer of Health, 2 June 2004)

Several Medical Officers of Health also took issue with territorial authorities whose draft bylaws included small owner-operated brothels and/or sex workers engaged in prostitution in their definition of a brothel, arguing that this was inconsistent with the definition of a brothel in the PRA (seven out of the 19 existing bylaws under the PRA existing at the time still included small owner-operated brothels under their provisions).

> It is important that solo prostitutes or small owner-operated brothels are *able to remain within the law* [emphasis in original] and are not forced to deny their activities. (Excerpt from a letter to the Policy Planner, Napier City Council from the Medical Officer of Health, Hawkes Bay commenting on a proposed variation and plan change, 20 December 2005)

Many of their submissions further argued that the effect of such an inclusive definition of a brothel and of zoning restrictions would be to drive such operations underground, compromise the ability of public health services to deliver either safe sex education/information and have a potential negative impact on human rights protection and occupational health and safety in the sex industry.

> Brothels will remain or become clandestine operations (and) deny those brothels' sex workers and their clients the protections provided by the Act. (Excerpt from the submission of the Medical Officer of Health, South Canterbury to the Timaru District Council, February 2004)

> Our concern as a public health organisation is that at least some of the brothels currently outside the restricted area will continue to operate anyway but will go 'underground' so they are not easily accessed for either safe sex education/information or for human rights protection and occupational health and safety. (Excerpt from the submission of Community and Public Health to Christchurch City Council, April 2004)

Formal submissions and informal approaches by Medical Officers of Health to territorial authorities had variable outcomes. For example, in the Auckland region, the strongly critical submissions by the Auckland Regional Public Health Service on the Auckland and Manukau City Councils' proposed bylaws appear to have had little impact (apart from on the communicable diseases provisions mentioned above) on the content of the bylaws that were passed. Indeed, the report of the Hearings Commissioners rejected the submitters' assertions that the bylaw's provisions were *ultra vires* or unreasonable (Auckland City Council, 2003).

In Hamilton, the Medical Officer of Health wrote to all council Chief Executive Officers when she became aware that bylaws were being considered, but found her intervention was not welcome, despite her statutory role.

> 'Let it be recorded that my letter was not well received. Interestingly nobody got back to me, but I heard informally from a regional council employee of great seniority that there had been some concern about my sticking my nose in there.' (Medical Officer of Health, Waikato)

By contrast, the approaches made by the Medical Officers of Health in Whangarei and Hastings seem to have helped persuade those territorial authorities not to enact bylaws, although they had considered doing so.

> Health and safety concerns have been raised by submitters not only for industry providers, but also for the community at large. By creating control, council forces individual industry providers into larger poorly controlled businesses. A potential solution is to provide for sole providers within the bylaw. Suggestion that the proposed bylaw goes against the primary intent of the Act. Same solution as above, or

remain as is, i.e. no bylaw established but wait and see effect of the Act on Whangarei. (Excerpt from summary of submissions on proposed bylaw under the Prostitution Reform Act. File ref:15/1/1 Whangarei District Council, 20 February 2004)

In other cases, both the Napier and Nelson City Councils accepted the recommendations made by their respective Medical Officers of Health regarding proposed changes to their district plan rules. The Medical Officer of Health for Hawkes Bay made a related argument in respect of small owner-operated brothels in his submission on a proposed plan change by the Napier City Council:

> I note in documentation concerning plan changes to the District Plan that there is no distinction made between large commercial sex premises and small owner-operated brothels. The latter are really people working from their own home or residence. A few days' perusal of 'Hawkes Bay Today' shows that there are three times as many prostitutes operating as solo workers (using only a cellphone) as there are brothels. (Excerpt from submission of the Medical Officer of Health, Hawkes Bay to the Napier City Council, 20 December 2005)

> '... I'm pretty sure it was taken on board. Um, we were just acknowledging that lots of people would have strong views about it and there needed to be a better way of assessing whether something was appropriate or not.' (Medical Officer of Health, Nelson)

Medical Officers of Health had not always made submissions on local bylaws. In some districts, such as Otago, none of the territorial authorities chose to enact bylaws, so no submissions were needed. In others, although Medical Officers of Health were aware of bylaws being proposed, they did not always feel their input was needed.

> 'At the time it seemed that the councils were essentially concerned with zoning issues and we decided to stay out of the discussions.' (Medical Officer of Health, Bay of Plenty)

In some cases, Medical Officers of Health were unaware that the territorial authorities in their region intended to enact bylaws until after the event.

> 'I do not think we made any submission about it at the time. Seems a bit slack but communication from the council is usually pretty poor and we may not have been informed about the bylaw at the time.' (Medical Officer of Health, Southland)

'No, now in terms of, um, when we became aware that city councils were starting to pass bylaws, we rang round all of the territorial local authorities in our region, and at that point, we discovered that Upper Hutt had already passed one.' (Medical Officer of Health, Wellington)

Conclusion

New Zealand's public health authorities have had a range of experiences with the implementation of the PRA. Most of their early involvement was in making submissions on proposed local bylaws and this has had variable impact, ranging from being unwelcome or ignored to being taken into account in decision making, including whether or not a bylaw was enacted. Aside from the initial provision of health information resources to the sex industry and the development of occupational safety and health guidelines for it, central agencies like the Ministry of Health and the Department of Labour have taken a largely 'hands-off' approach. The same has been true at a local level, where Medical Officers of Health and public health services have responded to complaints, rather than initiating an inspection regime, largely because of limited resources and competing priorities. Complaints to public health authorities under the PRA have been infrequent and few, if any, have resulted in prosecution. Most complaints concerned either unsafe sex or unhygienic premises, sometimes both, and almost all complainants were anonymous, limiting the ability to proceed with prosecutions.

Despite this, there is still a desire on the part of regulatory officers to take a more proactive health promotion approach to health and safety in the sex industry. Medical Officers of Health are comfortable with their role under the PRA and feel their involvement is appropriate and necessary, despite it having initially come as something of a surprise. All those interviewed were positive about their relationships with other regulatory agencies and the NZPC in particular. Most also felt that implementation of the PRA had had a positive impact on health and safety on the sex industry, although there were reservations about its impacts on the wider public health.

This study has identified a number of potential barriers to implementation of the roles of public health authorities under the PRA, many of which have been overcome in practice. One of the more crucial barriers – lack of specific funding for this regulatory activity – has resulted in a reactive, complaint-driven approach being taken, despite the expressed wish of regulatory officers to take a more proactive health promotion approach to working with the sex industry. The lack of priority given to the enforcement of the PRA by both the Ministry of Health and Department of Labour has been reflected in lack of funding for local education and enforcement activities by regulatory officers. This is hardly surprising, given that the original legislation was a Private Member's Bill, and that the policy work that would usually have been done regarding implementation of a government Bill was lacking. That at least some proactive work has taken place, despite under-resourcing, has largely been down to the commitment and enthusiasm of individual public health officers.

The problem of inter-agency cooperation in enforcement is also a potential barrier. This is a perennial one and the PRA is not the only example of New Zealand legislation where the roles of the Ministry of Health and Department of Labour potentially overlap. Yet those interviewed for this study were still mostly positive about inter-agency relationships at a local level, although acknowledging that levels of comfort with work under the PRA still varied between agencies and officers and made some, particularly from the Department of Labour, reluctant to exercise their role.

The reluctance of regulatory officers to take up their roles under the PRA might have been a barrier to its enforcement, but making Medical Officers of Health inspectors of brothels seems to have been a successful strategy. Having a background in health or public health work has contributed to a willingness to see work with the PRA and the sex industry in a matter-of-fact way, with little embarrassment or discomfort being expressed by those interviewed. While all Medical Officers of Health are doctors and some Department of Labour inspectors have a nursing background, it would not be unexpected that former factory inspectors, for example, might feel awkward dealing with some of the issues encountered in inspecting brothels and aspects of sex work.

The apparent logistical barrier to enforcement of the PRA posed by the lack of any requirement for central or local registers of sex industry premises has been largely overcome by public health agencies using local resources like phone books, advertisements and the local knowledge of NZPC staff. Nonetheless, there could be some advantages in a licensing regime for brothels analogous to that under the 1989 Sale of Liquor Act, which requires Medical officers of Health to report on all new on-licences and licence renewals. If all new brothels were to be inspected, it would provide an opportunity for education of managers and sex workers in their responsibilities under the PRA, and licence renewals could also be an opportunity to review compliance. Although it could assist in further improvements to health and safety in the sex industry, this would, of course, require additional resourcing. This is unlikely to be forthcoming, given the many competing priorities for public health funding and the argument that the overall public health gain would be limited.

References

Auckland City Council (2003) Report to the council from Hearings Commissioners, Draft Brothel and Commercial Sex Premises Bylaw, 10 December.

Ministry of Health (2003a) *Public health service handbook 2003/04*, Wellington: Ministry of Health, www.moh.govt.nz/moh.nsf/0/B13E45ADA9BC8943CC 256EC4000A8749/$File/2003-04Handbook.pdf

Ministry of Health (2003b) *Prostitution Reform Act 2003: Information for public health services and medical officers of health*, 19 August.

Ministry of Health (2003c) *Prostitution Reform Act 2003: Draft enforcement guidelines*, 16 December.

Ministry of Health (2003b) *Prostitution Reform Act 2003: Health and safety information for operators of businesses of prostitution*, 22 December, www.healthed.govt.nz/uploads/docs/HE1505.pdf.

TWELVE

The media and the Prostitution Reform Act

Lisa Fitzgerald and Gillian Abel

'I think it's salacious [media reporting on sex work]. I think they like it because it's ear pricking, you know, it's eye popping, it's attention grabbing, you know. I don't think they care about sex workers. They just like the downside of it. You know, they like, recently there was that murder of a woman, who supposedly had worked in the sex industry. Even though her murder, it turns out, had nothing to do with sex work, but more domestic violence, I mean it's, they, everyone's going after their angle, you know. I think anyone who targets sex work is lazy because we're just easy targets anyway, you know. I think the media still portray us as, yeah, sleazy, dark, yeah, it's just by, it's just trying to, yeah, trying to get headlines through, yeah, sleaziness and like making, making out it is, even though it's not. It's more like, to me sex work's more like a service.' (Dora, street worker, transgender)

Introduction

This chapter examines the role of the media in the context of the implementation of the 2003 Prostitution Reform Act (PRA), policy that was developed to protect the human rights of sex workers and minimise the amount of harm incurred by their occupation. As highlighted in previous chapters, the PRA indicated a shift in policy, from a moralistic to a public health and human rights approach. This chapter considers whether the media coverage of the PRA reinforced existing moral discourses of sex work, or developed new discourses in this new policy context. It does this through a content analysis of print media reporting on the PRA, exploring messages communicated in and by print media in New Zealand between 2003 and 2006, and qualitative analysis of in-depth interviews with 58 sex workers about their experiences of the media coverage surrounding the PRA. The chapter highlights how, although most print media was descriptive and neutral, the print media did draw on dominant moral discourses of sex work. Print media reporting that did draw on moral discourses was particularly acknowledged by sex workers and described as reinforcing existing stigmatisation surrounding sex work. A key feature of this chapter is to recognise and describe how sex worker participants resisted dominant discourses in their everyday practices.

Background

The media plays a significant role in western contemporary society. It provides resources that people draw on as part of their construction of personal identity, in the 'telling the story of their selves' (Seale, 2003, p 514). It is an important conduit through which relationships between individuals and groups in society are facilitated and/or denied. Through its role in the sharing of images, ideas and meanings, the media facilitates relationships as well as prejudices (Silverstone and Georgiou, 2005). Research has highlighted the powerful role of the media in preserving existing social relationships and how people draw on media representations in the crafting of their identities (Seale, 2003; Hodgetts and Chamberlain, 2006; Hodgetts et al, 2006; Hallgrimsdottir et al, 2008). They are primary sources for the general public's understandings of health and medical issues, from the definition of health-related social issues to the formation of health policies (Hodgetts and Chamberlain, 2006; Clarke and van Ameron, 2008). As media studies research has highlighted, all media depictions are social constructions (Seale, 2003). A key role for health social scientists is to critically examine the media to illustrate 'which stories get told and which are suppressed and in how members of the media audience ... respond to mediated health messages' (Seale, 2003, p 514).

Cultural theorists have highlighted the role of the media in the production and reproduction of dominant discourses about particular social groups and in the defining of public issues and influences that shape policy decisions (Hall et al, 1978; Kitzinger, 2000; Seale, 2003; Champion and Chapman, 2005; Hallgrimsdottir et al, 2006). The media creates understandings between different social groups through what has been described as media 'framing' (Gitlin, 2003; Hallgrimsdottir et al, 2006). Media framing is an analytic tool where frames are explored as 'shared cultural tools for the interpretation and meaning in context' (Koteyko et al, 2008, p 226). In the media, framing involves selecting 'some aspects of a perceived reality' and making them 'more salient in a communicating text, in such a way as to promote a particular problem definition, causal interpretation, moral evaluation, and/or treatment recommendation for the item prescribed' (Entman, 1993, p 52). Due to the hidden and marginalised nature of the sex industry, it is through the media that most people gain knowledge about the sex industry, meaning that '[t]he (mis)representations of sex workers found in mainstream media outlets thus have the potential to shape both the day-to-day interactions sex workers have with the public and their clients as well as legal and policy environments that shape their lives' (Hallgrimsdottir et al, 2008, p 120).

An important area in which the media has an influence is health policy. Research has highlighted how the media has an important influence over public opinion, politicians and the policy process, through the selection and repetition of particular themes, values and assumptions and the reliance on certain sources of information over others throughout the policy process (Hertog and Fan, 1995; Mutz and Soss, 1997; Niven, 2002; Tompsett et al, 2003). The media is central in defining social issues and legitimating specific approaches to these issues (Hodgetts and Chamberlain, 2006), and is an integral element in policy formation, as media representations are often taken to reflect public opinion regarding policy issues. These representations hold power and can influence policymakers, as Tompsett et al (2003, p 242) articulate: '[a] false perception of the collective opinion derived from biased media coverage could prove particularly detrimental when it is held by those with power to shape social policy'. What is important to note is how the media can play an important part of the disciplinary regime for marginalised groups such as sex workers, reinforcing disciplinary policy and control strategies (Hall, 1997; Taylor, 2008). The media has become a basis for authoritarian solutions to specific issues that can then drive policy solutions (Hall et al, 1978; Taylor, 2008). It constructs stories of threat and risk around such marginalised groups that require punitive policy solutions. The media has consistently depicted and marginalised sex workers as the 'other', belonging to an underworld associated with crime and drugs, and this narrative has been linked to the regulation of sex work (Hubbard, 1998).

The literature that has examined the media and sex work across different countries and policy settings highlights how the media often reinforces existing stereotypes and images of the sex work industry and people who are associated with this industry. Dominant discourses of sex work have tended to be utilised that are based on moral discourses that construct oppositional discourses of 'us' from 'them' (Sibley, 1995; Hodgetts et al, 2006), utilising metaphors such as 'dirty' and 'social festering boil' to signify the industry (Stenvoll, 2002; O'Neill and Campbell, 2006). They tend to ignore broader social and structural factors that underlie sex work and downplay any harm minimisation aspects (Mendes, 2005). The problems experienced by sex workers in their everyday lives and their treatment by the law are rarely addressed (Kantola and Squires, 2004). Most media depictions of sex work tend to make little use of evidence (Scott, 2003). With its focus on the more visible street-based sector, the media accentuates moral geographies that are focused on the regulation of the moral aesthetic of city spaces even in decriminalised and legalised environments (Hubbard, 1999; Scott, 2003). This accentuation of moral geographies reinforces disciplinary and regulatory policy frameworks.

Such an approach compounds stigmatisation experienced by sex workers (Hallgrimsdottir et al, 2008). Link and Phelan (2001, p 367) define stigma as existing 'when elements of labelling, stereotyping, separation, status loss, and discrimination occur together in a power situation that allows them'. The media in particular can play a role in structural stigma. Structural stigma is 'formed by socio-political forces and represents policies of private and government institutions that restrict the opportunities of the groups that are stigmatised' (Corrigan et al, 2005, p 551). When the media frames groups such as sex workers in a negative way, it propagates discrimination. As Hallgrimdottir et al (2008) articulate, stigmas are constructed within specific socio-cultural environments and, because of the unequal power relationship that often exists between the media and its audiences, media narratives of sex work can become insulated from alternative discourses.

The research literature rarely examines understandings of sex workers themselves or the framing of their own experiences of the media, such as the ways in which media representations are taken up in their lives (Hallgrimsdottir et al, 2006). Hodgetts et al (2006, p 498) emphasise a 'lack of media research into the experiences of marginalised subjects of media representations'. Previous studies have highlighted the power of media representations but if we are to understand the processes of mediation in everyday life and the importance of the media in people's constructions of their identities, we need to understand how sex workers take up and often resist media representations (Munoz, 1999).

Analysis of print media stories surrounding the implementation of the PRA, 2003-06

In New Zealand, the newspaper market is relatively unsegmented, with main city newspapers being major sources of information (Lawrence et al, 2008). Major city newspapers in New Zealand include the *New Zealand Herald*, which is based in Auckland and has one million readers, *The Evening Post*, which is based in Wellington and has a readership of 255,000, and *The Press*, a Christchurch-based newspaper that is the most widely read newspaper in the South Island with 237,000 readers. New Zealand has a concentrated ownership of print media, with two large overseas media and investment corporations owning most of New Zealand's newspapers (Rosenberg, 2008). The duopology of ownership comprises John Fairfax Holdings Ltd, whose titles, including the *Dominion Post* and *The Press*, account for nearly half of all daily newspaper circulation (48.9%), and APN News and Media, whose titles, including the *New Zealand Herald*, account for 42.4% of daily newspaper coverage (Rosenberg, 2008).

It is acknowledged that New Zealand has both a deregulated media market and public service charter legislation that requires state and privately owned broadcasters to 'educate, entertain, inform and broadcast material reflecting New Zealand culture and identity including minority interests' (Hodgetts and Chamberlain, 2004, p 47). Hodgetts and Chamberlain (2004, p 47) suggest that limited funding for the public service charter has resulted in a 'conservative approach where minority faces have been identified as an "audience turn off" and "political" and social topics are treated as distinct and separate domains in large news outlets, which constrains democratic deliberations regarding links between political processes, ethnic diversity, social conditions and health'. Various studies have examined the New Zealand print media reporting on marginalised populations including homeless people, Maori and Pacific Islanders, highlighting negative depictions of minority groups in the New Zealand media and how prejudices of the majority inform media frames. There is often a lack of minorities' own voices and a prevalence of negative media portrayals (Hodgetts and Chamberlain, 2004; Loto et al, 2006).

It would be very useful to examine the print media before decriminalisation, to make a comparison of media discourses before and after decriminalisation, but this was not the purpose of this research. One might postulate that sex work was reported on in a similar fashion to other minority groups, but this needs to be confirmed with further research. The aim of this study was to examine print media coverage immediately after decriminalisation and through the first three years of implementation, and this is explored in this section of the chapter.

The print media coverage of the PRA from 2003 to 2006 consisted of 218 news articles, 115 published letters to the editor and 28 editorials. (For a more comprehensive discussion of the methods used in the content analysis, see Chapter Ten.) An analysis of the content of the articles highlighted that the majority (60%) of all articles in New Zealand newspapers were neutral in disposition, with 29% negative and 11% positive towards the PRA (Pascoe et al, 2007). The most numerous articles were those that described, outlined or presented coverage of the PRA in a neutral tone, where the PRA and sex workers were exemplified by headlines such as 'One vote makes sex trade legal' (Nick Venter, *Dominion Post*, 26 June 2003). Such articles were common shortly after the Act was passed, reporting on the passing of the Act, presenting comments from various parties and discussing issues of implementation and compliance arising from the implementation of the Act. Examples of compliance issues covered in the print media included tax collection from sex workers, the compliance of brothels with occupational safety and health guidelines and issues around town planning, and typically used headlines such as 'Council to discuss brothel bylaws, rules' (Alison Rudd and New Zealand Press Association (NZPA), *Otago Daily Times*, 11 July 2003) and 'Council restricts zone for brothels' (Sean Scanlon, *The Press*, 21 December 2003).

Although most of the articles were descriptive, concerning the passing and implementation of the Act, there were a number of media narratives in all article types that described sex work as a 'threat to dominant morality' and a 'public nuisance' and sex workers as 'victims' (see Figure 12.1). Print media articles included much speculation as to what was going to happen after the passing of the Act. There were many articles where people made assertions/assumptions about the effects and implications of decriminalisation, with 29% of all articles making negative assumptions. Examples of these negative assumptions included that decriminalisation would attract more under-age workers and create more crime associated with the industry (70% of all negative news articles), and that the PRA would result in more street-based workers (10% of all negative news articles). The majority of letters to the editor were concerned with a supposed increase in under-age sex workers following the enactment of the PRA.

A smaller number of articles contained more positive narratives towards the PRA and the sex industry, such as arguments for sex workers' rights and a backlash against moral conservatism. However, these were mainly in letters to the editor in response to letters and news articles focusing on sex work as a threat to the dominant morality. The positive assumptions featured in print articles included that sex work was/would be better controlled (56%) and safer (33%) post-PRA. Few letters to the editor expressed positive views to the PRA.

Figure 12.1: Themes from all articles

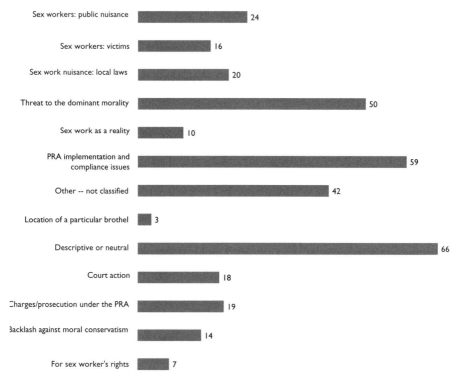

There were differences in newspapers across the country. The largest number of newspaper articles about the PRA appeared in the *The Press*, which published 35% of the total number of articles (population of Christchurch: 360, 400). *The Press* ran a series of investigative reports and two editorials between 21 and 28 February 2004 about a purported increase in under-age workers on the streets of Christchurch (Claridge, 2004a, 2004b, 2004c, 2004d, 2004e; Jones, 2004a, 2004b, 2004c; McNeil, 2004; Scanlon, 2004; *The Press*, 2004a, 2004b). They failed to acknowledge that under-age sex workers existed in Christchurch (and other centres in New Zealand) before the passing of the PRA. Nineteen letters decrying the PRA were published between 24 February and 4 March 2004 in response to this exposé, compared with only four refuting the stance taken by *The Press* and one that was neutral. The most common theme arising from the negatively disposed letters was that sex work was a threat to the dominant morality.

McNeil (2004), in his report on under-age sex work in Christchurch, described the general public as being 'decent folk' and 'victims of a social disaster which infects our streets every day'. As Weitzer (2007, p 448) states, 'the imputed scale of a problem ... far exceeds what is warranted by the available evidence'. The use of words such as 'explosion' and 'invasion' were extensively used to heighten public fear that the 'problem' posed a growing threat (Stenvoll, 2002). Claridge (2004a) in her opening statement 'expos[ing] the extent of the city's burgeoning under-age sex industry', claimed that the child sex trade in Christchurch was 'exploding' and that people as young as 12 were selling 'themselves for money, drugs, food, and booze'. This reporting gave little credence to evidence (Scott, 2003). The research described in this chapter, which involved a number of counts of sex workers across five locations in New Zealand including Christchurch, highlighted no increase in the numbers involved in the sex industry, including young people (Abel et al, 2009). Claims made by individuals that were unsubstantiated by research were cited as fact (Scott, 2003). Neither Claridge nor the other journalists involved in the exposé provided any sound foundation for their stories other than anecdotal evidence of community organisations and politicians who opposed the passing of the PRA. Reports were written laying the blame for under-age sex work at the door of the PRA. Even denials by the police that there were no more under-age sex workers on the streets of Christchurch in comparison with pre-decriminalisation days (Anon, 2004) did little to sway the *The Press* from its stance.

The problems sex workers experience in their everyday lives and their treatment by the law is rarely addressed in public debates (Kantola and Squires, 2004). The print media often ignores the broader social and structural factors that underlie sex work and downplay harm minimisation aspects (Mendes, 2005). Similarly, while the aims of the PRA are largely driven by public health concerns, there was no reporting of sex work in New Zealand as a public health issue (Pascoe et al, 2007) after the passing of the Act. The most frequently cited individuals in all articles in New Zealand were politicians, with sex workers cited least frequently (see Table 12.1). Health workers and academics with a public health focus were also cited infrequently.

Table 12.1: Parties cited in the media

Party	All articles Number (%)	News articles Number (%)	Letters to the editor Number (%)	Editorials Number (%)
Politicians	69 (29)	53 (28)	5 (17)	11 (65)
Local body politicians	28 (12)	27 (14)	1 (3.5)	0 (0)
Academic or legal experts	23 (9)	18 (9)	2 (7)	3 (18)
NZPC	20 (9)	16 (8)	4 (14)	0 (0)
Local body officials	14 (6)	14 (7)	0 (0)	0 (0)
Members of the public	15 (6)	14 (7)	1 (3.5)	0 (0)
Police	14 (6)	12 (6)	2 (7)	0 (0)
Brothel owners/managers	13 (5)	12 (6)	0 (0)	1 (6)
Government departments	11 (4)	10 (5)	1 (3.5)	0 (0)
Health workers	7 (3)	6 (3)	1 (3.5)	0 (0)
Religious bodies	7 (3)	2 (1)	5 (17)	0 (0)
Other moral authorities	7 (3)	2 (1)	5 (17)	0 (0)
Sex workers	7 (3)	7 (4)	0 (0)	0 (0)
Newspaper commentators	4 (2)	0 (0)	2 (7)	2 (11)

Sex workers' experiences of the media reporting of the PRA

Sex workers who participated in in-depth interviews described their experiences of all media forms following the passing of the PRA and the ways in which they drew on or resisted these media representations. Although the majority of print media reporting on sex work after decriminalisation was neutral, the participants in our study recognised and drew on the negative reports. The main theme to come out of participants' discussion of the media was that although in some cases the media portrayed some positive stories about sex work, participants' perceptions were that most of the media portrayals surrounding the PRA perpetuated stereotypes of sex workers, sensationalised the industry, often misrepresented the realities of the industry and ignored broader social issues. Participants articulated the focus of the media on sex workers as victims and the emphasis on street-based sex work, under-age sex workers, drugs and the association between sex work and crime.

Participants expressed a variety of experiences of the media depictions of the PRA and sex work more generally. Some were very articulate about the media and discussed particular television documentaries and print media depictions of sex work; others expressed little personal insight of media depictions of sex work. A small number of participants had been interviewed for the print media and for television documentaries following decriminalisation. Whereas some participants had found the experience beneficial, for example because it provided them with 'free advertising' or allowed them to reflect the realities of sex work by 'putting my real age in the article', others, in particular street-based sex workers, had more negative experiences. Some street-based sex workers had been filmed for television without their consent and described stories of younger street-based sex workers who had been manipulated into being interviewed for television documentaries.

> 'I thought, "What the hell is this?". I thought it was simply the blooming laser gun thing, and I was like, "What the hell?". And in the end I stormed over to the car. There were three people in the car with a camera, and like they didn't ask me if they could put me on TV and that ... my family's seen that on TV. I've got children.' (Sarah, street worker, female)

The initial media coverage following the passing of the PRA and its early implementation did not correspond with participants' experiences of what was happening in the industry at the time. As has been highlighted in other chapters in this book, many participants were keen to describe the positive effects of decriminalisation in terms of increased empowerment and human rights. But participants discussed how this was not reflected in the media at the time. Many described a sense of contradiction between a feeling of increased empowerment post-PRA and increased stigmatisation by the media through what they saw as increased media 'hype'.

> 'So I see it on the news and I think, "Oh fuck, good on them", and you know, I'm really glad for New Zealand that they're pressing their way forward with these issues and realising that, you know, human rights is an issue even if you are a prostitute. But it's still the general, um, view of everyone that, you know, prostitutes should keep to the streets and, you know, out of the way of everyone else, cause they're embarrassing.' (Vicky, managed worker, female)

There was some fear articulated that the negative media would provide impetus for repealing the PRA:

> 'Negative press, yeah, just makes me feel sad and scared that, you know, people may want to repeal if something, you know – it hasn't been that long. Who knows, they might, they could, I don't know.' (Dora, street worker, transgender)

Participants described 'media stereotypes' of the sex industry and many recognised dominant moral discourses of sex work. Although the print media analysis highlighted how a majority of the print media articles were descriptive in their coverage of the PRA (Pascoe et al, 2007), most participants did not discuss these neutral or descriptive articles. Instead, their focus was on what they recognised as negative media depictions of the PRA, sex industry and sex workers. Many discussed the media focus on sex workers as 'victims' of crime. Around the time of data collection there had been high media interest in the murders of two sex workers. Participants discussed their anger with the media for depersonalising the women who had been murdered.

> 'The one bit in the media that I noticed that struck me and really annoyed me was, and still annoys me, is when the sex workers have been murdered, in that, "Blah blah blah street worker. Blah blah blah prostitute". You know, not somebody's daughter, somebody's mother, somebody's … it's because of what it is, it's great gossip, and of course it sells. Things like that sell, newspapers, you know, "People want to know your dirty business". And that's, it's that demeaning thing, isn't it And it adds to, adds to the story, doesn't it? (Maureen, private worker, female)

> 'I think that they've got a bloody nerve plastering "prostitute". It doesn't matter who she is, where she comes from, what she did for a job. The point is that there was foul play and something happened to her that shouldn't have happened, you know, regardless. I mean, do any, if a secretary is killed, do they turn around and say, "Oh she was

a secretary" in quite the same frame, and in quite the same context? No, they do not. It's not fair, it's discrimination … it hurts, it hurts. It's like it's a label and it's a what's the word for it – it's an accusation. It's an accusation, it's a label, and it's like more or less saying, "Well this horrible thing has happened to this person, but she was a prostitute, so she was, she was looking for it", type thing, you know.' (Marge, managed worker, female)

Associated with this description of sex workers as 'victims' was recognition that the media often portrayed sex workers as lacking in agency. Participants described how the media focused on street-based sex work and associated this sector with crime, under-age workers and drugs, which reinforced and escalated the 'victimisation' of sex workers.

'Well, all sort of, like it's derogatory, you know, towards sex workers honing on, sort of you know, not attitudes, just more about under age or something like that, or still feel like sex workers are sort of you know, lifestyle. "Sex worker, you know, she's a type of sex worker." … I try to remove the stigma. I'll, I mean, if it's been a derogatory sort of profession, it's a profession like any other profession (Pat, managed worker, female)

It is important to recognise that although participants described the negative and stigmatising nature of the media narratives surrounding the PRA, many did not passively accept this imagery. As Barnett et al (2007, p 307) highlight, the appropriation of media images by marginalised people, or those lacking symbolic power and recognition, is an 'ongoing and socially negotiated process'. Participants negated stereotypical images of sex workers:

'It's just such crap, and I get sick of hearing you know, "Oh I do this because I need to pay for my drug habit". Well, it was your fucking choice to take drugs. Don't blame it on society. You knew what you were taking, so why stand there now and say, "Oh but you've made me be a prostitute because I take drugs". It's bullshit. It's just pathetic, and the media never, ever, ever go and find a working girl that treats her job seriously, that is respectful of her clients, that likes what she does, and that makes good money. They never go and find somebody like that. They always have to find the worst possible example of a working girl and splash that across the paper and go, "Oh look at these poor girls standing on street corners because they're all drug addicts". Well, excuse me, if you really want to find working girls, they're not that hard to find…. So, I mean, I'm not going to say – I mean, I know prostitution attracts drug addicts. I'm not that naïve. But I mean, if they're going to do a story, get a cross-section…. Stop picking the victims out and turning some more into victims…. 'Cause, I mean, to me all they're doing at the moment is they're actually making us into bigger victims, "Oh look, you know, these girls need help. They need a law change. They need this, they need that". They don't need that at all. What they need is basic respect … and then the media goes out and finds the worst possible example and says, "Oh look, victim, victim".' (Cathy, managed worker, female)

'I think the only thing I hear anything in the media about sex workers is that don't label us just that…. We are so many other things as well as a job. It's not our life … what about mother and treasurer of pony clubs, soccer club you know…. [Even though the law has changed] there's still stigma.' (Karen, managed worker, female)

Foucault (1990, p 95) stresses that 'where there is power, there is resistance, and yet, or rather consequently, this resistance is never in a position of exteriority in relation to power'. There has been much academic writing and critique about resistance (Sharp et al., 2000; Raby, 2005), but the concept of resistance recognises oppositional behaviour as political and informed (Giroux, 1983). According to Munoz (1999), our subjectivities are constituted through our identifications with others, identifications that are socially constructed, fragmented, multiple and intersecting. Munoz articulates a concept of disidentification, where marginalised people fashion a situational strategy for survival in hostile environments. He describes disidentification as a:

> … mode of dealing with dominant ideology, one that neither opts to assimilate within such a structure nor strictly opposes it; rather, disidentification is a strategy that works on and against dominant ideology. Instead of buckling under the pressures of dominant ideology (identification, assimilation) or attempting to break free of its inescapable sphere (counter identification, utopianism) this 'working on and against' is a strategy that tries to transform a cultural logic from within, always laboring to enact permanent structural change while at the same time valuing the importance of local or everyday struggles of resistance. (Munoz, 1999, p 148)

Disidentification is a way of taking dominant signs, roles and discourses and redeploying them in new ways that disrupt the dominant messages. It provides ways of thinking about resistance which acknowledges 'that we are interpellated into dominant ideological apparatus, but that we can insulate ourselves into them, distort them and come away with something different at the time' (Raby, 2005, p 166). Resistance 'can manifest where our temporary, fragmented, constituted and shifting selves "see through" contradictory discursive formations' (Raby, 2005, p 167). Participants articulated 'everyday acts of resistance' (Scott, 1985; Hollander and Einwohner, 2004) to the media imagery surrounding sex work. Many dismissed the media accounts as uninformed. Some participants actively rejected negative media narratives of what it is to be a sex worker and constructed and drew on other identities to define themselves outside of the dominant discourses. These participants tended to be those with the most resources, managed and private workers. They refused dominant narratives through constructing alternative constructions of themselves as professional people and good citizens (including paying taxes) and as being an integral resource for family members and friends.

Participants discussed how the 'sensational' aspects of the media coverage surrounding the implementation of the PRA was of no surprise to them, as this was the way sex work was portrayed in the media. Many articulated their understanding of the workings of the media and their focus on more sensational aspects of media storytelling. They stressed that they took the negative and ill-informed stories with 'a grain of salt', yet any media coverage of the sex industry was better than none, as it was making the sex industry visible.

> '… they have a sense in sensationalising everything, so I tend to read everything like that with a bit of a grain of salt, because I know they're trying to sell the paper and sell the story. It is good in a way that it's, some of it is kept in the public eye because they'll realise that this will not go away. You cannot push it under the rug and just pretend it doesn't exist, and you know, women will just stop doing it, because, you know, "Oh everybody can have jobs now, you know, whereas they weren't able to a hundred years ago". Yeah, we can, but this is still the highest paying one there pretty much is, especially when you're younger or maybe you weren't as educated for whatever reason. Or just you maybe had an illness or something, which stopped you from getting further ahead on the career ladder than you might have been able to. And there's so many, so many different reasons.' (Sheila, managed worker, female)

Recognition that the media coverage of the PRA ignored the realities of sex workers' everyday lives and the diversity of people working within the sex industry and attended instead to 'misrepresentations' was discussed. The fact that people such as politicians with no expertise in this area were most frequently called on to provide commentary on the state of the sex industry post-decriminalisation was recognised by participants in this study.

> 'Misrepresentations also as in people getting on there talking about the sex industry, when I don't really feel they know anything about it. Making comments and talking about how it's got out of hand and there's more prostitutes now than ever. (Petal, private worker, female)

Discussion

The PRA took a harm minimisation approach and aimed to protect the human rights of sex workers, yet this has been largely ignored in the print media. The themes debated did not include sex work as a public health issue and the parties cited included very few people who might know, in an objective or professional sense, about public health as it applies to the sex industry in New Zealand. The group that was quoted the greatest number of times was politicians, both local and national, who articulated their own views as a matter of individual conscience. Politicians have taken particular positions on what is portrayed in the media as a major social issue. This is consistent with the agenda-setting effect that the media has been found to have elsewhere (Colby and Cook, 1991; Iyengar and Simon, 1993; Hertog and Fan, 1995). Sex workers and their representative organisation, the New Zealand Prostitutes' Collective, were rarely used as a source of information for reports on the PRA. As the group arguably most affected by the change in the laws surrounding sex work, theirs would be a crucial opinion to seek out. Public health professionals were also rarely sought for their understandings of the Act.

The lack of public health focus in the media may in part be due to the fact that there was, at that stage, little quantifiable evidence regarding the success of the PRA as a public health measure. Although most of the media coverage was neutral towards the passing of the PRA, there were a large number of articles that focused on more controversial, sensational and extreme aspects of effects of the PRA. The extensive media coverage of the PRA may have served to stifle active debate by those whose opinions differed from those who claim to be the (often moral) majority. The over-representation of politicians' viewpoints over others highlights how privileged socio-cultural groups have most access to the media (Niven, 2002).

Most of the print media coverage was neutral towards the Act and could be understood as reporting on the 'facts' at hand. Yet it was the negative underlying media frames drawing on contextual discourses of sex work that sex workers targeted in their understandings of the media and sex work. The most common negative theme in the print media coverage of the PRA was that sex work was a threat to the dominant morality, even though there was no empirical evidence to support this claim. Such a position is consistent with Hubbard's (1998) findings from Britain that the media represents sex workers as the 'other', belonging to a social underworld associated with drugs and crime. Hubbard asserts that media coverage can use deeply held ideas of immorality and deviance in order to reassert moral order. The metaphors that he found in the British media associating sex work with conspicuous sex, disease and crime were also found in New Zealand, particularly the linking of sex work and crime. In some cases, the media made use of a template (Kitzinger, 2000) that, once established, incorporated the same overarching set of assumptions, values and perspectives set out at the beginning of reporting. This is particularly evident in the 'investigative' reporting on child sex work in *The Press*, in which articles built on one another, taking the assumptions and assertions made in previous stories as given. Lupton's assertion that the media prefers extreme views over more moderate, well-thought out-opinions is consistent with the reporting of this story, where the police and social services agencies were reported as disagreeing with the assertions made in the articles, but were implicitly portrayed as being wrong or downplaying the problem (Lupton, 1994).

This chapter also highlights the importance of the media in maintaining and constructing moral geographies associated with sex work, where the more conspicuous street-based sector received most negative media coverage. The connection between the media and the construction of moral geographies tied into many local body attempts to regulate and restrict the spatiality of street-based sex work at the time, highlighting the role of the media in the construction of structural stigma and power. Local media representations of sex work were part of the construction of moral geographies in particular places. Even with decriminalisation, there was an ongoing issue of street-based workers in public spaces and the desire to construct disciplinary regimes within these public settings. A number of local bodies have attempted to regulate street-based sex work within particular settings, but these have all been overturned at court level for contradicting the human rights and public health aims of the PRA (see Chapter Nine).

Individuals take abstract concepts reported in the media (usually in the form of specific examples) and integrate them into their own sense of self-identity, in order to justify their own position (Hodgetts and Chamberlain, 2006). Participants outlined how they negotiated meanings of media representations in the context of their personal experiences. This chapter highlights the importance of mapping acts of resistance, however mundane. Although participants described stigma resulting from the increased focus on the sex industry at the time, many discussed how they resisted negative media frames by constructing and emphasising other aspects of their identit(ies). Those with access to more resources were better able to do this successfully (Abel and Fitzgerald, 2008). This is discussed in more detail in Chapter Fourteen. Street-based sex workers were less able to resist dominant media frames. By gaining sex workers' own experiences, the research provided a more complex understanding of how stigma works in their everyday lives, and how they negotiate and resist stigmatised messages such as those contained in the media. Such an approach informs the increased focus on stigma and public health (*Social Science and Medicine*, 2008, no 67).

In the first three years following decriminalisation, there were few examples of positive media discourses of the sex industry that highlighted the realities of the sex industry. This may be due to the power of prevailing moralistic discourses that serve to stigmatise the sex industry and those associated with it. Stigma and the sex industry will be discussed in more detail in Chapter Fourteen. It may take time for existing media discourses to be challenged by a more realistic portrayal of the sex industry, and New Zealand with its public service charter is well placed to articulate alternative discourses in the media. Hodgetts and Chamberlain (2008, p 61) found that decisions journalists make about which stories to cover and how to cover them are influenced by a complexity of factors, including 'taken for granted cultural meanings, professional norms, editorial processes, notions of public interest, and perceptions of the audience'. Countries such as New Zealand do have continuing traditions of public service, where 'a "journalism of conversation" is also evident and raises broader responsibilities for journalists to ensure that the concerns of both minority and majority interests are included in political and social debates and the formation of policy responses' (Hodgetts and Chamberlain, 2008, p 62). The decriminalised New Zealand context has much potential to provide alternative media framings of sex work that could be circulated globally, drawing on empirical evidence of sex work in a decriminalised context. There is a role for public health researchers to inform public conversations rather than just disseminate findings and for critical public health researchers to be involved in the telling of broader stories as a form of media advocacy. There is also growing recognition within sex worker organisations of the vital role of media advocacy. Examples include the US-based sexworkerawareness.org media training programme, and the authors of this chapter participated in a workshop in Victoria, British Columbia, Canada in 2009 on how to inform the media about the realities of sex work, where representatives of sex worker groups, academic, government and the media gathered to discuss effective media advocacy for sex work issues.

Conclusion

The media plays a powerful role in society. It constructs identities and relationships, and plays a role in structural stigma and symbolic power. Marginalised groups lack access to symbolic power and voice in the media, and have to attend to media framing and representations about themselves. It is important to remember, however, that mediation is a political process and dominant media discourses and images can be resisted through everyday tactics. Public health researchers have a key role to play in collaborating with marginalised populations, community groups, government organisations and policy makers to advance particular public health agendas and policy change, and working with the media to promote research findings around public health issues (Hodgetts and Chamberlain, 2006). This would take us beyond the mapping of moral geographies and the role the media plays to thinking about how we can construct new moral geographies that include the input of sex workers.

References

Abel, G. and Fitzgerald, L. (2008) 'On a fast-track into adulthood: an exploration of transitions into adulthood for sex workers in New Zealand', *Journal of Youth Studies*, vol 11, no 4, pp 361-76.

Abel, G., Fitzgerald, L. and Brunton, C. (2009) 'The impact of decriminalisation on the number of sex workers in New Zealand', *Journal of Social Policy*, vol 38, no 3, pp 515-31.

Barnett, A., Hodgetts, D., Nikora, L., Chamberlain, K. and Karapu, R. (2007) 'Child poverty and government policy: the contesting of symbolic power in newspaper constructions of families in need', *Journal of Community and Applied Social Psychology*, vol 17, pp 296-312.

Champion, D. and Chapman, S. (2005) 'Framing pub smoking bans: an analysis of Australian print news media coverage, March 1996-March 2006', *Journal of Epidemiology and Community Health*, vol 59, pp 679-84.

Claridge, A. (2004a) 'Child prostitution', *The Press*, 21 February.

Claridge, A. (2004b) 'Dyson defends CYF's handling of child prostitution allegations', *The Press*, 25 February.

Claridge, A. (2004c) 'Prostitution reform MP wants enquiry', *The Press*, 24 February.

Claridge, A. (2004d) 'Police "could purge teen sex workers"', *The Press*, 25 February.

Claridge, A. (2004e) 'Child sex warnings ignored', *The Press*, 28 February.

Clarke, J. and van Ameron, G. (2008) 'Mass print media depictions of cancer and heart disease: community versus individualistic perspectives?', *Health and Social Care in the Community*, vol 16, no 1, pp 96-103.

Colby, D. and Cook, T. (1991) 'Epidemics and agendas: the politics of nightly news coverage of AIDS', *Journal of Health Politics*, vol 16, no 2, pp 215-49.

Corrigan, P., Watson, A., Gracia, G., Slopen, N., Rasinski, K. and Hall, L. (2005) 'Newspaper stories as measures of structural stigma', *Psychiatric Services*, vol 56, no 5, pp 551-6.

Entman, R. (1993) 'Framing: towards clarification of a fractured paradigm', *Journal of Communication*, vol 43, pp 51-8.

Foucault, M. (1990) *The history of sexuality*, New York, NY: Vintage Books.

Giroux, H. (1983) 'Theories of reproduction and resistance in the new sociology of education: a critical analysis', *Harvard Educational Review*, vol 53, no 3, pp 257-93.

Gitlin, T. (2003) *The whole world is watching: Mass media in the making and unmaking of the left*, Berkley, CA: University of California Press.

Hall, S. (ed) (1997) *Representation: Cultural representation and signifying practices*, London: Sage Publications.

Hall, S., Critcher, C., Jefferson, T., Clarke, J. and Robert, B. (eds) (1978) *Policing the crisis: Mugging, the state and law and order*, London: Macmillan.

Hallgrimsdottir, H., Phillips, R. and Benoit, C. (2006) 'Fallen women and rescued girls: social stigma and media narratives of the sex industry', *Canadian Review of Sociology and Anthropology*, vol 43, no 3, pp 265-80.

Hallgrimsdottir, H., Phillips, R., Benoit, C. and Walby, K. (2008) 'Sporting girls, streetwalkers, and inmates of houses of ill repute: media narratives and the historical mutability of prostitution stigmas', *Sociological Perspectives*, vol 51, no 1, pp 119-38.

Hertog, J. and Fan, D. (1995) 'The impact of press coverage on social beliefs: the case of HIV transmission', *Communication Research*, vol 22, no 5, pp 545-74.

Hodgetts, D. and Chamberlain, K. (2004) 'Narrativity and the mediation of health reform agendas', in C. Seale (ed) *Health and the media*, Oxford: Blackwell.

Hodgetts, D. and Chamberlain, K. (2006) 'Developing a critical media research agenda for health psychology', *Journal of Health Psychology*, vol 11, pp 317-27.

Hodgetts, D. and Chamberlain, K. (2008) 'Constructing health news: possibilities for a civic-oriented journalism', *Health: An Interdisciplinary Journal for the Social Study of Health, Illness and Medicine*, vol 12, pp 48-66.

Hodgetts, D., Hodgetts, A. and Radley, A. (2006) 'Life in the shadows of the media: imaging street homelessness in London', *European Journal of Cultural Studies*, vol 9, no 4, pp 497-516.

Hollander, J. and Einwohner, R. (2004) 'Conceptualising resistance', *Sociological Forum*, vol 19, no 4, pp 533-54.

Hubbard, P. (1998) 'Sexuality, immorality and the city: red-light districts and the marginalisation of female street prostitutes', *Gender, Place and Culture*, vol 5, no 1, pp 55-72.

Hubbard, P. (1999) *Sex and the city: Geographies of prostitution in the urban West*, Aldershot: Ashgate.

Iyengar, S. and Simon, A. (1993) 'News coverage of the Gulf crisis and public opinion: a study in agenda setting, priming and framing', *Communication Research*, vol 20, no 3, pp 365-83.

Jones, H. (2004a) 'Childhood lost for $200 a time', *The Press*, 21 February.

Jones, H. (2004b) 'Dominatrix focus on paedophiles', *The Press*, 25 February.

Jones, H. (2004c) 'Reports ignite prostitution reform debate', *The Press*, 28 February.

Kantola, J. and Squires, J. (2004) 'Discourses surrounding prostitution policies in the UK', *European Journal of Women's Studies*, vol 11, no 1, pp 77-101.

Kitzinger, J. (2000) 'Media templates: patterns of association and the (re) construction of meaning over time', *Media, Culture and Society*, vol 22, no 1, pp 61-84.

Koteyko, N., Nerlich, B., Crawford, P. and Wright, N. (2008) '"Not rocket science" or "no silver bullet"? Media and government discourses of MRSA and cleanliness', *Applied Linguistics*, vol 29, no 12, pp 223-43.

Lawrence, J., Kearns, R., Park, J., Bryder, L. and Worth, H. (2008) 'Discourses of disease: representations of tuberculosis within New Zealand newspapers 2002-2004', *Social Science and Medicine*, vol 66, pp 727-39.

Link, B. and Phelan, J. (2001) 'Conceptualizing stigma', *Annual Review of Sociology*, vol 27, pp 363-85.

Loto, R., Hodgetts, D., Chamberlain, K., Waimarie Nikora, L., Karapu, R. and Barnett, A. (2006) 'Pasifika in the news: the portrayal of Pacific peoples in the New Zealand Press', *Journal of Community and Applied Social Psychology*, vol 16, pp 100-18.

Lupton, D. (1994) 'Analysing news coverage', in S. Chapman and D. Lupton (eds) *The fight for public health: Principles and practice of media advocacy*, London: BMJ Publishing Group.

McNeil, J. (2004) 'Prostitution law mess', *The Press*, 25 February.

Mendes, P. (2005) 'Harm minimisation vs zero tolerance: a comparative study of press reporting of the Victorian street prostitution debate', *Social Work Review*, vol 16, no 3, pp 15-21.

Munoz, J. (1999) *Disidentifications: Queers of colour and the performance of politics*, Minneapolis, MN: University of Minnesoto Press.

Mutz, D. and Soss, J. (1997) 'Reading public opinion: the influence of news coverage on perceptions of public opinion', *Public Opinion Quarterly*, 61, pp 431-51.

Niven, D. (2002) 'Bolstering and illusory majority: the effects of the media's portrayal of death penalty support', *Social Science Quarterly*, vol 83, no 3, pp 671-89.

O'Neill, M. and Campbell, R. (2006) 'Street sex work and local communities: creating discursive spaces for *genuine* consultation and inclusion', in R. Campbell and M. O'Neill (eds) *Sex work now*, Cullompton: Willan.

Pascoe, N., Fitzgerald, L., Abel, G. and Brunton, C. (2007) *A critical media analysis of print media reporting on the implementation of the Prostitution Reform Act, 2003-2006*, Christchurch: University of Otago, Christchurch School of Medicine.

Press, The (2004a) 'City of sin', Editorial, 23 February.

Press, The (2004b) 'Pity the children', Editorial, 28 February.

Raby, R. (2005) 'What is resistance?' *Journal of Youth Studies*, vol 8, no 2, pp 151-71.

Rosenberg, B. (2008) 'News media ownership in New Zealand', http://canterbury. cyberplace.org.nz/community/CAFCA/publications/Miscellaneous/ mediaown.pdf

Scanlon, S. (2004) 'Probe of teen-sex industry', *The Press*, 27 February.

Scott, J. (1985) *Weapons of the weak: Everyday forms of peasant resistance*, New Haven, CT: Yale University Press.

Scott, J. (2003) 'Prostitution and public health in New South Wales', *Culture, Health and Sexuality*, vol 5, no 3, pp 277-293.

Seale, C. (2003) 'Health and media: an overview', *Sociology of Health and Illness*, vol 25, no 6, pp 513-31.

Sharp, J., Routledge, P. and Philo, C. (2000) *Entanglements of power: Geographies of domination, /resistance*, London: Routledge.

Sibley, D. (1995) *Geographies of exclusion: Society and difference in the west*, London: Routledge.

Silverstone, R. and Georgiou, M. (2005) 'Editorial introduction: Media and minorities in multicultural Europe', *Journal of Ethnic and Migration Studies*, vol 31, no 3, pp 433-41.

Stenvoll, D. (2002) 'From Russia with love? Newspaper coverage of cross-border prostitution in Northern Norway, 1990-2000', *Journal of Women's Studies*, vol 9, no 2, pp 143-62.

Taylor, S. (2008) 'Outside the outsiders: media representations of drug use', *Probation Journal*, vol 55, pp 369-87.

Tompsett, C., Toro, P., Guzicki, M., Schlienz, N., Blume, M. and Lombardo, S. (2003) 'Homelessness in the US and Germany: a cross-national analysis', *Journal of Community and Applied Social Psychology*, vol 13, pp 240-57.

Weitzer, R. (2007) 'The social construction of sex trafficking: ideology and institutionalization of a moral crusade', *Politics and Society*, vol 35, no 3, pp 447-75.

THIRTEEN

Risk and risk management in sex work post-Prostitution Reform Act: a public health perspective

Gillian Abel and Lisa Fitzgerald

Introduction

In many countries, including New Zealand, harm minimisation has been the predominant philosophy informing public health policy and underpinning the control of HIV/AIDS and other sexually transmitted infections (STIs). Among the sex worker population, the priority has been to reduce disease transmission through advice on safe-sex practices and to help in the implementation of such practices. Such traditional harm minimisation approaches assume that educating sex workers on HIV/AIDS and informing them of their responsibility in preventing transmission would mean that they would then make rational choices to protect themselves and others (Chan and Reidpath, 2003). Yet the assumption that sex workers are vectors of diseases serves to marginalise and blame sex workers without taking into account issues of poverty, gender, public fear and the law (Chan and Reidpath, 2003). Such structural and political issues need to be taken into account and integrated with health education for a more effective health promotion approach to the sex industry (Scambler and Scambler, 1995; Chan and Reidpath, 2003; Frieden et al, 2005).

Public health workers have, therefore, been challenged to take a more holistic approach to health promotion for sex workers (Wolffers and van Beelen, 2003). As well as HIV and other STIs, occupational health and safety issues, which include sexual and mental health, physical violence and coercion, are major health and safety concerns for sex workers and thus the protection of sex workers' human rights needs to also be addressed for successful harm minimisation. This would necessarily require a harm minimisation approach to also take a human rights approach and encompass law reform to create safer working environments (Sanders, 2004a). Some harm reductionists have endeavoured to take a neutral approach (Lenton and Single, 1998), not taking any stance on decriminalisation or legalisation. These practitioners have, however, tended to take a very narrow view of harm minimisation, focusing on the medical means of promoting health and have been less concerned with structural social issues that also contribute to the overall health and well-being of sex workers (Sanders, 2004a).

It was with a broad and encompassing view of harm minimisation that decriminalisation of the sex industry was advocated by public health workers in New Zealand. It was envisaged that by repealing the laws that criminalised all activities associated with sex work, sex workers' autonomy, as well as their capacity to protect themselves, would be increased. It has been theorised that under a decriminalised system, with human rights for sex workers realised, set standards for working environments would enhance the health and safety of sex workers (Overs and Druce, 1994; Brewis and Linstead, 2002). This theory has not been adequately tested, as few countries have adopted such legislative reform and there has been little research done to support or discredit this theory. This chapter addresses whether there have indeed been any gains for sex worker health and safety in a decriminalised environment.

Sex workers' perception of risk varies according to which sector of the sex industry they are working in (Whittaker and Hart, 1996; Sanders, 2005). It has been contended that sex work is a segmented industry (Plumridge and Abel, 2001). Sex workers are not a homogenous population (Campbell and O'Neill, 2006) and the environments in which they work vary greatly, highlighting the 'importance of structural location in influencing and constructing people's experience of work and their exposure to risk' (Whittaker and Hart, 1996, p 412). Sex workers working in street-based, managed and private settings offer different accounts of risk. The main threats to health and safety identified by the participants in this study (the methodology and methods for which are detailed in Chapter Ten) were risks to sexual health, risks of violence and exploitation and, to a much greater extent, risk to emotional health.

Risk to sexual health

Because public health researchers have historically taken a very narrow view of harm minimisation, they have tended to focus on sexual health when exploring the health and safety of sex workers. However, it is argued that this focus ignores other dimensions of sex workers' lives that pose a far greater risk to their health (Alexander, 1999). Indeed, risks to sexual health are viewed as minor by sex workers, as they have well-maintained strategies to ensure condom use and this is viewed as a controllable feature of their work (Sanders, 2004a). Sex workers are acknowledged in all developed countries to be knowledgeable on safe-sex issues and to report high levels of condom use (McKeganey and Barnard, 1992; Ward and Day, 1997; Ward et al, 1999; Benoit and Millar, 2001; Plumridge and Abel, 2001; Fox et al, 2006). Similarly, in New Zealand post-decriminalisation, there were few reports of unprotected sex with clients in the previous 12 months for vaginal or anal sex (see Table 13.1). Managed participants were the most likely to report using protection for all sexual activities, a finding comparable with other studies (Vanwesenbeeck, 2001; May and Hunter, 2006). The working environment has a part to play in the use of condoms in commercial sex encounters (Vanwesenbeeck, 2001). Sex workers who work indoors under a system of management may be

Table 13.1: Condom use by sector*

	Total % (s.e†.)	Street workers % (s.e.)	Managed indoor % (s.e.)	Private indoor % (s.e.)	Comparison across sectors
Unprotected vaginal sex in last 12 months (n=747)	5.5 (0.9)	12.1 (2.8)	4.1 (1.1)	5.1 (1.9)	χ^2 =26.0; df=2; p<0.0001
Unprotected anal sex in last 12 months (n=744)	2.1 (0.5)	5.1 (1.9)	0.6 (0.4)	3.5 (1.3)	χ^2 =33.2; df =2; p<0.0001
Unprotected blow jobs in last 12 months (n=745)	11.0 (1.3)	20.5 (3.3)	5.3 (1.2)	16.1 (3.1)	χ^2 =80.0; df =2; p<0.0001
Unprotected going down in last 12 months (n=739)	13.2 (1.5)	15.7 (3.3)	9.9 (1.6)	17.9 (3.4)	χ^2 =22.5; df =2; p<0.0001

Notes: * Weighted estimates to account for variation in probability of selection and response.
† s.e. = standard error

more likely to consistently use condoms than street-based workers if management makes the use of condoms an imperative, but the amount of control sex workers have over their environment is also likely to play an influential role.

Prior to decriminalisation, if sex workers in New Zealand were stopped by police and they had condoms in their possession, these could be used as evidence to pursue charges on prostitution-related offences. Most surveyed participants were aware that under the 2003 Prostitution Reform Act (PRA) they now had occupational safety and health rights (see Table 13.2). However, less than half had seen the occupational safety and health (OSH) guidelines published by the Department of Labour (2004). Two-thirds of surveyed participants had seen the Ministry of Health (MoH) pamphlets giving information on the safe-sex requirements stipulated under the PRA (www.healthed.govt.nz/resources/healthandsafetyinformationforsexwo.aspx). Participants in the managed sector were significantly more likely than participants in the other sectors to have seen both publications.

Managed and private participants referred to the OSH manual and MoH pamphlets as being valuable tools in their negotiation of safe sex with clients and reinforced their knowledge of their rights regarding safe sex.

'We always have those pamphlets out in places where they're pretty obvious, so the clients see them. They're always right by our products, right by the side of the table on the side of the bed. There are times where – I haven't as yet had to basically tell them 'no' and hand them the pamphlet – but I have referred to the pamphlet and referred to the information on the pamphlet if ever they have suggested unprotected sex. Usually it's a "no" straight away, and if they bug me, then I refer to that, and usually then they shut up quite fast. But I've been lucky enough not to have anyone that wants to push the subject any further.' (Trish, private worker, female)

Table 13.2: Sex workers' perceptions of rights under the Act and knowledge of health and safety publications, by sector*

	Total % (s.e†.)	Street workers % (s.e.)	Managed indoor % (s.e.)	Private indoor % (s.e.)	Comparison across sectors (df=2)	
					χ^2	p
We have no rights (n=739)	8.4 (1.1)	18.8 (3.3)	6.4 (1.3)	7.0 (2.2)	45.5	<0.0001
We have employment rights (n=681)	92.0 (1.1)	89.9 (2.3)	91.9 (1.6)	93.4 (1.9)	3.7	0.2
We have legal rights (n=729)	95.9 (0.8)	96.3 (1.6)	96.1 (1.1)	95.5 (1.5)	0.5	0.8
We have OSH health and safety rights (n=645)	93.8 (1.0)	90.9 (2.1)	95.0 (1.3)	92.9 (2.2)	7.8	0.02
Have seen the OSH manual (n=766)	40.7 (2.1)	26.6 (3.7)	46.3 (2.7)	38.0 (4.3)	38.2	<0.0001
Have seen the MoH pamphlets (n=761)	67.1 (2.0)	38.2 (4.1)	80.2 (2.1)	58.5 (4.4)	207.2	<0.0001

Notes: * Weighted estimates to account for variation in probability of selection and response.
† s.e. = standard error

The majority of participants told clients who requested sex without a condom that it was the law to use condoms. Decriminalisation has enabled workers to insist on condom use, something that has been argued would improve working conditions (Overs and Druce, 1994). Street-based participants maintained that they had always been good users of condoms, but that the law had made it far easier for them to negotiate with clients on their use.

> 'You cannot do a job without using protection. The law has changed so much. It's made people think a lot more.' (Joyce, street and private worker, female)

> 'It's always been my own sort of morals. Like I have morals out there. I won't do sex without protection, I won't put myself in jeopardy or, you know, like that. And it's the law now, which is really good and I say that to them and they can't – yeah, they might get offended and be like, "Oh well I don't want you", sort of thing and go somewhere else. But at least I know I'm safe, and I know, you know, I've given them a reasonable explanation and that it's the truth.' (Sally, street worker, female)

Participants not only informed their clients on the need for safe sex, but also took the responsibility for educating their clients on their rights under the PRA.

'They don't, they say, "Ooh, really?", "Yes, remember it's now law. It's part of the law. It's not just the fact it's been made law so you can safely come and see us and you won't get prosecuted coming to see us. You know, other things have changed as well when it comes to wearing condoms and not wearing condoms and how you treat a woman. You can't rough her up any more and you know, she's not going to go to the cop station and not nark on you."' (Liz, private and managed worker, female)

'I think it's fantastic [the OSH manual]. I think it's really good. I don't know that you could improve it. I actually, I really like it. It's great for clients to see as well. It's very handy. It gives you, as a worker, it makes you official almost. Like, "Hang on, this is, you know, this is the occupational safety and health manual. This is how it works. So, you know, I'm sorry, I have to work within these guidelines." I like it, it works well. It's always handy having one lying around, because it, people still think of it, um, as, you know, being a bit dodgy. But to have something like that, yeah, it puts it into that category of respectable almost.' (Jack, private worker, male)

Increased legal rights with regard to safe sex was seen by all participants as empowering and afforded some legitimacy to their occupation. It was a way of regaining some credibility and respectability and could be used as a counter to the stigma attached to sex work. Although all participants gave accounts of being responsible in ensuring safe sex prior to decriminalisation, legislative change provided a powerful stage from which to negotiate.

Risk of violence and exploitation

Although it is acknowledged that sex work is a dangerous occupation, it is not inherently violent and the majority of commercial sex transactions go without incident (Brewis and Linstead, 2000; Lowman and Atchison, 2006). The managed sector is regarded as the safest sector and studies have found that few managed sex workers have experienced serious violent incidents while working (Pyett and Warr, 1997, 1999; Brents and Hausbeck, 2005; Perkins and Lovejoy, 2007; Sanders and Campbell, 2007; Kinnell, 2008), while the street-based sector is acknowledged as the sector most susceptible to violence (Douglas, 1986; O'Neill, 1996; Pyett and Warr, 1999; Lowman, 2000; Benoit and Millar, 2001; Plumridge and Abel, 2001; Valera et al, 2001; Vanwesenbeeck, 2001; Sanders, 2004b). This is no different from sex work in New Zealand in a decriminalised environment. Since the passing of the PRA until August 2009, three sex workers have been murdered, all of whom were street-based workers in Christchurch. Two of the murders have resulted in the perpetrators being sentenced to life imprisonment and the third remains unsolved. Some in New Zealand have claimed that the murders have shown that the PRA has failed to reduce violence in the sex industry. However, these claims are unjustified, as the realisation of employment and legal rights has given many sex workers confidence to avert or react to situations that hold the potential for violence.

Sanders and Campbell (2007) argue that placing the responsibility on sex workers to ensure their own safety is a victim-centred approach where the state does not take responsibility for ensuring the safety of sex workers. Encouraging sex workers to report attacks is a reactive approach to violence, rather than a proactive preventative strategy. In this way, women are blamed for putting themselves in the position of being attacked, 'rather than the cause and subsequently the prevention of violence located with the perpetrator' (Sanders and Campbell, 2007, p 13). They argue that the position of sex workers being responsible for their own safety holds more legitimacy in a legal environment that enables equal rights to protection, labour rights and full citizenship. Survey participants indicated that they had rights under the PRA, although significantly more street-based workers than managed and private workers reported that they had no rights (see Table 13.2). Most spoke of the empowerment that they felt because of the increased human rights they now enjoyed following the decriminalisation of the industry.

> 'Well it definitely makes me feel like, if anything were to go wrong, then I'm, then it's much more easier for me to get my voice heard. And I also, I also feel like it's some kind of hope that, um, there's slowly going to be more tolerance perhaps of you know, what it is to be a sex worker. And it affects my work, I think, because when I'm in a room with a client, I feel like like I'm, like I feel like I am deserving of more respect because I'm not doing something that's illegal. So I guess it gives me a lot more confidence with a client because, you know, I'm doing something that's legal, and there's no way that they can, you know, dispute that. And, you know, I feel like if I'm in a room with a client, then it's safer, because, you know, maybe if it wasn't legal, then, you know, he could use that against me or threaten me with something, or you know. But now that it's legal, they can't do that.' (Jenny, managed worker, female)

Under decriminalised or legalised conditions, the right to legal protection is a feature that enhances perceptions of safety (Pyett and Warr, 1997). Almost all surveyed workers knew that they had legal rights under the PRA and this differed little across sectors (see Table 13.2). In qualitative interviews, participants from all sectors reported that legal rights had improved since the PRA had been enacted.

> 'So yeah, so say just the power it's given us as the professionals, that we have the law behind us and we can say, "Look if you do this, we can prosecute you", like any other place where they break, you know, the law.' (Sheila, managed worker, female)

'It surely must give us rights. We're not invisible people. We are human beings, and if we're being attacked, we have the right also to the same protection as anyone else. I must say when the law changed, it did turn, it did make it even easier because you could just ring the police and just say, you know, and they'd be up there like a shot.' (Josie, private worker, female)

The risk of violence was not perceived as an issue by managed and private sex workers as most had never experienced violence. Some had been physically assaulted, such as having hair pulled or being thrown off the bed, but they reported these as being minor events. Managed workers ensured their safety by making it clear to clients prior to going into the room what they could expect in the transaction. This was something that was not possible prior to decriminalisation for fear of entrapment on soliciting charges. Misunderstandings by clients of what can be expected with regard to sexual acts can lead to violent attacks on sex workers (Kinnell, 2008). Being able to explicitly state the services they were prepared to provide enabled sex workers to avoid the problem of unmet expectations leading to volatile situations.

'You know, whereas now, cause I like being very upfront and honest, I can say in the lounge, "Look, X, Y and Z because of X, Y and Z", and it's all upfront. Everybody knows what's going on, there's no innuendo, you're not going to get as many, I would expect, problems in the room, because you sorted everything out beforehand, ' cause you can be open and honest as to what's going on. And then once you get in the room, you can just have fun and be relaxed, rather than, you know, if you haven't discussed things in the room, and then you get – I mean in the lounge – and then you get into the room and they're expecting certain things, then that can get a little bit awkward.' (Sheila, managed worker, female)

The rights afforded to sex workers through OSH regulations and their ability to openly negotiate with clients with the backing of the legal system has the potential for reducing the possibility of violence in their workplace. The more control sex workers have over the location in which they have sex with the client, the less likely they are to experience violence from the client (Trotter, 2007). Increasing safety in an indoor environment has been found to be more successful because of the presence of formal and informal controls (Sanders and Campbell, 2007). Security within the managed sector is enhanced by supportive management, the proximity of other workers and other security features, such as alarms and security cameras (Pyett and Warr, 1997, 1999; Benoit and Millar, 2001; Sanders, 2006; Perkins and Lovejoy, 2007; Sanders and Campbell, 2007). In this study, management was identified by sex workers working in the managed sector as an important source of support in ensuring safe working conditions.

More pertinent to managed workers, especially prior to decriminalisation, was the risk of exploitation from management. Participants who had been working prior to decriminalisation reported that it was easier to refuse to have sex with a client since the law had changed (see Table 13.3). Significantly fewer private and managed female workers in Christchurch reported having to accept a client when

Table 13.3: Ability to refuse clients in last 12 months, by sector*

	Total % (s.e‡.)	Street workers % (s.e.)	Managed indoor % (s.e.)	Private indoor % (s.e.)	Comparison across sectors (df=2)	
					χ^2	P
Felt that they had to accept a client when they didn't want to in last 12 months (n=768)	35.3 (2.0)	41.7 (4.0)	37.5 (2.6)	29.1 (3.9)	18.6	<0.0001
Refused a client within the last 12 months (n=768)	69.8 (2.0)	85.5 (2.9)	61.3 (2.7)	77.1 (3.9)	78.7	<0.0001
Participants who had refused a client in last 12 months and who were penalised (n=540)	10.5 (1.4)	9.5 (2.6)	12.4 (2.2)	8.3 (2.4)	6.0	0.05
More able to refuse a client since law change (n=493†)	64.8 (2.5)	61.9 (4.8)	67.3 (3.3)	62.7 (5.1)	3.3	0.2

Notes: *Weighted estimates to account for variation in probability of selection and response.
† Includes only participants who had been working prior to enactment of PRA.
‡ s.e. = standard error

Table 13.4: Ability to refuse clients in last 12 months, for Christchurch female 1999 and 2006 samples

	Christchurch 1999 %	Christchurch 2006 %	Comparison across samples (df=2)	
			χ^2	P
Felt that they had to accept a client when they didn't want to in last 12 months	53	44	1.3	0.3
Street workers	58	45	4.0	0.05
Managed workers	63	38	6.0	0.01
Private workers				
Refused a client within the last 12 months	85	82	0.3	0.6
Street workers	47	68	11.1	0.0009
Managed workers	77	77	0.01	0.9
Private workers				

they did not want to in 2006 than in 1999 (see Table 13.4). Managed workers were also significantly more likely to have reported refusing to do a client in the previous 12 months in 2006 than in 1999. This provides some evidence that there may be an improvement in management practices following the PRA. This was supported by the qualitative interviews.

Interviewer 'So before the law changed, with those sorts of clients, would you have gone to get your boss?'

H 'Yes, I would have, and I would not, I would have refused the job. I would have got in trouble and probably been fined, but I still wouldn't do the job without the protection.'

Interviewer 'So the boss used to fine, the bosses used to fine ...'

H 'Yeah, we used to get fined all the time.'

Interviewer 'Yeah, tell me about that. Has that changed?'

H 'Oh that's totally changed up here. I don't know if it's changed anywhere else, but up here it has totally changed. We don't get fined or anything like that now. It's, you know, it's, if we don't want to do a job, we don't have to do it.'

Interviewer 'And that's changed since the law changed?'

H 'That has changed, yeah, because before we had to always do it, no matter what, how we felt, we still had to do the job. Because he's paid for your time, you've got to give him that time, and it's like, "But I don't want to use, you know", "I'm not going to do it without protection". And you know, back then it was like, "Mate, you're just going to do, you know, as you're told", sort of thing. But since it's become legal and since I've been working up here, we don't, if we don't want to do the job, we don't do it, just like that.' (Hilda, managed worker, female)

Weitzer (2007) argues that the conditions of work in brothels that run under a legalised or decriminalised system provide the safest working environment for sex workers, maintaining that under such conditions, sex work is not inherently dangerous and risks can be minimised and sex workers more empowered. Following decriminalisation, there was a perception by many managed participants interviewed that there had been an improvement in their employment rights. The majority of surveyed managed participants reported that they had employment rights under the PRA (see Table 13.2). Even when management was resistant to change, some participants talked of the knowledge of their rights and what they could insist on.

> 'It also made the owners absolutely awful because you had no rights as such, as in like you worked 14-hour shifts, they fined you, they bonded you; just all these real small things that made the sex industry quite unpleasant. But some, the majority of the places that I had worked at, the bosses were really good to their staff and that was before the law reform. But I have friends that worked for other places that were brothels, massage parlours then, rap parlours, and they were treated like dogs. Made to work ungodly hours, weren't allowed to leave, their money was fined off them. So they could earn like $600 a shift and go home with $200, because $400 of that was lost in fines. And I think with the PRA it's made it easier for people from, say, NZPC [New Zealand Prostitutes' Collective], also from the health sector, as in Auckland Sexual Health etc, easier for them to get into the premises to see the workers, because the PRA has a provision in there that the Medical Officer of Health is allowed to come in. They also have OSH or the Labour Department that can come in and inspect the premises and make sure that it's up to scratch with the health and safety aspects. Some places I have heard of and actually been there but not worked there, they don't launder their towels properly, and with that you're liable to end up with skin infections and many other little nasty things. And it's made them appreciate their staff because without the staff, well, you know, they really don't have a business unless they're going to do it themselves.' [Laughs] (Becky, managed worker, female)

Street-based workers are not unaware of the dangers of their environment, but they are often more fatalistic in their acceptance of violence as a condition of working. This is especially the case in countries where they are working within a criminalised environment where legal rights for sex workers are compromised (Pyett and Warr, 1999). Many sex workers see violence as a normal part of their job (WHO, 2005) and, even in a decriminalised environment, the street-based workers in this study accepted their susceptibility to violence. Joyce described the danger of working on the street but maintained that there was "nothing much you can do about it". Working on the street meant having to accept the possibility of violence. But she went on to clarify that after decriminalisation, the streets had become safer.

> ''Cause there is some clients out there that do watch the news and see everything that's going on. So I reckon it changed it quite a bit. Made

the street more safe.... Well it just, like when, when I was working out there before it got legalised, we, it was like we had some real dodgy people, real dodgy people coming down that street. And the police weren't around as much. But when it got legalised the police were everywhere. We always have police coming up and down the street every night, and we'd even have them coming over to make sure that we were all right and making sure our minders, that we've got minders and that they were taking registration plates and the identity of the clients. So it was, it changed the whole street, it's changed everything. So it was worth it.' (Joyce, street and private worker, female)

It is argued that 'respectable' women are expected to avoid situations that are risky and compromise their safety and thus women who are involved in sex work are discredited (Malloch, 2004). Such women, who place themselves at risk through their actions, are often faced with perceptions that they deserve violence (Vanwesenbeeck, 2001; Sanders and Campbell, 2007). Vanwesenbeeck (2001) argues that the increased incidence of violence among street-based workers compared with indoor workers cannot be attributed solely to the nature of the work, but to the stigma attached to street-based workers. In our study, street-based workers endured abuse from the general public that was often in the form of verbal abuse, but also included having objects thrown at them from cars. Some participants perceived that the heightened media attention following decriminalisation (as discussed in Chapter Twelve) made them more visible and exacerbated these attacks.

'But what they're actually doing now is going round in carfuls and throwing bottles. And that was something that never yeah, that was a rare thing to ever happen. Now it's happening like maybe four times a night on the weekends. 'Cause we're more visible, because of the law. Yes, I think that's what it is. I think that it's like some, some part of society don't want us, don't want to see us at all, so they want to force us back into the, um, shadows where we can't be seen.' (Kyra, street worker, transgender)

Much of the violence sex workers experience is not reported to the police (Pyett and Warr, 1997; Lowman, 2000) and research has documented a number of reasons for this. The most common reasons for this are sex workers' belief that they will not be taken seriously by the police and the courts because of their occupation (Campbell and Kinnell, 2000/2001; Lewis and Maticka-Tyndale, 2000), perceived attitudes that police think that sex workers get what they deserve when they are attacked (Lewis and Maticka-Tyndale, 2000), fear of their occupation being made public (Campbell and Kinnell, 2000/2001), fear of reprisal from perpetrators (Campbell and Kinnell, 2000/2001) and, under a criminalised system, fear of arrest for sex worker-related offences (Pyett and Warr, 1997; Campbell and Kinnell, 2000/2001).

More than half of survey participants who had been working prior to the implementation of the PRA thought that police attitudes had changed for the better since the law had changed (see Table 13.5). Street-based workers and private workers were significantly more likely than managed workers to report this. A third of all survey participants reported that the police had visited their workplace in the past year. Street-based workers were the most likely to report this. The majority of street-based workers said that the police were just 'cruising' or passing by to check on things. Many street-based workers talked about this increased contact in the qualitative interviews and the majority talked of more tolerance shown by the police post-law reform.

> 'But now for the last couple of years, the police have been really good, really on to it. So we've been having more patrol cars going down the street and then hangouts. So that's, that's real good. Yeah, yeah, now they actually care. Before [law change] they just didn't care. You know, if a girl, if a worker gets raped or, you know, anything like that, there wasn't much, then there wasn't much they could do. But now that the law's changed, it's changed the whole thing.' (Joyce, street and private worker, female)

> 'They don't harass now. Like I, like when I was working, I've never had a problem with them. But I've seen them harass other girls when

Table 13.5: Sex worker perceptions of police attitudes and policing, by sector of work*

	Total % (s.e‡.)	Street workers % (s.e.)	Managed indoor % (s.e.)	Private indoor % (s.e.)	Comparison across sectors
Police care for safety of sex workers: (n=657)					
Most concerned	17.2 (1.7)	23.7 (3.5)	16.4 (2.3)	15.1 (3.2)	χ^2=17.1
Some concerned	60.0 (2.3)	50.7 (4.2)	63.1 (3.0)	59.1 (4.7)	df=4
None concerned	23.0 (2.0)	25.4 (4.1)	20.5 (2.5)	25.8 (4.2)	p=0.002
Police attitudes changed for better following PRA (n=417†)	57.3 (2.8)	65.8 (4.6)	48.8 (4.0)	64.2 (5.5)	χ^2=27.5 df=2 p<0.0001
Visit of police to workplace in last year: (n=693)	31.3 (1.9)	74.5 (3.6)	32.8 (2.8)	9.9 (2.3)	χ^2=422.0 df=2 p<0.0001

Notes: * Weighted estimates to account for variation in probability of selection and response.
† Includes only participants who had been working prior to enactment of PRA.
‡ s.e. = standard error

before the law change come out. And, you know, like, you know, just questioning and, you know, just being a nuisance and hanging around so the clients can't stop, you know. Whereas now it's like they're more understanding. They'll just keep driving. You know, they won't stop and harass, and sometimes if they look under-age or something, they might stop and talk to the girls. But I think, I think they're a lot more, maybe, I'm not sure, but to me more open to it. To like, you know, that this is a job and that, you know, we're just as welcome as any other person that works in the workplace.' (Sally, street worker, female)

Despite the good relationship, there still was reluctance by some to report incidents to the police. This was not out of fear of being treated indifferently by the police, but a concern about their occupation being publicised. The stigma associated with their occupation created an obstacle to contacting the police. As Sanders (2005) found, the stigma associated with their name and occupation being made public was not only a risk to their personal identity, but also held the potential to interfere with their personal relationships.

'I think now it's more easier to actually go to the police, but I don't think I would. It depends what happens. I mean, God forbid, nothing. You know, yeah, but like I said, it depends what the bad thing is, you know. So far I've been lucky. And would it be a hassle? If it's a hassle of having to, and would it work out, and would it go my way, and would it be in the newspapers for start, you know. Would I have name suppression? If my name's in the newspaper, I'd feel so stink. So.... Because, you know, people might think, "Oh, I know her. I know that name", you know, and then like I said, not a lot of people know what I do, and then the others might say, "See, I knew, I heard right, see, I knew she was a hooker".' (Dee, managed worker, female)

However, many participants maintained that they would not hesitate to report any adverse incidents to the police.

'I think now I would be more happy to go and talk to them [the police] now, whereas before the law changed, I definitely wouldn't have. From what I hear now from a lot of girls saying things, they're much more friendlier.' (Delia, private worker, female)

There have been many gains in minimising the harm experienced by sex workers in relation to experiences of violence and exploitation. The knowledge of their rights and improved relationships with police have enabled sex workers to feel more secure in their work environment. Yet ongoing perceptions of stigmatisation continue to impede the full realisation of their rights.

Risks to emotional health

In qualitative interviews, participants generally reported that they enjoyed good health overall, but many identified the emotional and mental strains of working in the sex industry. The shift nature of the work played a large part in the experience of stress and burn-out.

> 'Yeah, I think, I think the other, like one of the big things for me that, like, made me really struggle with it was the length of the shifts. You know, that they make you work, like, 11-hour shifts. And it's, for me, like to lose a whole night's sleep like that, you know, like coming home at 7 or 8 in the morning, and then having a few hours' sleep during the day, and then, you know, trying to catch up, you know, leave me like really, really tired for quite a few days after that. You know, and they never let you go home early. And not eating properly as well, and you know, having to like drink lots of coffee just to keep awake. And I think that really, really affected my health.' (Jenny, managed worker, female)

Inability to predict or control pace of work causes stress as well. A sex worker may wait all night and fail to attract a client. But in the time of waiting, there is no possibility of switching off, as they have to remain vigilant.

> 'I just get a bit stressed out when I don't get any work, you know. I just get a bit down in the dumps and that's where girls in an agency don't have that. They've got each other to talk to and, you know, I don't have anybody. I just, you know, well fall apart sometimes.' (Kate, private worker, female)

Burn-out is not unique to sex work and has been found in other occupations that involve shiftwork. Several studies that have looked at nursing shortages have found that many nurses report emotional exhaustion and burn-out as a reason for leaving, or intending to leave, their profession (Aiken et al, 2001, 2002; Finlayson et al, 2007). It was recognised by many participants in this study and they discussed how they actively managed their emotional and mental health.

> 'Other health matters, well of course there's always mental health as well and emotional health. You know, because if, I truly believe that if it's not in your heart to be able to care for different people on an individual basis regularly like that, if you're not a caring person, then it's going to take you down. You know, like mentally, emotionally and then ultimately hanging yourself or topping yourself or something physically, you know. It's only a matter of time if you're, if you're not comfortable with what you're doing..... Oh I say it to everybody, I say it to every worker I know, you have to have at least one day off

a week, at least one. You know, ultimately if you can afford it, two in a row, like a normal worker's weekend sort of thing, you know. It's really important, you've got to have your time out. Free yourself, you know, to go home and, you know, put candles all round the bath and, you know, nurture yourself, you know. It's so important, and cleanse with all that. Oh I've always done it, always done it. It's so important. You just end up slowly, slowly, slowly going down if you don't do it, 'cause you get exhausted for a start, keeping those rotating hours happening. You can't do that forever. No one can. You've got to take your breaks.' (Paul, street worker, male)

Some studies have sought to draw comparisons between the mental health of the sex worker population and the general population. In British Columbia, Canada, this differed considerably (Benoit and Millar, 2001). Around half of sex workers reported depression compared with less than 6% of the general population. A large part of sex workers' generally poor mental health was attributed to the stigmatisation they experienced. In Queensland, Australia, the SF–36 scale, which assesses self-rated perceptions of health, was used to assess sex workers' mental health (Prostitution Licensing Authority, 2004). The study reported that (illegal) street-based workers experienced significantly poorer mental health than (legal) brothel and private workers. Sex workers overall experienced significantly poorer mental health than the general population. In contrast to these arguments of poorer mental health among sex workers were the findings from a small study of sex workers in two cities in New Zealand prior to decriminalisation that reported that sex workers did not experience poorer physical or mental health, lower self-esteem or impaired social relationships compared with the participants from the general population who completed the Otago Women's Health Survey (Romans et al, 2001).

Survey participants in the present study completed questions on general health, mental health and energy and vitality from the SF–36 scale. There was little difference in perceptions of health in all three areas between street, managed and private workers, although private workers were slightly more likely than street-based workers to perceive higher levels of general health (see Table 13.6). Comparisons of crude rates were made between male and female workers in this study and the general population of New Zealand using data collected in the New Zealand Health Survey (Public Health Intelligence, 2004). This survey also made use of the SF–36 scale, which made comparisons possible. With regard to general health and energy and vitality, there were no significant differences between either males or females in the sex worker survey and the general population (see Table 13.7). There were significant differences, however, in perceptions of mental health, with both males and females in this study reporting lower perceived levels of mental health than the general population.

It was not possible to compare age-adjusted estimates directly, as different age bands were collected across the two studies. Table 13.8 presents self-rated perceptions of health from the New Zealand Health Survey for the age groups used in its analysis and Table 13.9 presents the data for the present study. There is a discernible gradient in perceptions of mental health across age bands in the general population and the sex worker population, with self-rated mental health improving with

Table 13.6: Self-rated perceptions of health, by sector*

	Total Mean (95%CI)	Street workers Mean (95%CI)	Managed workers Mean (95%CI)	Private workers Mean (95%CI)
General health (n=743)	74.5 (72.7-76.4)	69.2 (65.5-72.9)	74.4 (72.1-76-6)	77.2 (73.2-81.1)
Mental health (n=742)	72.6 (71.0-74.1)	69.5 (66.4-72.6)	73.0 (70.9-75.0)	73.3 (70.1-76.5)
Energy and vitality (n=744)	64.0 (62.5-65.6)	60.7 (57.3-64.1)	64.2 (62.1-66.2)	65.4 (62.3-68.5)

Note: * Weighted estimates to account for variation in probability of selection and response.

Table 13.7: Self-rated perceptions of health for sex worker and general populations, by gender*

	Total female sex workers Mean (95% CI)	General population females[†] Mean (95% CI)	Total male sex workers Mean (95% CI)	General population males[†] Mean (95% CI)
General health	74.3 (72.3-76.3)	75.4 (74.7-76.2)	75.5 (69.0-82.0)	75.6 (74.8-76.4)
Mental health	72.3 (70.6-74.1)	82.1 (81.5-82.6)	74.8 (69.8-79.8)	84.6 (84.0-85.2)
Energy and vitality	63.5 (61.8-65.3)	62.8 (62.1-63.4)	67.0 (62.3-71.7)	67.6 (66.8-68.5)

Notes: * Weighted estimates to account for variation in probability of selection and response.
† Ministry of Health, 2004.

age in both populations. Even though age bands do not align well, differences between the populations hold across age bands. Although differences between age bands among the sex worker population were not significant, younger female sex workers perceived lower levels of mental health than older female sex workers.

Some studies have found that older workers are more able to cope with their work and exhibit lower levels of emotional exhaustion than younger workers (Vanwesenbeeck, 2001). This appears to be supported by the findings of the present study. The majority of younger workers in this study worked in the street sector and most were poorly educated and had poor family connections. Although they articulated managing safe sex competently, they were exposed to greater risks in their work environment in the form of violence than participants in other sectors. Although the work environment and the shift nature of the work are important contributors to mental and emotional exhaustion, the stigma attached to sex work also has an important part to play in the mental health of sex workers (McKeganey,

2006; Day and Ward, 2007). Studies carried out looking at the stigma experienced by sex workers have suggested associations between stigma and mental health problems (McKeganey, 2006; Day and Ward, 2007), including increased levels

Table 13.8: Self-rated perceptions of health for the general population, by age°

	15-24 yrs	25-34 yrs	35-44 yrs	45-54 yrs	55-64 yrs	65-74 yrs	75+ yrs
Females							
GH*	71.6	77.1	78.9	77.2	74.8	72	71.4
	(69.6-73.7)	(75.5-78.6)	(77.5-80.3)	(75.6-78.7)	(73-76.6)	(69.8-74.1)	(69.4-73.3)
MH†	78.2	81.7	81.7	83	84	84	85.1
	(76.7-79.7)	(80.6-82.8)	(80.8-82.7)	(82-84.1)	(82.8-85.2)	(82.5-85.5)	(83.6-86.6)
EV‡	61.4	62.4	62.8	64.2	65	63.2	59.3
	(59.5-63.3)	(60.8-63.9)	(61.4-64.2)	(62.5-65.8)	(63.2-66.9)	(61.1-65.3)	(56.9-61.6)
Males							
GH*	78.5	78.3	77	75.7	73	69.9	67
	(76.6-80.4)	(76.7-79.9)	(75.3-78.7)	(73.8-77.7)	(70.6-75.3)	(67.2-72.5)	(64.1-69.9)
MH†	83.1	83.5	84.2	84.8	86	87	87.2
	(81.5-84.7)	(82.2-84.7)	(83-85.5)	(83.6-85.9)	(84.6-87.4)	(85.3-88.7)	(85.3-89.1)
EV‡	70.5	67.6	68	67.4	67.6	66.5	59.9
	(68.4-72.7)	(65.8-69.4)	(66.4-69.6)	(65.5-69.3)	(65.2-70)	(64-69)	(56.7-63.1)

Notes: ° Ministry of Health, 2004.
GH* General Health
MH† Mental Health
EV‡ Energy and Vitality

Table 13.9: Self-rated perceptions of health for the sex worker populations, by age°

	<18 yrs	18-21 yrs	22-29 yrs	30-45 yrs	>45 yrs
Females					
GH*	63.2	70.0	73.3	77.5	75.4
	(52.3-74.1)	(66.4-73.7)	(69.6-77)	(74.1-80.8)	(67.6-83.2)
MH†	63.5	69.4	71.3	73.8	77.8
	(53.8-73.2)	(65.4-73.4)	(68.1-74.6)	(71.1-76.4)	(72.6-83)
EV‡	41.3	64	62.2	64.4	67.8
	(31.7-50.9)	(60.2-77.7)	(59-65.4)	(61.8-67)	(60.7-74.9)
Males					
GH*		71.8	71	75.6	89
		(66.2-77.5)	(63.9-78)	(70.2-81)	(76.4-100)
MH†		74.4	70.3	71.8	83.5
		(68.7-80.1)	(63.6-76.9)	(66.8-76.8)	(69.1-97.9)
EV‡		65.1	59.9	59.4	66.1
		(59.2-71.1)	(52.5-67.2)	(54.3-64.5)	(44.1-88.1)

Notes: ° Ministry of Health, 2004.
GH* General Health
MH† Mental Health
EV‡ Energy and Vitality

of burn-out (Vanwesenbeeck, 2005), post-traumatic stress disorder (Farley and Barkan, 1998;Valera et al, 2001) and depression (Benoit and Millar, 2001). Stigma is discussed in more detail in the following chapter.

Conclusion

The hierarchy of risks as perceived by sex workers runs counter to that perceived by many public health professionals. Risk to emotional health as a result of the stigmatisation attached to their occupation was paramount in sex workers' overall conceptualisation of the risks attached to sex work. Risks of violence and exploitation were seen as less problematic and risks to sexual health were regarded as minor. Decriminalisation has reinforced the ability to ensure safe sex and secure sex workers' environment through the provision of occupational, employment and legal rights. However, the emotional risks attached to sex work have not lessened to the extent of these other risks in a decriminalised environment.

Although there were no differences in self-rated perceptions of general health and energy and vitality between survey participants in this study and the general population, sex workers' perceptions of their mental health were significantly lower than those of the general population. Although burn-out due to the shift nature of their work could account for some of this difference, the stigma attached to their occupation was regarded by most participants in the in-depth interviews as being detrimental to their emotional health.

References

Aiken, L., Clarke, S., Sloane, D., Sochalski, J., Busse, R., Clarke, H., Giovannetti, P., Hunt, J., Rafferty, A. and Shamian, J. (2001) 'Nurses' reports on hospital care in five countries', *Health Affairs*, vol 20, no 3, pp 43-53.

Aiken, L., Clarke, S., Sloane, D., Sochalski, J. and Silber, J. (2002) 'Hospital nurse staffing and patient mortality, nurse burnout, and job dissatisfaction', *JAMA:The Journal of the American Medical Association*, vol 288, no 16, pp 1987-93.

Alexander, P. (1999) 'Health care for sex workers should go beyond STD care', *Research for Sex Work*, Issue 2, pp 14-15.

Benoit, C. and Millar, A. (2001) *Dispelling myths and understanding realities:Working conditions, health status, and exiting experiences of sex workers*, Victoria, British Columbia: University of Victoria.

Brents, B. and Hausbeck, K. (2005) 'Violence and legalized brothel prostitution in Nevada: examining safety, risk, and prostitution policy', *Journal of Interpersonal Violence*, vol 20, no 3, pp 270-95.

Brewis, J. and Linstead, S. (2000) '"The worst thing is the screwing" (2): context and career in sex work', *Gender, Work and Organization*, vol 7, no 3, pp 168-80, http://web.ebscohost.com/ehost/pdf?vid=3&hid=112&sid=d4d02f66-0e6c-475e-8bb0-9bf62bc8dd7c%40sessionmgr104

Brewis, J. and Linstead, S. (2002) 'Managing the sex industry', *Culture and Organization*, vol 8, no 4, pp 307-26.

Campbell, R. and Kinnell, H. (2000/2001) '"We shouldn't have to put up with this": street sex work and violence', *Criminal Justice Matters*, vol 42, pp 12-13.

Campbell, R. and O'Neill, M. (2006) 'Introduction', in R. Campbell and M. O'Neill (eds) *Sex work now*, Cullompton: Willan.

Chan, K. and Reidpath, D. (2003) '"Typhoid Mary" and "HIV Jane": responsibility, agency and disease prevention', *Reproductive Health Matters*, vol 11, no 22, pp 40-50.

Day, S. and Ward, H. (2007) 'British policy makes sex workers vulnerable', *British Medical Journal*, vol 334, p 187.

Department of Labour (2004) *A guide to occupational health and safety in the New Zealand sex industry*, Wellington: Department of Labour.

Douglas, M. (1986) *Risk acceptability according to the social sciences*, London: Routledge and Kegan Hall.

Farley, M. and Barkan, H. (1998) 'Prostitution, violence, and posttraumatic stress disorder', *Women and Health*, vol 27, no 3, pp 37-49.

Finlayson, M., Aiken, L. and Nakarada-Kordic, I. (2007) 'New Zealand nurses' reports on hospital care: an international comparison', *Nursing Praxis in New Zealand*, vol 23, no 1, pp 17-28.

Fox, J., Tideman, R., Gilmour, S., Marks, C., Van Beek, I. and Mindel, A. (2006) 'Sex work practices and condom use in female sex workers in Sydney', *International Journal of STD and AIDS*, vol 17, pp 319-23.

Frieden, T., Das-Douglas, M., Kellerman, S. and Henning, K. (2005) 'Applying public health principles to the HIV epidemic', *New England Journal of Medicine*, vol 353, no 22, pp 2397-402.

Kinnell, H. (2008) *Violence and sex work in Britain*, Cullompton: Willan.

Lenton, S. and Single, E. (1998) 'The definition of harm reduction', *Drug and Alcohol Review*, vol 17, no 2, pp 213-20.

Lewis, J. and Maticka-Tyndale, E. (2000) 'Licensing sex work: public policy and women's lives', *Canadian Public Policy – Analyse de Politiques*, vol 26, no 4, pp 437-49.

Lowman, J. (2000) 'Violence and the outlaw status of (street) prostitution in Canada', *Violence Against Women*, vol 6, no 9, pp 987-1011.

Lowman, J. and Atchison, C. (2006) 'Men who buy sex: a survey in the Greater Vancouver Regional District', *Canadian Review of Sociology and Anthropology*, vol 43, no 3, pp 281-96.

Malloch, M. (2004) '"Risky" women, sexual consent and criminal justice', in M. Cowling and P. Reynolds (eds) *Making sense of sexual consent*, Aldershot: Ashgate.

May, T. and Hunter, G. (2006) 'Sex work and problem drug use in the UK: the links, problems and possible solutions', in R. Campbell and M. O'Neill (eds) *Sex work now*, Cullompton: Willan.

McKeganey, N. (2006) 'Street prostitution in Scotland: the views of working women', *Drugs: Education, Pprevention and Policy*, vol 13, no 2, pp 151-66.

McKeganey, N. and Barnard, M. (1992) 'Selling sex: female street prostitution and HIV risk behaviour in Glasgow', *AIDS Care*, vol 4, no 4, pp 395-407.

Ministry of Health (2004) *An indication of New Zealanders' health*, Wellington, Ministry of Health.

O'Neill, M. (1996) 'Researching prostitution and violence: towards a feminist praxis', in M. Hester, L. Kelly and J. Radford (eds) *Women, violence and male power: Feminist activism, research and practice*, Buckingham/Philadelphia, PA: Open University Press.

Overs, C. and Druce, N. (1994) 'Sex work, HIV and the state: an interview with Nel Druce', *Feminist Review*, vol 48, pp 114-21.

Perkins, R. and Lovejoy, F. (2007) *Call girls: Private sex workers in Australia*, Crawley: University of Western Australia Press.

Plumridge, L. and Abel, G. (2001) 'A "segmented" sex industry in New Zealand: sexual and personal safety of female sex workers', *Australian and New Zealand Journal of Public Health*, vol 25, no 1, pp 78-83.

Prostitution Licensing Authority (2004) *Selling sex in Queensland 2003*, Brisbane: Prostitution Licensing Authority.

Public Health Intelligence (2004) *A portrait of health: Key results from the New Zealand Health Survey 2002/2003*, Wellington, Ministry of Health.

Pyett, P. and Warr, D. (1997) 'Vulnerability on the streets: female sex workers and HIV risk', *AIDS Care*, vol 9, no 5, pp 539-47.

Pyett, P. and Warr, D. (1999) 'Women at risk in sex work: strategies for survival', *Journal of Sociology*, vol 35, no 2, pp 183-97.

Romans, S., Potter, K., Martin, J. and Herbison, P. (2001) 'The mental and physical health of female sex workers: a comparative study', *Australian and New Zealand Journal of Psychiatry*, vol 35, pp 75-80.

Sanders, T. (2004a) 'A continuum of risk? The management of health, physical and emotional risks by female sex workers', *Sociology of Health and Illness*, vol 26, no 5, pp 557-74.

Sanders, T. (2004b) 'The risks of street prostitution: punters, police and protesters', *Urban Studies*, vol 41, no 9, pp 1703-17.

Sanders, T. (2005) *Sex work: A risky business*, Cullompton: Willan.

Sanders, T. (2006) 'Behind the personal ads: the indoor sex markets in Britain', in R. Campbell and M. O'Neill (eds) *Sex work now*, Cullompton: Willan.

Sanders, T. and Campbell, R. (2007) 'Designing out vulnerability, building in respect: violence, safety and sex work policy', *British Journal of Sociology*, vol 58, no 1, pp 1-19.

Scambler, G. and Scambler, A. (1995) 'Social change and health promotion among women sex workers in London', *Health Promotion International*, vol 10, no 1, pp 17-24.

Trotter, H. (2007) 'Navigating risk: lessons from the dockside sex trade for reducing violence in South Africa's prostitution industry', *Sexuality Research and Social Policy: Journal of NSRC*, vol 4, no 4, pp 106-19.

Valera, R., Sawyer, R. and Schiraldi, G. (2001) 'Perceived health needs of inner-city street prostitutes: a preliminary study', *Journal of Health Behavior*, vol 25, p 1.

Vanwesenbeeck, I. (2001) 'Another decade of social scientific work on sex work: a review of research 1990-2000', *Annual Review of Sex Research*, vol 12, pp 242-89.

Vanwesenbeeck, I. (2005) 'Burnout among female indoor sex workers', *Archives of Sexual Behavior*, vol 34, no 6, pp 627-39.

Ward, H. and Day, S. (1997) 'Health care and regulation: new perspectives', in G. Scambler and A. Scambler (eds) *Rethinking prostitution: Purchasing sex in the 1990s*, London: Routledge.

Ward, H., Day, S. and Weber, J. (1999) 'Risky business: health and safety in the sex industry over a 9 year period', *Sexually Transmitted Infections*, vol 75, pp 340-43.

Weitzer, R. (2007), 'Prostitution: facts and fiction', *Contexts*, 6: 4, 28-33.

Whittaker, D. and Hart, G. (1996) 'Research note: managing risks: the social organisation of indoor sex work', *Sociology of Health and Illness*, vol 18, no 3, pp 399-414.

Wolffers, I. and van Beelen, N. (2003) 'Public health and the human rights of sex workers', *The Lancet*, vol 361, p 1981.

WHO (World Health Organization) (2005), *Violence against women and HIV/AIDS: Critical intersections*, Geneva: Department of Gender, Women and Health, WHO.

FOURTEEN

Decriminalisation and stigma

Gillian Abel and Lisa Fitzgerald

This chapter further examines the emotional health of sex workers, as discussed in the previous chapter, in light of the stigma that sex workers continue to experience post-decriminalisation. We draw on and develop theories of stigma and examine how sex workers themselves actively manage stigma through constructing alternative identities.

Experiences of stigmatisation prevail among sex workers, brought about through negative social reactions to their occupation (Vanwesenbeeck, 2001). Moral discourses place sex workers in the category of 'deviant' – not conforming to the norms of society. It has been argued that sexuality is able to cause moral panic because it is fundamental to the general population's worldview (Sibley, 1995). Sex workers, and most especially female sex workers, do not conform to ideals of 'normal' sexuality with its accompanying presumptions of female passivity in the sexual domain. They are, therefore, as Sibley (1995) has termed, 'othered' – different from 'normal' decent citizens, framed as 'deviant' and generally stereotyped as involved in drug use, gang activity, crime, spread of sexually transmitted infections and with threatening the moral fabric of society. Identifying norms and labelling difference, stereotyping and connecting the labelled to undesirable traits and separating them into 'others' – different from 'us' – are all part of the process in which stigma is generated (Link and Phelan, 2006). This process has been used worldwide in attempts to exclude sex workers from society, leading to loss of status and the reproduction of inequalities (Link and Phelan, 2006). It is within this milieu that sex workers must justify their actions.

Goffman (1990) argued that if an individual fails to maintain norms, it has an impact on the defaulter's acceptability in social situations. Such difference or 'deviance' leads to feelings of shame, which create a 'spoiled identity' – stigma being mapped on to people resulting in them being devalued by society (Goffman, 1990). However, in recent years, Goffman has been critiqued as providing an analysis of stigma that is too individualised and fails to account for the structural conditions that lead to the reproduction of inequality and exclusion (Riessman, 2000; Link and Phelan, 2001; Parker and Aggleton, 2003; Scambler, 2007; Scambler and Paoli, 2008). Parker and Aggleton (2003, p 15) proposed that Goffman's theorising suggests that stigma is a 'static attribute' rather than a 'constantly changing (and often resisted) social process'. Scholars have argued that power and control are essential in the production of stigma (Link and Phelan, 2001, 2006; Parker and Aggleton, 2003; Bayer, 2008). Within the hierarchical structure of society, those in positions of power have greater ability to dominate and impose stigma on those who are relatively powerless and already socially vulnerable, which reinforces inequalities (Parker and Aggleton, 2003; Bayer, 2008; Phelan et al, 2008). Parker and Aggleton (2003, p 18) therefore argue that rather than thinking of stigma as happening in some 'abstract manner', as Goffman suggests, it is instead 'part of complex struggles for power that lie at the heart of social life'.

Stigmatisation and discrimination is considered to be an important contributor to health disparities (Stuber and Meyer, 2008). The link between stigmatisation and public health came to the fore in the context of the AIDS epidemic in the 1980s (Bayer, 2008). Early interventions to try to prevent the spread of AIDS were ineffective as a social-psychological or individualised perspective of stigma dominated over a social-structural perspective and its broader notions of power and domination (Parker and Aggleton, 2003; Bayer, 2008). Moral judgements and hostility towards gay men, who were initially identified as most vulnerable to contracting AIDS, and towards all those who contracted the disease, affected the choices people made as to whether they were tested for the disease, disclosed the disease to others or sought help for their physical, psychological and social needs (Herek and Glunt, 1988). The exercise of power and reinforcing of inequalities has very clear implications for public health. The discrimination identified by participants in this study (the methodology and methods of which are described in Chapter Ten) had a direct impact on the broader determinants of health, most notably on their employment options outside of the industry, their ability to both rent and purchase houses, their accessing of health and other essential services and for many, especially street-based workers, social networks, which were constricted and mostly comprised other sex workers.

Sheila, like others, spoke of the discrimination that she thought she would experience if she were exposed as having worked in the sex industry and how this would limit her chances of gaining employment outside of the sex industry.

> 'And like I said before, because it's a society, that does sort of, could impact on my career choices in the corporate environment, and ironically shut me back into the world, you know, into the prostitutes' world, of which they, you know, they don't want you in there, but because they know you were there, you're kind of stuck there 'cause now they won't let you out. Which is really, really stupid, but it's the way it is.' (Sheila, managed worker, female)

Wendy spoke of how the body corporate that oversaw her apartment complex tried to evict her and threatened to call the police, even though she was legally permitted to work in the industry post-decriminalisation.

> 'And because the apartments that I lived in, my landlady rang me up and said, you know, if I – she wasn't saying that I was – but if I was in

> prostitution, that you know, to stop because the whole complex was not happy about it.' (Wendy, private worker, female)

Many participants highlighted these and other forms of discrimination they endured as a consequence of being 'othered' by society. A rights-based approach to reducing stigmatisation and discrimination in which such practices would no longer be tolerated is argued as the only viable option (Parker and Aggleton, 2003), yet clearly the participants in this study continued to experience stigmatisation in a decriminalised environment. Goffman (1990) described various types of stigma – felt stigma, courtesy stigma and enacted stigma – and these definitions have been utilised by other researchers to describe the stigma that sex workers' experience (Hallgrimsdottir et al, 2006, 2008).

Felt stigma

The change to a decriminalised system in New Zealand did not bring with it social acceptance of sex workers by all in society. The participants in in-depth interviews recognised this and reluctantly accepted that possibly there would never be a time when they would be on an equal footing with workers in other occupations. They were cognisant of the fact that laws had little or no impact on social perceptions of their job as "no laws have the power to do that. The people have to change" (Petal, private worker, female).

Goffman (1990) suggested that stigmatised individuals internalised their negative image and feared being discriminated against on the grounds of their social unacceptability, a concept he termed 'felt stigma'. Felt stigma, however, has been contested by other scholars, who argue that Goffman neglected to explicate how individuals may resist stigmatisation (Anspach, 1979; Crocker and Major, 1989; Riessman, 2000; Link and Phelan, 2001; Parker and Aggleton, 2003; Bayer, 2008; Scambler and Paoli, 2008). Scambler and Paoli (2008, p 1851) suggest that far from internalising shame and blame, stigmatised people often form positive strategies and tactics to avoid 'enacted stigma' (discussed later) without succumbing to 'felt stigma', something they term 'project stigma'.

Participants in this study accepted that they operated outside the norms of society and acknowledged that they were therefore stigmatised by society. But most participants did not internalise shame and were angry at the perceived injustice and contravention of their human rights to be able to choose and work within an industry without discrimination. Some, like Trish, would not accept the representations people had of her. She voiced her indignation at a local mayor, whom she perceived as implying that sex workers were "dogs", "pieces of shit" and "not human", instead of "real people" who "deserve to be treated with respect".

> 'You know, you're just trying to make a living just like anyone else. But recently I have seen a news what was it, a news article, not news article, something on television where, you know, they were tying

little ribbons on lines to support escorts that have been hurt or abused. And I think being able to actually put it out there and say that, you know, they're real women, these sex workers are actually real people, real women, and regardless of what job they do, they deserve to be treated with respect just like anyone else. So I really quite liked that option as well that's out there. Otherwise, and actually I was a bit disgusted. There was, oh the mayor of Manukau had an interview on the radio and was talking about, pretty much talking about how disgusted he was with prostitution in Manukau. How, you know, you know, street hookers especially, even though he never referred to street hookers, he was talking, I think he was talking about how, you know, how dirty they are, because they leave their condoms all over the place. And the way that he was talking about them, like they were just dogs, you know, they were just pieces of shit, you know, they were not human, they're not a woman, they're not nothing. That outraged me, because, you know, I am an escort and I am educated, and I am a businesswoman, and I'm professional. And I have my good days and bad, but I'm not a piece of shit, and I'm not a dog, and I should not have to have some stranger make assumptions of other, certain people's actions as a collective idea of what we are or what we do or, yeah. So, you know, I mean there's the good and the bad, I guess. I mean there's always going to be people who support and the people who don't. So flinging shit's a natural thing really.' (Trish, private worker, female)

Resistance to stigma meant not internalising the stereotypical labels, but speaking out against those who tried to stigmatise, turning their discourses around to lay blame on the stigmatiser (Riessman, 2000). Contrary to Goffman's depiction of 'felt stigma', shame was not internalised; rather, the negative images of sex workers were redefined as ignorance (Buseh and Stevens, 2007).

Sex workers provide strong justifications for the importance of their role in society (Sanders, 2005c). The justifications they provide function as a counter to the stigmatisation they experience from their occupation. Many of the participants in this study turned what Riessman (2000, p 128) termed a 'flaw' into an 'attribute' by arguing that their role in society meant that there would be fewer violent attacks on other women. In addition, men who through disability, illness or personal characteristics had no other outlet for their sexual needs were catered for in a caring way. It was also argued that many marriages remained intact when husbands used the services of a sex worker as opposed to finding a mistress.

'Yeah, we're doing a service, we're doing, we're actually doing a service. We're keeping the rapists off the street, and the married men married, and the single guys from 18 years of maintenance. That's how I feel about it.' (Philippa, private worker, female)

'It's not about me. It's about what's best for everyone. You know, if it makes someone, who has like a, like a disease, Parkinson's or a mental illness, feel free and able to come and see me, well then that's good. If a rapist or something like that can come and see me rather than commit that crime, that's good, yeah. If it's going to benefit other people with it being legal, I'm down with that, man.' (Wendy, private worker, female)

These participants presented, thus, a benevolent discourse of being useful and productive members of society in opposition to the dominant public discourse of 'pariah' and 'moral deviant'. Goffman (1990, p 29) proposed that some stigmatised individuals may approach situations with 'hostile bravado' while others may vacillate between 'cowering and bravado'. Yet some participants in this study were vocal in their resistance to societal stigmatisation by articulating being open and unashamed about their occupation.

'I think people will only stigmatise you if you stigmatise yourself. I mean I'm proud of what I do. I'm very good at what I do. I make a lot of money at what I do. And so why do I need to be ashamed of it? I'm one of the best people in New Zealand at my profession, so why should I be ashamed of it? Because if I was a lawyer, I'd be singing it from the rooftops. If I was a doctor, I'd be, you know, singing it from the rooftops, so why should I be any different? And so if I go into a pub and someone says, "Hi, (Cathy), how are you?", I go, "Hi, I'm good, thanks. How are you?". And if I run away and hide and go, "Don't look at me, don't look at me," and sit there like I'm all embarrassed about suddenly being seen out in public, then they're going to think, "Well she's really ashamed of what she does, so I'm going to treat you like you should be ashamed of what you do." If you don't behave like you're ashamed of what you do, then people aren't going to treat you like you should be.' (Cathy, managed worker, female)

Although Cathy strongly asserted that she did not allow anyone to stigmatise her and that she was unashamed and open about her profession, she went on to describe how, under certain circumstances, she would not offer information about her occupation as a form of respect for her husband. In addition, she did not disclose out of respect for herself because she did not want to be "their entertainer".

'But if, I mean, if I'm just like, oh if it's a work dinner or something with my husband and we were all sitting there having dinner and someone said, "What do you do?", I'll just say, "Nothing". Because they really *don't* need to know. And I don't really feel like being anyone's entertainment at a work dinner. We're having a little drink and, "Oh guess what, we've got a hooker here". [Laughs.] I won't be their entertainer. And then I kind of think it's quite disrespectful to my husband too. I mean he doesn't want to go to work and have all the guys go, "Oh so, your missus is a working girl", "So oh undo the trousers", you know. He doesn't – and I mean not that he would get that, 'cause he doesn't give away that persona either. But it's kind of, it's up to us to tell people, and how and when and who we tell is our business as well.' (Cathy, managed worker, female)

Although Cathy resisted being personally stigmatised by society and was not ashamed of what she did, through concern for her husband she was less forthcoming about her occupation in certain situations in order to protect him from stigma by association.

Courtesy stigma

Goffman (1990) proposed that stigma by association, or 'courtesy stigma', occurs when relatives, friends or associates are obliged to share some of the discredit of a stigmatised person. Being linked by some relationship to a sex worker may affect that person's standing in society with accompanying negative consequences.

Because all sex workers in this study acknowledged that they were members of a stigmatised population, they were then faced with the dilemma of how to manage this and still present as credible individuals. Stigma is managed through controlling information (Goffman, 1990; McVerry and Lindop, 2005; Sanders, 2005b, 2005c) and this is an important tool for psychological survival (McVerry and Lindop, 2005; McKeganey, 2006). Sex workers have to carefully conceal their occupation from some people, while systematically exposing themselves to others, such as clients. When they have to keep their stigma secret, it affects intimate relationships with others and may lead to admission of occupation to the intimate or feelings of guilt for not doing so. The possibility of disclosure could potentially lead to personal and emotional loss and this risk can be seen as less controllable than all other risks that sex workers face (Sanders, 2004). Sanders (2005b) describes her participants controlling information on a 'need-to-know basis'. This was similar to many participants in this study, who selectively chose who they would take into their confidence and who they would leave in ignorance.

'But just the stigma that is attached to it nowadays, which I think is starting to go a little bit, 'cause most of my friends know, and they don't have an issue with it. But having said that, I wouldn't tell my mum, mainly cause she's of an older generation and I don't think she'd react to it in that way, rather than actually, you know, sitting down with me and talking about why I decided to do this and why I'm still doing it. She'd just go, "Oh my God", you know, and all the horror stories again that the media loves to pander is the first thing that's going to come into their mind.' (Sheila, managed worker, female)

As in other studies (Pyett and Warr, 1997, 1999; Plumridge, 1999a; Vanwesenbeeck, 2001), less than half of the survey participants in this study told family members and partners of their occupation (see Table 14.1). Street-based survey participants were more likely than managed and private participants to report that they told others of their occupation. Transgender participants in particular were more likely to reveal their occupation to family members, close friends and health workers than either male or female participants (see Table 14.2). This may be because they were already members of a stigmatised population because of their gender identity and this 'otherness' was clearly evident.

In in-depth interviews, the majority of participants of all genders and all sectors described careful concealment of their occupation. The participants who were in private relationships had to make the decision on whether to disclose their occupation to their partners or keep it a secret. Regardless of the choice they made, they had to contend with the emotional consequences of this decision. Some participants elected to keep their occupation secret because they were scared

Table 14.1: Sex workers' confidants, by sector*

	Total % (s.e†.)	Street workers % (s.e.)	Managed indoor % (s.e.)	Private indoor % (s.e.)	Comparison across sectors (df=2)	
					χ^2	P
Who do you tell that you work in the sex industry? (n=746)						
Any family member	46.0 (2.1)	63.6 (3.4)	40.3 (2.7)	47.5 (4.5)	48.9	<0.0001
Any close friend	72.4 (2.0)	84.5 (3.1)	67.9 (2.6)	74.4 (4.2)	28.7	<0.0001
Partner	46.8 (2.1)	50.5 (4.2)	46.0 (2.8)	46.5 (4.5)	9.7	0.05
Health workers	66.2 (2.1)	70.1 (3.6)	62.3 (2.7)	70.7 (4.2)	14.0	0.0009
Youth workers	9.5 (1.2)	21.5 (3.1)	7.3 (1.6)	7.6 (2.2)	56.6	<0.0001

Notes: * Weighted estimates to account for variation in probability of selection and response.
† s.e. = standard error

Table 14.2: Sex workers' confidants, by gender*

	Female workers % (s.e†.)	Male workers % (s.e.)	Transgender workers % (s.e.)	Comparison across gender (df=2)	
				χ^2	P
Who do you tell that you work in the sex industry? (n=746)					
Any family member	43.2 (2.4)	52.1 (7.2)	75.1 (5.1)	57.3	<0.0001
Any close friend	69.9 (2.3)	83.3 (5.4)	91.3 (3.1)	46.9	<0.0001
Partner	46.0 (2.4)	57.5 (7.2)	42.4 (6.0)	38.3	<0.0001
Health workers	63.7 (2.3)	77.1 (6.1)	84.3 (3.9)	39.4	<0.0001

Notes: * Weighted estimates to account for variation in probability of selection and response.
† s.e. = standard error

that the disclosure would result in the end of the relationship. Other participants were more open with their partners, but they worried about the psychological hurt they were inflicting on their partners by working. Vicky had conflicting emotions with regard to sex work. She maintained that she was proud of what she did when speaking about it with friends who knew of her occupation, but in the presence of her partner, who was also aware that she was a sex worker, she had to change demeanour and not talk about it in positive terms in order to protect him.

> 'Yeah, it's hard, it's hard to explain. I'm very proud of what I do, and I'm proud of how I handle myself, and I'm proud of what I've done in regard with other girls in teaching other girls to not be ashamed of what they are or to stick up for themselves, because it's always what I've done. But in the same regards it's like I'm not openly happy about the fact that I work with my partner, because he would be upset about it. You know, so with certain people I don't talk about it, but with my girlfriends who know or girlfriends who work, you know, it's like we're free and open about it. And we'll talk about it in public, you know, in a café, and you know, if anyone hears and looks at us like, "Huh?", then we just look at them going, "Well why are you eavesdropping?".'
> (Vicky, managed worker, female)

There is no guarantee of complete anonymity regarding social identity as there is always the chance that someone (a client) may greet the sex worker in a social situation, leading to the possibility of disclosure (Goffman, 1990). Sometimes somebody from the private life enters the domain of the working life. Alternatively, sex workers may be in the realm of the private life when they meet a client from the working life. Most often a pact of secrecy is entered into, as both stand to lose from any disclosure (Sanders, 2005c). In the smaller cities, ensuring anonymity is even more difficult. The possibility of meeting a client in a social situation is greater than for those living in larger cities. To protect against the shame of being publicly exposed, Mandy often terminated social evenings early when she spotted a client.

> 'I find it probably more in a social situation if I'm at the pub. I do freak out a bit because it's a small town. I think, mmm, 'cause I see a lot of my clients around. Like I'd be out just having a few beers sitting outside a sharp club in the smoking part. So I'd be sitting there and it would be like four clients may walk past and I'm like, "Oh, I hope", 'cause I think, "Ooh". And I actually end up going home early 'cause I think, "Ooh, after a few, you know, a bit of alcohol, are they going to start, are they going to start, you know – 'cause they're with guys – are they going to start mouthing off, "Oh yeah, she's a ….", "Oh yeah, I've done her". It does worry me a little bit because I'm yeah, it's just that it worries me a little bit cause I don't want my friends

to be embarrassed. I don't want to be embarrassed, or I just think I don't want people to get the wrong impression of me.' (Mandy, private worker, female)

Enacted stigma

Sex workers fall into what Goffman (1990) has described as a 'discreditable' group, as their stigma is not obviously apparent[1]. He therefore argues that the issue is not about managing tension through social contacts with 'normals', but about managing the information of their failing. He described 'enacted stigma' as a fear of being subject to abuse because of not conforming to societal norms. The possible reaction of others to the revealing of their occupation was always a concern to participants in this study and governed whether this information was divulged or not.

Jenny, a young woman in her mid-twenties, who was a student and mother, epitomised society's ideal of 'normal'. However, she was aware that her occupation was seen as a failing and having to admit her 'inferior status' as a sex worker raised risks of discrediting herself and incurring discrimination. She therefore chose to conceal her 'failing' in dealings with certain people.

> 'So after, yeah, after I'd been talking to this woman about everything, that I was studying at university, and that I was a parent, and you know, all the things I was involved in, I just felt like it was too hard for me to say that I was a sex worker, because I just felt like it was going to discredit everything, you know, all the other wonderful things that I was doing in my life. And you know, you always have that fear that they're going to feel sorry for you and, you know, I don't want to be felt sorry for. Yeah.' (Jenny, managed worker, female)

Shame is experienced when people perceive that they are different and do not possess the attributes of the 'normal' (Goffman, 1990; Sanders, 2005c). They feel guilt and shame, not because they are causing harm to anyone, but because they believe that the behaviour is wrong (Sanders, 2005c).

Participants in this study did acknowledge that they fell outside of the norms of society, but most provided discourses of active resistance to their stigmatisation. Although few internalised shame, most were concerned about protecting family and friends from the consequences of their actions (courtesy stigma) and feared reprisals in the form of abuse and being judged by others through exposure of their occupation (enacted stigma). Goffman (1990, p 84) suggested that '[t]he stigma and the effort to conceal it or remedy it become "fixed" as part of personal

---

[1] Goffman argues that people with observable characteristics, such as physical or mental disabilities, comprise members of a 'discredited' group. Their differentness is clearly evident and in social contacts the issue for such people is to manage tension generated because of their 'failing'.

identity'. Yet Scambler (2007) argues that people are multiple selves and in the case of sex workers, stigma is only confined to one set of identities. In his study, he found that the sex workers he met:

> … *were* and *were not* in the trade, so the felt stigma they experienced was and was not at the core of their self identities. They were able to sign in and out of petit narratives with a degree of equanimity. (Scambler, 2007, p 1091, italics in original)

But leading a double life and managing double lives is stressful and can have adverse consequences for well-being (Vanwesenbeeck, 2001; Sanders, 2006; Scambler, 2007;). Emotional consequences of the discovery of their occupation prevail among sex workers (Sanders, 2004; 2005c). The double life that they endured through keeping their work and their private life separate was an emotional stress to most of the participants interviewed in our study. They identified that this posed a risk to their mental and physical health and required the adoption of different roles.

Sex work as performance

People present themselves in multiple ways, defined by context with constantly shifting boundaries (Kondo, 1990). Goffman (1959) proposes that people actively construct preferred ways of being viewed by others and convey these through verbal and performative cues. Most often people switch between roles when changing settings unconsciously, convinced that the reality that they are presenting is 'real' (Goffman, 1959). However, when one of the roles a person plays is antithetical to societal values and carries with it a stigma, it may not be as easy to switch unconsciously between roles.

Constructing a public and private role

Studies have highlighted the different roles sex workers adopt within the public and private environments (Browne and Minichiello, 1995; Warr and Pyett, 1999; McVerry and Lindop, 2005; McKeganey, 2006; Day, 2007; Day and Ward, 2007). While in the public environment, the sex worker takes on the role of 'other', but in the private realm, most sex workers actively construct an identity of 'normality' that fits the accredited values of society (Goffman, 1959).

Day (2007, p 43) described sex workers in her study as articulating 'two bodies that lay inside and outside the person, oriented to different activities and relationships, endowed with distinctive attributes and values'. Similar to Day's (2007) findings, participants in the present study sometimes spoke of themselves as two different people. Some participants talked of their public role using their working name, emphasising like Sally, that this was a "totally different person" from the person presenting in the private domain.

'The person I turn into [at work], I'm a totally different person. I'm not me. I'm different, I'm [Sally], I'm a different woman.' (Sally, street worker, female)

Sheila accomplished throwing the switch between roles through the use of routine. Routine acts in one setting were distinctly different from those used in the other setting, which enabled her to accomplish the change in persona from "that person" to "me".

'And I definitely have my little routine at work that before I go into work, I have my little routine. So, you know, I set up to go to the personality of that person, and then when I get home I have my little routine to wind down. I don't think it's too dissimilar from a lot of other jobs. You know, people will come home, they'll put their bag down, they might take off their shoes and change out of their work clothes, have a glass of wine. It's that sort of shifting from work to home mentally.' (Sheila, managed worker, female)

In constructing a public identity, sex workers most frequently take on a working name and a fictitious background (McVerry and Lindop, 2005; Sanders, 2005b; McKeganey, 2006). This provides some form of protection for their family life but also acts as a prop in acting their role and maintaining a barrier between public and private identities (Sanders, 2005b, 2005c). In Sanders' (2005a, 2005b) study, all participants used pseudonyms, but for some there came a time where identities started to merge, which caused some anxiety. It has been argued that attempts to construct a boundary between private and public life can sometimes create difficulties in reconciling the two (Hubbard, 2002) and that inevitably sex work becomes the entire life (Brewis and Linstead, 2000). This may apply to the most vulnerable of sex workers as found in the present study, but for the majority there were strategies used to distance self from role as sex worker.

Separation of self from public role

Hochschild (1983) argued that people are able to effectively separate self from the role they play at work. Some occupations require individuals to display emotions that may conflict with internal feelings. People working in such occupations have been referred to as engaged in 'emotional labour' (Hochschild, 1979, 1983). The management of emotions can be viewed as a dramatic performance in which individuals' behaviour is understood as either 'surface acting' or 'deep acting'. Surface acting requires individuals to act in a way known to be false in an effort to delude others, to create a display or an illusion of self. Emotional *expressions* are regulated in surface acting. In deep acting, individuals make use of remembered emotions to provide a convincing performance, where pretending is unnecessary.

In other words, it involves a transformation of feelings and a need to disassociate from self.

Some researchers have drawn on Hochschild's concepts of deep and surface acting to examine emotional labour among sex workers (Brewis and Linstead, 2000; Browne and Minichiello, 1995; Plumridge, 1999b; Sanders, 2005b; Sanders, 2005c; Shaver, 1994; Vanwesenbeeck, 2005). Plumridge (1999b), in her unpublished report, states that arguably for sex workers, the threats and risks to selfhood are greater than for any other worker engaged in emotional labour. In using Hochschild's (1983) argument that those engaged in emotional labour have to deal with managing the estrangement between self and feeling, and self and display, Plumridge argues that sex workers have to face the challenge of deep acting, using and transmuting private experiences for use in the work environment, and yet maintain a sense of selfhood outside of the job. They have to maintain a sense of honour in work where the potential for disrespect and dishonour is greater than in any other form of emotional labour.

Many professions require individuals to take on a role in which they distance themselves emotionally from their work (Vanwesenbeeck, 2001). In caring professions (such as nurses, doctors, social workers), professional distancing is used as emotional protection (Shaver, 1994; Grandey, 2000; Vanwesenbeeck, 2001). Such professions require workers to distance themselves from the bodies and the private lives of their clients (Shaver, 1994).

Some participants in this study recognised the parallels with other occupations that require professional distancing. Sheila acknowledged that it took a special type of person to achieve this:

> 'I mean, there is a few mental boundaries that you need to put up because you are so close physically to a person. And that doesn't happen too much in other jobs apart from, say, nursing, or maybe working as a mortician, you know. And I'm sure those people, you know, nurses get attached to their patients, and it is especially, I'd say working with children can be extremely difficult. So they would also need to put up their mental boundaries and say, "Look, this is work. You know, I'm going to have to, this kid's screaming in pain, but I still need to inject whatever it is into them because that's your job".' (Sheila, managed worker, female)

The ability to construct identity is dependent on specific circumstances, including the biography of the individual and the location of work (Brewis and Linstead, 2000; Sanders, 2005b). Multiple identities, or different selves, can be more easily sustained if 'role and audience segregation are well managed' (Goffman, 1990, p 81). Trish described the challenge of sustaining a separation of her role as sex worker from her other roles, as she saw clients privately in her own home. There was no longer the clear demarcation of the different 'stage' or setting on which to assume the role of sex worker. She spoke of the difficulties she had in preventing the merging of identities.

'I guess when you're working in a normal job, you know, you're performing for someone else. You are doing a particular job where you get to keep some of yourself away from the work. And I think in the industry, in the sex industry, as much as can close a part of yourself down and you create maybe an alter ego or alternative sort of person, I think that there is so much more emotional and psychological connections that sex work can get to that in employment can't. You know what I…. Yes, I can, I can go to work and have a good day and be said, "You've done a good job" and "Have you done this, have you done that?" and I can go home and then be myself as well. But a sex worker, I found doing privately, especially if there's a, if these clients are coming into my home, it's very, very hard to decipher between your working name and you, apart from just … I mean just your name, you know, like I found that me and [Trish] were different. But because of what we do, because of the intimacy, and because of the connection, and because of the touching, because of the yeah, that sometimes we blend. Where at work I can be different, and in a normal job I can be a certain role. I can be a manager or something, and then I come home and then I'm me. It's very hard to, I think that's one of the challenges, to be able to separate without um losing yourself completely.' (Trish, private worker, female)

As Sanders (2005a) and Brewis and Linstead (2000a) argue, location plays a part in how successful sex workers are in maintaining a separation of roles. For some private workers, this may be more difficult because the act of going to another location could provide the impetus for the mental switch between roles. In this study, most managed and private workers emphasised the compartmentalised nature of their work and described the multi-faceted nature of their lives. They actively constructed a private self that included 'normal' activities. For these participants, the role of sex worker was seen as separate from their other roles, which included being a partner, friend, parent, student and child.

'I play darts. I have my friends. At the moment I'm going back to the gym and things like that, so I make sure there's some other things in my life other than sex. I get out of the house. Something I've learnt, 'cause when I first started at a place, it's the one I had a lady working with me. But when I was by myself for about a year, I found I used to get so stagnated and I was doing nothing, putting a lot of weight on, being miserable, that I had to get out. And so you have to. You can not just do this job 24/7, it's just not worth your health. So yes, I play, I play my darts, I have friends, I go out and I sometimes go to

the pictures. I go round to see people for coffee and things like that.'
(Liz, private and managed worker, female)

Paul provided an account of the numerous 'normal' social events he took part in in his private life, but also noted that sometimes his roles did merge when he met another man in the realm of his private life who ended up in the realm of the public life.

> 'Music's hugely important to me. So much of my spare time at home is spent on the piano. I just love it, absolutely love it, and I sing. And away from work, I also like to have like a social life with neighbours and stuff. Like I do have my mates that I've developed where I live, you know, and we do get together and take the table and chairs outside on the deck, and you know, have a few drinks and sort of chips and dips and things like that. You know, just have a normal social occasion, so to speak, you know. I love swimming. Absolutely love swimming. I love gymnastics, but because of the skeletal stuff, I had to give that up. I love dancing, although I'm over nightclubs, absolutely over nightclubs. I love hitch-hiking through the country. It's amazing who you can meet hitch-hiking, it really is. I've had some awesome adventures hitch-hiking. I've met a couple of clients hitch-hiking. I pretty well love everything. I love life. You know, I'm so lucky to be alive and I'm so pleased to be alive, you know, and I just think life's fabulous.'
> (Paul, street worker, male)

Male street-based workers are possibly more adept at maintaining a distinction between their private and public roles than female street-based workers. Maintaining a separation of public and private roles was problematic for those female street-based workers in this study who were working to fund their drug use. They had no ability to craft an identity that did not include drugs and sex work. Joan found the interviewers' questioning about other aspects of her life that were important to her extremely difficult to answer.

> J 'That's a hard question because I don't do anything else. I think that's a hard question. No, it really is a hard question because I don't do anything. I mean, I have no goals. Well the only goal I have at the moment is detox, because I mean I'm just, I'm ready to do that now, you know, but I don't do anything. I mean, I just laze around at home, and so, yeah. That's a very hard, that's one of the hardest questions you've asked me.'

> Interviewer 'So do you see your life as, you know, do you see yourself, what do you see yourself as? What, what do you – you see yourself

as a sex worker, you see yourself – what else do you see yourself as? What do you say you are?'

J 'Oh shit, I don't know. I mean even that's a hard question because I mean, yeah, I see myself as a person that has a drug problem, and I come out to work to support it, and I don't want to do that any more. But yeah, I don't know, even that's a hard question.' (Joan, street worker, female)

Others provided similar accounts.

'My life is really just sex work, because all I do is go to work, get my drugs and I'm well, sleep during the day, and then get ready, go to work again. It's the same shit every day.' (Sarah, street worker, female)

For some sex workers, strategies to manage their emotions are not totally effective and they resort to drugs and alcohol to cope (Brewis and Linstead, 2000; Sanders, 2005c). Work roles may be separated from private roles through the use of substances to create a personality change and distance oneself from reality (Brewis and Linstead, 2000; Day, 2007).

Table 14.3: Substance use, by sector*

	Total % (s.e†.)	Street workers % (s.e.)	Managed indoor % (s.e.)	Private indoor % (s.e.)	Comparison across sectors
How often have drugs been taken before or during work in previous two weeks? (n=764)					
Never	60.5 (2.0)	24.0 (3.3)	66.6 (2.6)	67.0 (4.0)	χ^2 =279.8
Rarely	10.8 (1.3)	10.0 (2.2)	10.3 (1.6)	12.1 (2.8)	df =8
Sometimes	14.9 (1.4)	30.6 (3.9)	12.7 (1.8)	11.5 (2.6)	p<0.0001
Most times	9.1 (1.1)	21.4 (3.5)	7.3 (1.4)	6.4 (1.7)	
Every time	4.7 (0.8)	14.0 (2.8)	3.1 (0.9)	3.0 (1.2)	
When drugs have been taken before or during work, what is the reason? (n=342)					
It helps you get through work	24.6 (2.5)	30.8 (4.2)	26.8 (4.1)	14.5 (4.3)	χ^2 =55.9
You like the feeling	24.7 (2.8)	23.7 (4.1)	20.3 (3.8)	33.5 (6.9)	df =10
It's part of your social life	21.3 (2.6)	16.0 (3.6)	26.1 (4.1)	18.6 (5.6)	p<0.0001
To socialise with the client	10.1 (2.0)	11.8 (3.7)	5.2 (2.1)	16.6 (5.1)	
To stay awake through the night	9.4 (1.8)	8.4 (2.8)	13.0 (3.1)	4.5 (2.4)	
Other	9.9 (1.9)	9.4 (2.8)	8.6 (2.6)	12.4 (4.5)	

Notes: * Weighted estimates to account for variation in probability of selection and response.
† s.e. = standard error

In this study, there were significant differences with the use of drugs either before or while working. While in total 60.4% of survey participants reported that they never took drugs while working, there were differences between sectors (see Table 14.3). Street-based participants were more likely than managed and private workers to report drug use while working – only a quarter reported not using drugs compared with around two thirds of participants in other sectors.

Sex workers who work from indoor venues are less likely to use drugs because of management restrictions (Plant, 1997; Sanders, 2006). Perhaps, as Sanders (2005b) claims, the emotion management strategies sex workers use are most effective for women who have entered sex work in the face of an array of other possibilities, but have freely chosen sex work as their career option. Street-based workers on the whole in this study did not have the array of choices of occupation that many managed and private workers had. Many were using drugs at the time of entry into sex work and started sex work to fund their drug use. It has been argued that demographic characteristics such as being young, unmarried, poorly educated and from working-class backgrounds are factors associated with alcohol and illicit drug use and these are characteristics also associated with most street-based workers (Plant, 1997). There were some street-based workers who spoke of the cycle of having to work to pay for their drugs in order to numb their emotions to work.

> T 'Yeah, as I said, some of the girls, you know, actually all of them, I would say, prefer to be out of it. The simple reason is because, you know, you feel more relaxed and it's 'cause of what you're doing for a job.'
>
> Interviewer 'Do you go out there straight sometimes?'
>
> T 'Yes, no, sometimes I have and like it sucks because I'm thinking, you know, "I really want to have something, but like I've got to get the money first to actually get something".' (Toni, street worker, female)

Interviews with Christchurch sex workers in the study prior to decriminalisation revealed that street-based workers had few strategies other than the use of drugs as a way of emotionally managing their work (Plumridge, 1999b). The use of drugs to provide psychological distancing is more common among street-based workers than indoor workers (Pyett and Warr, 1997; Brewis and Linstead, 2000; Sanders, 2007). A third of street-based workers in the present study who used drugs while working in the previous two weeks reported that they did this to help them get through work and a quarter reported that they liked the feeling (see Table 14.3). Some street-based workers also discussed in in-depth interviews how they utilised drugs as a strategy to numb their emotions and perform the role of sex worker. These participants were less able than their indoor counterparts to maintain the separation of their public and private identities and for many, sex work (and drugs) became their entire life and they could not define themselves as anything other than 'sex worker'. Although a few managed and private workers did utilise drugs while working, they did this for a different purpose. The long shifts required them to stay awake for extended times and although drugs were sometimes used to do this, they did not require the drugs to manage their emotions. The other strategies they had at their disposal were more relevant.

> 'But I use party pills if I, you know, if I'm working days and all of a sudden I have to do two nights. I can't physically sleep during the day, so I'll try, you know, I'll even take sleeping pills. But at night to keep me awake, I'll use caffeine pill or I use party pill, you know. Does that mean that I'm using drugs? Or some girls just drink ridiculous amounts of coffee to the same effect. Some illegal substances are always going to be there, but they're definitely not encouraged, and girls that are caught with it are fired or fined.' (Vicky, managed worker, female)

Radical feminists argue that separation of self from the sex worker role is inherently damaging and creates a false sense of control (Barry, 1995). Yet, it is disputable whether separation of self from role (distancing) is damaging or whether it is in fact an effective strategy to manage emotions. Opposing arguments have been made conceptualising sex work as role play and distancing self from role as less an act of denial than a valuable strategy or tool for managing emotional risk (Chapkis, 1997; McVerry and Lindop, 2005; Sanders, 2005a, 2005c). Chapkis (1997) argues that the danger lies not in the separation of self from role, but in identifying too closely with the role. Most participants in this study were able to achieve this separation. The conceptualisation of themselves as providing a performance in their work life is a psychological safeguard to provide a strict separation of home and work life (McVerry and Lindop, 2005).

Conclusion

Participants in all sectors were cognisant of the fact that they were a stigmatised population and thus regarded by society as 'inferior', yet managed and private participants were better able to manage the emotional risks posed by their stigmatisation than street-based participants through the adoption of various strategies.

Most participants provided accounts of managing stigma through controlling information about their occupation, being selective about whom they disclosed this information to. They constructed different roles within the public and private domains of their lives and most distanced themselves from the sex worker role they played. In referring to themselves in this role, they often spoke of 'that person' as being distinctly different from 'me'. Some, predominantly female, street-based workers were unable to maintain this separation of roles. For these participants, substances were used in an attempt to distance themselves from the sex worker role. However, they described a cycle of drug taking and work that left little space to separate the 'me' from the sex worker role and they could not construct an identity that did not include sex work.

Although separation of self from the sex worker role has been argued as being damaging (Barry, 1995), for the majority of participants in this study, it was an effective protective strategy. By disassociating themselves with that role and conceptualising it as a part they played, much as an actor in a theatre production, they could then construct a private role that fulfilled all the ideals and values held by mainstream society. In other words, they were then able to identify as 'normal'. In doing so, they could actively resist the stigma attached to their occupation.

This study highlights that even after decriminalisation, sex workers still experience stigmatisation and they have to contend with this in their everyday lives. The media, as discussed in Chapter Twelve, has continued to draw on moral discourses that perpetuate stereotypes of sex workers and contribute to their ongoing experiences of stigmatisation. Yet, on the other hand, many of our participants discussed how decriminalisation and the realisation of employment, legal and health and safety rights had provided them with a legitimacy that had aided their resistance of stigmatisation (see also Chapter Thirteen). Many indicated that they felt empowered through their increased rights. Indeed, there has been some positive shift in social perceptions towards sex workers by many in New Zealand society. As sex workers become more confident in exercising their rights and standing up to and challenging negative stereotypes, it will be interesting to see whether experiences of stigmatisation decrease in this population.

References

Anspach, R. (1979) 'From stigma to identity politics: political activism among the physically disabled and former mental patients', *Social Science and Medicine*, vol 13, pp 765-73.

Barry, K. (1995) *The prostitution of sexuality: The global exploitation of women*, New York: New York University Press.

Bayer, R. (2008) 'Stigma and the ethics of public health: not can we but should we', *Social Science and Medicine*, vol 67, pp 463-72.

Brewis, J. and Linstead, S. (2000) '"The worst thing is the screwing" (1): consumption and the management of identity in sex work', *Gender, Work and Organization*, vol 7, no 2, pp 84-97.

Browne, J. and Minichiello, V. (1995) 'The social meanings behind male sex work: implications for sexual interactions', *British Journal of Sociology*, vol 46, no 4, pp 598-622.

Buseh, A. and Stevens, P. (2007) 'Constrained but not determined by stigma: resistance by African-American women living with HIV', *Women and Health*, vol 44, no 3, pp 1-18.

Chapkis, W. (1997) *Live sex acts: Women performing erotic labor*, New York, NY: Routledge.

Crocker, J. and Major, B. (1989) 'Social stigma and self-esteem: the self-protective properties of stigma', *Psychological Review*, vol 96, pp 608-30.

Day, S. (2007) *On the game: Women and sex work*, London: Pluto Press.

Day, S. and Ward, H. (2007) 'British policy makes sex workers vulnerable', *British Medical Journal*, vol 334, p 187.

Goffman, E. (1959) *The presentation of self in everyday life*, London: Anchor Books.

Goffman, E. (1990) *Stigma: Notes on the management of spoiled identity*, London: Penguin Books.

Grandey, A. (2000) 'Emotion regulation in the workplace: a new way to conceptualise emotional labor', *Journal of Occupational Health Psychology*, vol 5, no 1, pp 95–110.

Hallgrimsdottir, H., Phillips, R. and Benoit, C. (2006) 'Fallen women and rescued girls: social stigma and media narratives of the sex industry', *Canadian Review of Sociology and Anthropology*, vol 3, no 3, pp 265–80.

Hallgrimsdottir, H., Phillips, R., Benoit, C. and Walby, K. (2008) 'Sporting girls, streetwalkers, and inmates of houses of ill repute: media narratives and the historical mutability of prostitution stigmas', *Sociological Perspectives*, vol 51, no 1, pp 119–38.

Herek, G. and Glunt, E. (1988) 'An epidemic of stigma: a psychologist's perspective', *American Psychologist*, vol 43, pp 886–91.

Hochschild, A. (1979) 'Emotion work, feeling rules and social structure', *American Journal of Sociology*, vol 85, no 3, pp 551–75.

Hochschild, A. (1983) *The managed heart: Commercialization of human feeling*, Berkeley, CA: University of California Press.

Hubbard, P. (2002) 'Sexing the self: geographies of engagement and encounter', *Social and Cultural Geography*, vol 3, no 4, pp 365–81.

Kondo, D. (1990) *Crafting selves: Power, gender, and discourses of identity in a Japanese workplace*, Chicago, IL: University of Chicago Press.

Link, B. and Phelan, J. (2001) 'Conceptualizing stigma', *Annual Review of Sociology*, vol 27, pp 363–85.

Link, B. and Phelan, J. (2006) 'Stigma and its public health implications', *The Lancet*, vol 367, no 9509, pp 528–9.

McKeganey, N. (2006) 'Street prostitution in Scotland: the views of working women', *Drugs: Education, Prevention and Policy*, vol 13, no 2, pp 151–66.

McVerry, S. and Lindop, E. (2005) 'Negotiating risk: how women working in massage parlours preserve their sexual and psychological health', *Health Care for Women International*, vol 26, pp 108–17.

Parker, R. and Aggleton, P. (2003) 'HIV and AIDS-related stigma and discrimination: a conceptual framework and implications for action', *Social Science and Medicine*, vol 57, pp 13–24.

Phelan, J., Link, B. and Dovidio, J. (2008) 'Stigma and prejudice: one animal or two?', *Social Science and Medicine*, vol 67, pp 358–67.

Plant, M. (1997) 'Alcohol, drugs and social milieu', in G. Scambler and A. Scambler (eds) *Rethinking prostitution: Purchasing sex in the 1990s*, London: Routledge.

Plumridge, E. (1999a) 'Making prostitution thinkable: transgression of romantic love or instrumental sex?', unpublished report, University of Otago, Christchurch School of Medicine.

Plumridge, E. (1999b) 'Making sex work doable: emotional labour', unpublished report, University of Otago, Christchurch School of Medicine.

Pyett, P. and Warr, D. (1997) 'Vulnerability on the streets: female sex workers and HIV risk', *AIDS Care*, vol 9, no 5, pp 539-47.

Pyett, P. and Warr, D. (1999) 'Women at risk in sex work: strategies for survival', *Journal of Sociology*, vol 35, no 2, pp 183-97.

Riessman, C. (2000) 'Stigma and everyday resistance practices: childless women in South India', *Gender and Society*, vol 14, no 1, pp 111-35.

Sanders, T. (2004) 'A continuum of risk? The management of health, physical and emotional risks by female sex workers', *Sociology of Health and Illness*, vol 26, no 5, pp 557-74.

Sanders, T. (2005a) 'Blinded by morality? Prostitution policy in the UK', *Capital and Class*, vol 86, pp 9-15.

Sanders, T. (2005b) '"It's just acting": sex workers' strategies for capitalizing on sexuality', *Gender, Work and Organization*, vol 12, no 4, pp 319-42.

Sanders, T. (2005c) *Sex work: A risky business*, Cullompton: Willan.

Sanders, T. (2006) 'Behind the personal ads: the indoor sex markets in Britain', in R. Campbell and M. O'Neill (eds) *Sex work now*, Cullompton: Willan.

Sanders, T. (2007) 'Protecting the health and safety of female sex workers: the responsibility of all', *BJOG An International Journal of Obstetrics and Gynaecology*, vol 114, pp 791-3.

Scambler, G. (2007) 'Sex work stigma: opportunist migrants in London', *Sociology*, vol 41, no 6, pp 1079-96.

Scambler, G. and Paoli, F. (2008) 'Health work, female sex workers and HIV/AIDS: global and local dimensions of stigma and deviance as barriers to effective interventions', *Social Science and Medicine*, vol 66, pp 1848-62.

Shaver, F. (1994) 'The regulation of prostitution: avoiding the morality traps', *Canadian Journal of Law and Society*, vol 9, no 1, pp 123-45.

Sibley, D. (1995) *Geographies of exclusion: Society and difference in the west*, London: Routledge.

Stuber, J. and Meyer, I. (2008) 'Stigma, prejudice, discrimination and health', *Social Science and Medicine*, vol 67, pp 351-7.

Vanwesenbeeck, I. (2001) 'Another decade of social scientific work on sex work: a review of research 1990-2000', *Annual Review of Sex Research*, vol 12, pp 242-89.

Vanwesenbeeck, I. (2005) 'Burnout among female indoor sex workers', *Archives of Sexual Behavior*, vol 34, no 6, pp 627-39.

Warr, D. and Pyett, P. (1999) 'Difficult relations: sex work, love and intimacy', *Sociology of Health and Illness*, vol 21, no 3, pp 290-309.

FIFTEEN

Conclusion

Gillian Abel and Lisa Fitzgerald

New Zealand was the first country to decriminalise all sectors of the sex industry and in this book we have provided some sound reasoning as to why and how this came about. The chapter on the history of the New Zealand Prostitutes' Collective (NZPC) highlights the strong non-government organisation sector within New Zealand and how it has been supported by government. The coming together of the original nine founding members and the development of the NZPC, within a non-hierarchical structure, were influential in highlighting the human rights violations brought about by the laws that criminalised sex workers. As an organisation, NZPC created an inclusive atmosphere that provided support for sex workers across all sectors of the industry. The New Zealand government appointed NZPC members on to key committees such as the National Council on AIDS and also provided funding for this organisation from October 1988. NZPC increasingly raised its profile and credibility in the public arena. Its key role in initiating the call for decriminalisation cannot be overstated, as undoubtedly this legislation would not have been on the agenda without its commitment. As NZPC is the only sex worker organisation in New Zealand, it presented a united front for sex workers in campaigning for decriminalisation. Perhaps this can be seen as a particular strength, as in countries such as Canada and Australia there are several sex worker organisations across the different states, some of which are not peer-run organisations. There are philosophical differences between such organisations that might make it difficult for them to work cohesively towards a goal of policy change.

NZPC's drive for decriminalisation was an intellectual one, driven from the boardroom as opposed to the streets. The danger of relying on street protests for law reform is that it could engender a backlash through raising the visibility of sex workers, creating anxiety and moral panic among the general public. Instead, NZPC negotiated at the highest level, often with very conservative organisations and politicians. Through its effective networking, it gathered increasing support for decriminalisation. The women's movement in New Zealand has been influential in the reform of many laws affecting women, including employment, domestic violence, matrimonial property and paid parental leave (Duncan, 2007). Many women's organisations worked alongside NZPC in lobbying for decriminalisation. Although there were some feminists arguing against decriminalisation from a radical perspective, this was not the dominant feminist voice coming through in New Zealand. In Chapter Six, Alison Laurie highlighted how traditionally conservative women's groups, such as the Young Women's Christian Association and the Maori Women's Welfare League, drew on liberal feminist ideas of equality and fair treatment for women. It is interesting that those feminists arguing for and against the Prostitution Reform Bill drew on international conventions of women's rights to support their stances; for example, both sides drew on the Convention for the Elimination of Discrimination Against Women, particularly Article 6 on suppressing trafficking and exploitation of women. Those opposing the Prostitution Reform Bill argued that decriminalisation would increase the trafficking of women and children into New Zealand to work in the sex industry, while those supporting the Bill maintained that it would decrease trafficking. Interestingly, there has only been a handful of reports of trafficking of sex workers in New Zealand prior to law reform and since the 2003 Prostitution Reform Act (PRA), immigration authorities have yet to uncover any instances of trafficked people despite proactive investigations (PLRC, 2008). Yet trafficking remains a hotly debated issue.

It took almost two decades of conceptualising and drafting the Prostitution Reform Bill, as well as networking and campaign building with a wide variety of organisations and individuals, before the Bill was finally enacted. The mixed-member proportional (MMP) system of government brought a diversity of politicians from different ideological positions into the mix. The Bill was introduced to parliament as a Private Member's Bill and was not voted on along party lines but on a conscious vote. Individual Members of Parliament could thus be persuaded by the public health and human rights arguments rather than voting along traditional party lines. As Tim Barnett suggests in Chapter Four, possibly the greatest benefit of MMP was its positive impact on the power and energy of the parliamentary institutions. Despite a growing right-wing conservative element in parliament, the Bill was finally voted on and enacted in June 2003.

Written into the PRA was the need to review the Act within five years. This is something unique to policy within New Zealand. A diverse committee was set up by the Ministry of Justice to undertake this review. The PRA was a departure from a moralistic stance to the regulation of sex work to one that considered the public health and human rights of sex workers. As highlighted in Chapter Seven, the Prostitution Law Review Committee (PLRC) was mindful of sticking to the purposes of the Act in considering the review of the PRA and not being drawn into moral arguments. It was their intent instead to base the review on sound research evidence. It commissioned and drew on evidence from empirical research in producing a report on the impact of the PRA. Part Two of this book highlighted some of the research findings that contributed to this review. After examining all the evidence, the PLRC concluded that the PRA has been effective in achieving its purpose and sex workers are better off in a decriminalised environment. Increased rights have had a positive impact on their health and safety, they have more power in their negotiations in dealings with clients and management and the law change has created an environment where they feel more supported by the legal system. Their confidence in being able to use the legal system is growing with more and more positive experiences of some sex workers in their dealings with police and the courts. Similarly, community agencies and brothel operators identified many improvements as a result of decriminalisation that align with those identified by sex workers. Some improvements need to be made with regard to eliminating poor management practices and protecting young people under the age of 18 entering sex work through improvements to social policies and services for this specific age group. Transgender youth are highlighted as being particularly vulnerable. More research needs to be carried out in New Zealand in this area.

Two different groups with key responsibilities under the PRA, Medical Officers of Health (MOoHs) and territorial authorities (TAs), interpreted their roles under the PRA in very different ways. MOoHs were designated as inspectors of brothels under the terms of the Act and were given powers of entry to sex work businesses. TAs were given bylaw-making powers to regulate signage and location of brothels within their districts. Whereas MOoHs were positive about the PRA and its purposes, some TAs sought to aggressively utilise their available powers in contravention of the intentions of the Act. As Dean Knight highlights in Chapter Nine, TA regulation became the centre of debate about regulating prostitution. This debate was framed by tensions between a national direction to ensure a safe and healthy environment for sex workers and strong views by some local communities against prostitution, with some uncertainty from the courts about how to mediate between these tensions. The media reports played on these tensions within the communities. Although most of the print media reporting on the PRA was neutral and descriptive, some sex workers reflected on the negative media framing of the sex industry and identified increased stigmatisation due to such coverage.

A strength of the research contained in this book is that it has moved beyond traditional public health perspectives of sex workers' health to gaining sex workers' own perspective on their health. This is a new public health approach to sex work, where the emphasis is less on individual risk factors, but has applied a sociological lens to examining how behaviour choices shape and are shaped by society, analysing these choices within the context of structural opportunities and constraints (Giddens, 1986; Lin, 2002). As discussed in Chapter Thirteen, the hierarchy of risks as perceived by sex workers runs counter to that perceived by public health professionals. Risk to safety and risk to emotional health were paramount in sex workers' overall conceptualisation of the risks attached to their occupation. They strategised, some more effectively than others, to manage these risks. Risks to sexual health were regarded as minor, as all sex workers had well-rehearsed, solid grounds for managing these. Brothel owners/managers, community agencies and sex workers all maintained that decriminalisation had had little impact on safer sex as most sex workers had already been practising safe sex prior to law reform. However, decriminalisation has further reinforced the ability to ensure safe sex as sex workers are now able to negotiate safe sex openly, are not afraid to have condoms and safe-sex literature on the premises and have the backing of the law if their clients attempt to enforce unprotected sex.

Decriminalisation has also provided sex workers with more tools to manage the environment in which they work. With knowledge of their employment rights, managed workers are more able to refuse to see certain clients. With legal rights ensured, they are also more able to report instances of violence to the police. There is evidence that relationships between the police and street-based workers in particular are improving, which increases the likelihood that reporting of incidents will continue increasing over time.

However, sex workers are less proficient at managing the emotional risks of their job than they are these other risks (Sanders, 2005). Emotional risks, unlike risks of violence and health-related risks, are not left behind in the working environment, but follow sex workers into the private realm, where they are vulnerable to having their public role exposed with sometimes dire consequences (Sanders, 2006). The emotional risks posed by their work have to be constantly guarded against and the participants in this study did strategise to manage these risks.

Decriminalisation brought with it increased rights for sex workers, but stigma still remains. In the qualitative interviews with sex workers, discussion on many topics, including the media and disclosure of occupation and mental health, stigma was a dominant theme. These findings reinforce the relationship between stigma and health and the need to develop conceptualisations of stigma. The research presented in this book demonstrates that sex workers are not passive recipients of stigma, but rather actively resist stigma by constructing alternative identities. This has implications for their emotional health.

Social perceptions are slow to change and it would possibly be many years before there is any major change in the stigmatisation experienced by most sex workers. The messages sex workers get from society, such as how they are presented in the media, how the requirements of the PRA are implemented and how their human and civil rights are attended to, will play a role in reinforcing or lessening their stigma.

The entire process of decriminalisation was a consultative one, with sex workers' perspectives incorporated in the design of the policy as well as the occupational safety and health guidelines and Ministry of Health pamphlets on safer sex. Having sex workers' voices incorporated in the process was always going to increase the likelihood of the success of decriminalisation. The NZPC played a large role in the development of the Act, ensuring that the various clauses within the Act would be acceptable and workable from the perspective of sex workers. They worked with researchers from the Christchurch School of Medicine in a partnership approach to the research discussed in Chapters Ten to Fourteen of this book, providing an important gatekeeper role to the sex worker population and ensuring the robustness of the research. They were also there to assist in the review of the Act. There were aspects of the PRA that they were uncomfortable with, most notably sections of the Act that dealt with its application to the 1987 Immigration Act. Whereas immigrants from other occupational groups, such as nurses, doctors, hairdressers and so on, are allowed to enter New Zealand and work in their particular trade, immigrants are not able to work as sex workers.

This has meant that people who have immigrated and who are working in the sex industry are working illegally, which makes them vulnerable to exploitation and violence and inaccessible to by health and social workers. This is an area that requires more research in New Zealand but would require a significant amount of relationship building by researchers to develop trust among this vulnerable group.

On the whole, the general public in New Zealand has accepted decriminalisation and as Paul Fitzharris pointed out in Chapter Seven, this was not brought up as an election issue in 2008, nor was the review of the Act that was released in this same year given any extensive news coverage. However, from time to time the issue of street-based work does attract media attention, especially in Manakau, which is part of the greater Auckland city region. There was a concerted effort by Manukau City Council to prohibit street-based sex work and, in 2005, it developed the Manukau City Council (Control of Street Prostitution) Bill. The Local Government and Environment Committee advised that the Bill was contradictory to the intentions of the PRA and would have a number of adverse effects. The Bill was voted down as a consequence. This issue has resurfaced periodically and is always given extensive media coverage. The five councils that make up the greater Auckland city region are currently in the process of amalgamating into one super-city council. There is the possibility that the newly formed council could pursue the issue of recriminalising street-based work, but there appears to be a resolve among the majority of legislators as well as the judiciary to adhere to the intentions of the PRA.

Sex workers in New Zealand do recognise their increased rights under the PRA, but in some cases, stigmatisation has impeded the achievement of their rights. However, if organisations like NZPC, youth organisations, religious leaders, sexual health professionals, police, court officials, TAs, the media and others give credence to the purposes of the PRA, this may have a positive impact on the ability of sex workers to achieve their rights. All have a part to play in changing attitudes, reducing the stigmatisation sex workers' experience and improving their health and safety.

NZPC is recognised in the PRA and in a post-decriminalisation environment is also consulted as the expert body on sex work and sex worker issues by many government authorities on how to deal with situations that are presented to them. They encourage the general public to get to know what sex work is from those who have experienced it rather than relying on dominant public discourses. They have encouraged people to come into their community drop-in centres with banners that read 'Don't talk about us … talk to us'. It is fitting, therefore, that this book should end with the voice of a New Zealand sex worker. The point of difference with decriminalisation in New Zealand is that it included street-based workers and as Joan articulates below, the Prostitution Reform Act was a law "for us".

'Well, it is legally for us a job…. So, you know, my opinion on it is now, now that the laws have changed, it is for us, it's a professional job and I don't see any bad things about it, 'cause you know, everyone in life goes through that stage where they go through so much.' (Joan, street worker, female)

References

Duncan, G. (2007) *Society and politics: New Zealand social policy*, Auckland: Pearson Education New Zealand.

Giddens, A. (1986) *Sociology: A brief but critical introduction*, London: Macmillan.

Lin, N. (2002) *Social capital: A theory of social structure and action*, Cambridge: Cambridge University Press.

PLRC (Prostitution Law Review Committee) (2008) *Report of the Prostitution Law Review Committee on the operation of the Prostitution Reform Act 2003*, Wellington: Ministry of Justice, www.justice.govt.nz/prostitution-law-review-committee/publications/plrc-report/index.html

Sanders, T. (2005) *Sex work: A risky business*, Cullompton: Willan.

Sanders, T. (2006) 'Behind the personal ads: the indoor sex markets in Britain', in R. Campbell and M. O'Neill (eds) *Sex work now*, Cullompton: Willan.

Index

Note: The abbreviations NZPC and PRA refer to the New Zealand Prostitutes' Collective and the Prostitute Reform Act respectively. The letters n and t following page numbers refer to notes and tables.

A

advertisements 77–8, 79
Aggleton, P. 240
AIDS *see* HIV/AIDS
Auckland 34, 35, 36
  bylaws 32, 146–7, 188–9, 191
  JB International v *Auckland City Council*
    [2006] 146–7, 149
  murders 40
  red-light district 30
  street-based workers 116
Australia
  Prostitutes' Collective of Victoria (PCV) 47,
    60
  regulation of sex work 7, 8–9
  system of certification 131
Australian Federation of AIDS Organisations
  77

B

Barnett, A. 206
Barnett, Tim 40, 62, 65, 82
  on the campaign and its outcome 66–9
Barry, K. 4, 89
Bay of Islands 27, 28
Belich, J. 27, 28
bonds 129–30
Bradbury, H. 161
Braun, V. 168
Britain *see* United Kingdom
brothel operators
  Crimes Act (1961) 75–6
  experiences of decriminalisation 120t, 121–2
    conditions of employment 129–31
    health information and services 126–7
    leaving the sex industry 132–3
    level of support for the PRA 123–5
    monitoring and enforcement 136–8
    operator certificates 131, 137
    preventing entry of under age sex workers
      135–6
    prosecutions regarding under-age sex
      workers 135
    research interviews content 122–3
    research methodology 120
    safe-sex practices 125–6
    sex workers' safety 127–9
    territorial authority responses to the PRA
      136
    under-age sex workers 133–6

and HIV prevention programme 59
  opposition to reform 64
  reaction to NZPC 50
brothels 121n
  advertisements for staff 79
  Crimes Act (1961) 75–6
  the gold rush 29
  inspectors of 80–1, 173, 174, 186
  local authorities' bylaws 70–1, 79, 136
    location 142–9
    signage 149–51
  see also massage parlours
burn-out 230–1
Business and Professional Women's Federation
  38, 53, 61, 87, 95
bylaws 70–1, 79, 109–10, 114, 116, 136
  19th century 32
  challenges to 144–9, 154–5
  location of brothels 142–9
  public health submissions 188–93
  signage of brothels 149–51

C

campaign *see* decriminalisation campaign
Campbell, R. 222
Cancian, F. 161
Canterbury 32, 33
Carmen 37, 105–6
Catholic Women's League of New Zealand 95
CATWA 89, 90
CEDAW 87, 89, 90, 91, 92–3, 94, 95, 99
certification system 81, 113, 131, 137
Chamberlain, K. 200, 210–11
Chapkis, W. 8, 86, 255
Chetwynd, J. 48
Christchurch
  bylaws 145, 189–90
  escort business 107
  'phone text' safety initiative 128–9
  sex work, 19th century 30, 31, 32, 33, 34
  sex workers and police relationship 69–70,
    128–9
  Willowford v *Christchurch City Council* [2005]
    145–6, 149
Christchurch School of Medicine (CSoM) 60,
  111, 113
  study methodology and methods 159–70
    community-based participatory research
      160–2

M

Macdonald, C. 30–1
Mackinnon, Catherine A. 89
male sex workers 46, 49, 252
Manukau City Council 156, 263
Maori Action Group 49
Maori feminists 95–6
Maori sex workers 27–8, 50, 96
Maori Women's Welfare League 61, 96
Margerison, Ruth 90
massage industry 61
Massage Institute 61
massage parlours 45, 46, 76, 107, 121n
  see also brothel operators; brothels
Massage Parlours Act (1978) 37, 45, 76, 107
Maticka-Tyndale, E 161, 162
Maxim Institute 62
Mazengarb Report 36
McKenzie, Flora 36
McNeil, J. 202
media 50–1, 62–3, 198–200, 211
  depiction of sex workers 199–200
  dominant discourses of sex work 199
  influence of 198–9
  see also print media reporting, analysis
medical certificates 78
Medical Officers of Health and the PRA
    80–1, 173, 174–6, 177, 178, 193
  dealing with complaints 182–4
  implementation of 179–82
  local authority bylaws, submissions on 190–3
  perceptions of impact of 186–7
  relationships with other agencies 184–5
  role of 185–6
  training 178–9
migrant sex workers 71, 80, 127
Ministry of Health, NZPC's contract with 48
Ministry of Justice 110, 111
Ministry of Women's Affairs 53
mixed-member proportional (MMP) system
    58, 67–8
moral discourses 199, 201, 202, 205, 210–11,
    239
*Mount Victoria Residents Association Incorporated
    v The Wellington City Council* [2009] 154–5
Munoz, J. 207
murders 40, 69, 221–2

N

National Collective of Independent Women's
    Refuges Inc. 87–8, 94
National Council of Women 35, 38, 52, 53, 61,
    86, 88, 92–3
National Council on AIDS 52
National Party 58, 60, 68
*Nature and extent of the sex industry in New
    Zealand: An estimation* (PLRC) 110
needle exchange programmes 49, 59
Nelson, bylaws 189, 192

New Zealand AIDS Foundation 48, 49, 61
New Zealand Herald 200
New Zealand Prostitutes' Collective (NZPC)
    37, 45–54, 87, 263
  background 45–6
  composition of 51
  condom distribution programme 48, 59
  expansion 48, 49–50
  government funding 46–9, 59
  health and safety guidelines collaboration 77
  HIV prevention programme 47, 48, 59, 125
  importance of 126, 185
  law reform, push for 51–4, 60
  and the media 50–1
  operator certificates 131
  Prostitution Reform Working Group 177
  reflection on campaign and its outcomes
    69–71
  sex industry's reactions to 50
  submissions to Select Committee 97–8
non-governmental organisations (NGOs) 53,
    63, 68
non-resident sex workers 71, 80, 127
North Shore City, signage regulation 151
Nunn, Pamela Gerrish 92
NZPC *see* New Zealand Prostitutes'
    Collective

O

occupational safety and health 77, 176–7
occupational safety and health guidelines 77,
    115, 126, 178, 187, 219, 221
occupational safety and health inspectors 179,
    184
Olssen, E. 30
Ongoing Network Transgender Outreach
    Project (ONTOP) 49
operator certificates 81, 113, 131, 137
opponents of law reform 62–4, 70
O'Regan, Katherine 40, 60, 62
Ostergren, P. 99

P

Palmerston North Women's Health Collective
    Inc. 95
Paoli, F. 241
Parker, R. 240
parliamentary system 58, 67
parlour owners *see* brothel operators
parlours *see* brothels; massage parlours
PCV (Prostitutes' Collective of Victoria) 47,
    60
Perez-y-Perez, Maria 97
'Phone Text' safety initiative 69, 128–9
Plumridge, E. 250
police 45–6, 106–7
  attitudes, changes in 228–9
  reporting violence to 128, 227–8
  seizing of condoms 52–3, 59, 76